DEMOCRACY AND PREBENDAL
POLITICS IN NIGERIA

AFRICAN STUDIES SERIES   56

GENERAL EDITOR
J. M. Lonsdale, *Lecturer in History and Fellow of Trinity College,
Cambridge*

ADVISORY EDITORS
J. D. Y. Peel, *Charles Booth Professor of Sociology, University of Liverpool*
John Sender, *Faculty of Economics and Fellow of Wolfson College,
Cambridge*

Published in collaboration with
THE AFRICAN STUDIES CENTRE, CAMBRIDGE

OTHER BOOKS IN THE SERIES

6 *Labour in the South African Gold Mines, 1911–1969*   Francis Wilson
14 *Culture, Tradition and Society in the West African Novel*   Emmanuel Obiechina
18 *Muslim Brotherhoods in Nineteenth-century Africa*   B. G. Martin
20 *Liberia and Sierra Leone: An Essay in Comparative Politics*   Christopher Clapham
23 *West African States: Failure and Promise: A Study in Comparative Politics*   John Dunn
24 *Afrikaners of the Kalahari: White Minority in a Black State*   Margo and Martin Russell
25 *A Modern History of Tanganyika*   John Iliffe
26 *A History of African Christianity 1950–1975*   Adrian Hastings
28 *The Hidden Hippopotamus: Reappraisal in African History: The Early Colonial Experience in Western Zambia*   Gwyn Prins
29 *Families Divided: The Impact of Migrant Labour in Lesotho*   Colin Murray
30 *Slavery, Colonialism and Economic Growth in Dahomey 1640–1960*   Patrick Manning
31 *Kings, Commoners and Concessionaires: The Evolution and Dissolution of the Nineteenth-century Swazi State*   Philip Bonner
32 *Oral Poetry and Somali Nationalism: The Case of Sayyid Muhammad Abdille Hasan*   Said S. Samatar
33 *The Political Economy of Pondoland 1860–1930: Production, Labour, Migrancy and Chiefs in Rural South Africa*   William Beinart
34 *Volkskapitalisme: Class, Capital and Ideology in the Development of Afrikaner Nationalism 1934–1948*   Dan O'Meara
35 *The Settler Economies: Studies in the Economic History of Kenya and Southern Rhodesia 1900–1963*   Paul Mosley
36 *Transformations in Slavery: A History of Slavery in Africa*   Paul E. Lovejoy
37 *Amilcar Cabral: Revolutionary Leadership and People's War*   Patrick Chabal
38 *Essays on the Political Economy of Rural Africa*   Robert H. Bates
39 *Ijeshas and Nigerians: The Incorporation of a Yoruba Kingdom, 1890–1970s*   J. D. Y. Peel
40 *Black People and the South African War 1899–1902*   Peter Warwick
41 *A History of Niger 1850–1960*   Finn Fuglestad
42 *Industrialisation and Trade Union Organisation in South Africa 1924–55*   Jon Lewis
43 *The Rising of the Red Shawls: A Revolt in Madagascar 1895–1899*   Stephen Ellis
44 *Slavery in Dutch South Africa*   Nigel Worden
45 *Law, Custom and Social Order: The Colonial Experience in Malawi and Zambia*   Martin Chanock
46 *Salt of the Desert Sun: A History of Salt Production and Trade in the Central Sudan*   Paul E. Lovejoy
47 *Marrying Well: Status and Social Change among the Educated Elite in Colonial Lagos*   Kristin Mann
48 *Language and Colonial Power: The Appropriation of Swahili in the Former Belgian Congo 1880–1938*   Johannes Fabian
49 *The Shell Money of the Slave Trade*   Jan Hogendorn and Marion Johnson
50 *Political Domination in Africa: Reflections on the Limits of Power*   edited by Patrick Chabal
51 *The Southern Marches of Imperial Ethiopia: Essays in History and Social Anthropology*   edited by Donald Donham and Wendy James
52 *Islam and Urban Labor in Northern Nigeria: The Making of a Muslim Working Class*   Paul M. Lubeck
53 *Horn and Crescent: Cultural Change and Traditional Islam on the East African Coast, 500–1900*   Randall J. Pouwels
54 *Capital and Labour on the Kimberley Diamond Fields 1871–1890*   Robert Vicat Turrell
55 *National and Class Conflict in the Horn of Africa*   John Markakis

DEMOCRACY AND PREBENDAL POLITICS IN NIGERIA

The rise and fall of the Second Republic

RICHARD A. JOSEPH

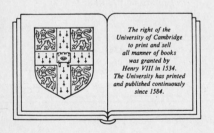

The right of the
University of Cambridge
to print and sell
all manner of books
was granted by
Henry VIII in 1534.
The University has printed
and published continuously
since 1584.

CAMBRIDGE UNIVERSITY PRESS

CAMBRIDGE

NEW YORK   NEW ROCHELLE   MELBOURNE   SYDNEY

Published by the Press Syndicate of the University of Cambridge
The Pitt Building, Trumpington Street, Cambridge CB2 1RP
32 East 57th Street, New York, NY 10022, USA
10 Stamford Road, Oakleigh, Melbourne 3166, Australia

© Cambridge University Press 1987

First published 1987

Printed in Great Britain at the University Press, Cambridge

British Library cataloguing in publication data

Joseph, Richard A.
Democracy and prebendal politics in
Nigeria: the rise and fall of the Second
Republic – (African studies series; 56).
1. Nigeria – Politics and government—1979–1983
I. Title II. Series
966.9′05 DT515.8

Library of Congress cataloging in publication data

Joseph, Richard A. 88-9180
Democracy and prebendal politics in Nigeria.
(African studies series; 56)
Bibliography.
Includes index.
1. Nigeria – Politics and government – 1979–1983.
I. Title. II. Series.
DT515.84.J67 1987 966.9′05 87-8314

ISBN 0 521 34136 1

TM

For my sons
Mark Vincent
Richard Anthony
Robert Lionel

Contents

		page	
List of maps			viii
List of tables			viii
Acknowledgements			ix

1 Introduction   1

Part I The problem of democracy   13
2 A democracy that works   15
3 Dilemmas of Nigerian democracy   30

Part II Nigeria's social dynamics and military rule   41
4 Politics in a multi-ethnic society   43
5 Clientelism and prebendal politics   55
6 Military rule and economic statism   69

Part III The return to tripartism in the Second Republic   91
7 Personality and alignment in Igbo politics   93
8 Ethnicity, faction and class in Western Nigeria   109
9 Northern primacy and prebendal politics: the making of the NPN   129

Part IV The crisis of Nigerian democracy   151
10 The challenge of the 1983 elections: a republic in peril   153
11 Electoral fraud and violence: the Republic's demise   170
12 Conclusion: democracy and prebendal politics in Nigeria   184

Notes   199
Select bibliography   224
Index   233

Maps

1 Nigeria's nineteen states   *page* ix
2 1979 presidential election   128

Tables

Nigerian General Elections, 1979   *page* 125
1 Senate election   125
2 House of Representatives   126
3 State Assembly   126
4 State Governors   127
5 Presidential election   127

Acknowledgements

There are three major sources for the ideas and factual information which have been incorporated in this book. The first is the individuals who were actively involved in the politics and political debates in Nigeria which the author was able to observe at close hand between 1976 and 1979, and for brief periods in 1983 and 1984. The openness of the political process during these years would match that of any country in the world. For that reason, the author obtained considerable access to the views of Nigerian politicians, higher civil servants, military officers, and journalists as well as to those of his academic colleagues. There will also be noted throughout the book the numerous official and private publications, the public speeches and televised broadcasts, as well as the personal interviews which provided a cornucopia of insights into, and information about, Nigerian politics and society. The democratic spirit of the Nigerian people is therefore implicitly reflected in the range and vitality of the oral and written materials that were available for such a study.

The second source of ideas and information was the Nigerians with whom the author interacted on a personal and professional basis while lecturing at the University of Ibadan from February 1976 until August 1979. To a considerable extent, the analytical framework of this book was provided, often unconsciously, by these Nigerians who conveyed the nature of the dynamics of their society and its politics. Special appreciation must be expressed for the several hundred Nigerian students whom it was my privilege to teach and for whom the classroom became an arena of confrontation between the ideas of Western political thinkers and the accumulated political practices of the Nigerian people. In a sense, the manner in which this book has been written reflects its germination within those classroom debates. A small indication of this indebtedness can be seen in the studies of re-emergent party politics, cited in Part III, which were carried out by some of the graduating seniors in the Department of Political Science at Ibadan in 1978–9.

The third source from which this book has been drawn is the teachers and colleagues who have fostered my continuing interest in political and social theory. Insights from lectures of two decades ago by Arthur M. Wilson of

Acknowledgements

Dartmouth College, by John Plamenatz, Isaiah Berlin and Anthony Quinton of Oxford, as well as ideas suggested more recently by my Dartmouth colleagues, Henry Ehrmann, Nelson Kasfir, and Vincent Starzinger, have been incorporated throughout the study. Jane Guyer and Sara Berry made incisive comments on the first drafts of Parts I and II, and Nelson Kasfir provided a constant critical challenge which resulted in the sharpening of a number of the arguments advanced. At crucial stages of the project, the following individuals were particularly helpful: Billy Dudley, Joseph Black, Femi Ogunsanwo, Allison Ayida, Dare Aguda, Bob Townsend, Odia Ofeimun, Richard Horovitz, Omo Omoruyi and Crawford Young. My research assistant in Nigeria, S. Balbahadur, deserves special recognition for his valuable services, and the same can be said for the unfailingly helpful staff of Baker Library, Dartmouth College. Individuals who helped with the typing at various stages until the acquisition of a word-processor are Audrey Borus of Harvard University, and Deborah Hodges, Sandy Masters and Evelyn Johnson of Dartmouth College. The contribution of my wife, Jennifer, from the inception to the conclusion of this study, is incalculable.

Financial support for various aspects of this study was generously provided by research grants from the Rockefeller Foundation, the Ford Foundation, The National Endowment for the Humanities and Dartmouth College. The Fulbright Program, by awarding me a Visiting Professorship in 1978–9, made it possible for me to remain in Nigeria and complete the first stage of the research. In 1981, the Center for International Affairs at Harvard University made their facilities available for unhurried reflection and writing. Finally, the many Africanist colleagues who listened to different aspects of this study at seminars and conferences during the four years of its gestation will now, I hope, derive some reward for their patience and encouragement.

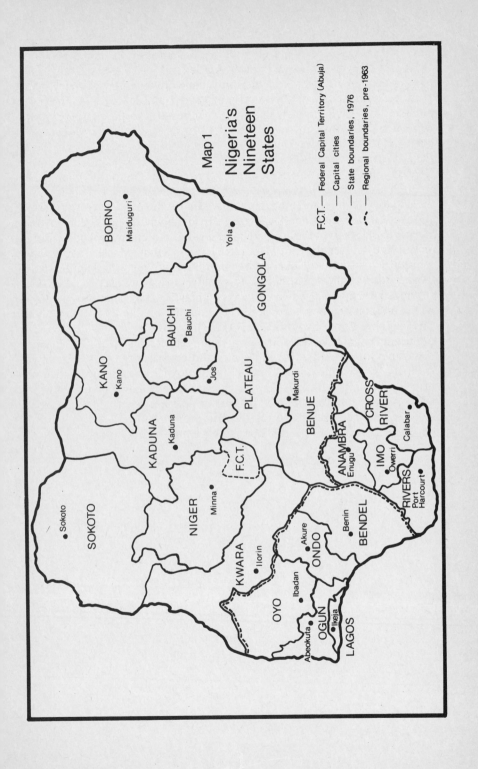

Map 1

Nigeria's
Nineteen
States

F.C.T. — Federal Capital Territory (Abuja)
● — Capital cities
〜 — State boundaries, 1976
〈 — Regional boundaries, pre-1963

1

Introduction

What is the nature of the fundamental processes of Nigerian political life? That is the question this study will attempt to answer. The further question of whether any renewed experiment with democratic party politics will succeed depends, ultimately, on whether such a system can be brought into congruence with these processes, and provide a means of transcending some of their harmful aspects. The arguments advanced here should apply to any political order, military or civilian, which might be imposed or attempted in Nigeria, whether the Second Republic of 1979–83 or its sequels. One basic contention of this study is that fruitful discussions about Nigeria's present and future depend upon a prior understanding of the nature, extent and persistence of a certain mode of political behavior, and of its social and economic ramifications.

Politics, as is often asserted, is fundamentally about the struggle over scarce resources. In some countries, that struggle is not focused in a continuous and insistent way on the state itself. Power, status and the major economic goods can often be procured through a variety of paths and from a multiplicity of sources. In Nigeria, however, the state has increasingly become a magnet for all facets of political and economic life, consuming the attention of traders, contractors, builders, farmers, traditional rulers, teachers, as much as that of politicians or politically motivated individuals in the usual senses of these terms. One important aim of this study, therefore, will be to elaborate a conceptual notion–prebendalism–which seems most appropriate for explaining the centrality in the Nigerian polity of the intensive and persistent struggle to control and exploit the *offices* of the state.

Any perceptive individual who listens closely to the commentaries by Nigerians, or to resident observers of Nigerian life, will quickly understand a certain logic about the dominant socio-political system:

> A man who supports the party in office will be rewarded with contracts for official projects, enabling him to pass on largesse to those further down the line who look to him for generosity.

> The system helps those in power to perpetuate their rule because they are at the fountainhead of wealth.[1]

1

Instead of formulating two quite different sets of statements, one by able journalists and another by social scientists, one of the aims of this study will be to develop and apply concepts which derive directly from – and can be applied without obfuscation to – the known experiential record of Nigerian political and economic life. My discussions about state power, class formation, ethnicity, patron-client ties and access to economic resources can be seen in one sense as filling out, in more formalized language, the fundamental understanding of the political process in Nigeria which guides the behavior of political actors and yields reasonable expectations concerning their actions.

The evidence adduced in support of the arguments advanced in this study will be of varying sorts: commentaries of other scholars, utterances of important political actors, data and reports of government and parastatal agencies. A specific decision was made to leave for the later chapters a discussion of the return to party politics in 1978–9 and to begin with the more problematic, but crucial, task of explaining what is perceived to be the underlying dynamic of that political life. Such a project leaves ample space for the conducting of survey research to test some of the hypotheses advanced, or to discover how arguments which apply generally can be explained in the light of more localized circumstances. The progress of social science depends on periodic attempts being made to formulate a systemic approach which can pull together the essential of accumulated micro-studies.

A NOTE ON COMPOSITION

This book was written in an order different from that in which the research was conducted. (It can also be read in different ways depending on the degree of interest of readers in the theoretical explorations as contrasted with the more empirical discussions.) The study of Nigerian party politics of 1978–9, discussed in Part III, was the real germination of the work. The intuitive recognition that the nature of party formation and recruitment was rooted in the dynamics of Nigerian societies motivated the exploration of those dynamics as set forward in Part II. This exploration took the unexpected form of a theoretical disquisition because what was problematic was no longer the nature of these dynamics – briskly stated in the first pages of Chapter 5 – but how this interpretation of Nigerian society related to the existing theoretical literature on "plural societies" and on the phenomena of clientelism and patrimonialism.

Reflections on democratic theory and on Nigeria's prior experiences with democratic government and party politics, which constitute Part I, made inevitable an examination of the alternative to these democratic experiments, namely the period of military rule from 1966 to 1979. It can be argued that those thirteen years were the most decisive in the shaping of the contemporary Nigerian polity. The major features of Nigerian government from the beginning of the civil war hostilities to the return to civil rule, i.e. the break-up of the regions into states and the concurrent centralization of power in the

2

federal government, the predominance of two bureaucratic corps, military and civil service, and the widening role of the state in the economy with the use of petroleum revenues, all served to alter greatly the context in which political power would be exercised when the civilians returned to the helm. Whereas the polity had undergone a geologic structural shift since 1966, however, the politicians could be little distinguished in their behavior from their predecessors (and in many cases their earlier selves) who had been ousted by the soldiers thirteen years previously. Moreover, the same could be said of the expectations of the Nigerian public regarding how their votes should yield immediate dividends to their communities and themselves in the apportioning of the "national cake."

If there is an abrupt transition from the discussion of the politics and economics of military rule in Part II to the frenetic process of party formation in Part III, such a transition partly mirrors the reality of that period. The re-civilianizing regime of General Olusegun Obasanjo (1976–9) was so skeptical of the ability of politicians to do any more than return the country to the days of electoral fraud, personality clashes, and ethnic conflicts, that it delayed the return to party politics until one year before power would be handed over to a successor regime (and ten months before a series of five national elections would be held). It is surely an anomaly that three years, 1975–8, would be devoted to the fashioning of a constitution for the Second Republic and less than a year to the legal phase of the creation of parties which had to organize and campaign for power – after a 13-year hiatus – in a country of 100 million citizens.

The elections of 1983 are discussed in Part IV in some detail because they throw much light on the ways in which power was exercised during the Second Republic. The decline in the moral stature, political thought and policy proposals of all the parties during the four years since the 1979 elections is starkly apparent. In writing those chapters I had returned to the starting point of my initial research project, i.e. of studying party and electoral politics. This time, however, it was largely a case of recording the nature of a system in decay, a democracy whose very name had become synonymous with austerity, insecurity and corruption. Finally, in the conclusion I return to where the roots of the Nigerian dilemma can be traced, namely, to the interaction between the fundamental social dynamics of the nation's constituent communities and the politics of the public arena.

DEMOCRACY IN NIGERIA

It may at first glance appear arbitrary to have chosen to discuss the political sociology of Nigeria within the context of democratic government. Yet, democracy is not a concern that has simply been imposed on Nigeria from without, although there is certainly a connection between that commitment and the official ideology of the former colonial power. More pertinently, it will be contended here that the underlying political and social system in Nigeria yields a continuing concern with how interests are represented and benefits distributed. The struggle against colonial rule included a demand for direct political representation and a rejection of the monopolization of state power by foreign rulers and their affiliated local agents. A further demand was that the economic product of the territory should be directly utilized for the benefit of indigenous producers rather than appropriated to meet the metropolitan needs of the colonial power and the many foreign firms. Government of, by and for the people was therefore a fundamental principle of the anti-colonial struggle, despite the fact that it is a principle which has been so much abused since independence by indigenous regimes. The unfulfilled demand for a democratic political process, together with a deep concern about the inequitable sharing of public wealth, will continue to render democratic theory and practice of great relevance to Africa.

Such a process of democratization will simultaneously include political and economic dimensions. In Nigeria, the presence of competitive regional and ethnic blocs of the population, a contest complicated by differences in language, religion and level of economic attainment, have rendered the issue of revenue allocation one of uncommon intensity. It is not a matter of chance that three of the most contentious issues in Nigeria in recent years have a common thread: the actual size of the population and its spacial distribution, the desirable number and size of the constituent states of the Federation, and the most equitable revenue allocation system. Each of these three issues can be shown to be linked to the struggle for an ever-greater share in state-power by individuals and groups and for access to the important resources controlled by the state. Nigerians are compelled to pursue democracy for the very reason that they are unable to rely on any government – or agency of the government – in which their particular subgroup of the population is not directly and effectively represented.

Such a contention can be further discussed in light of the debate among Western academics on the need to revise the normative provisions of "classical democracy" as well as the more recent discussions concerning consociational democracy. The gap between the preference for democratic procedures, and the still-limited development of a sense of nationhood in Nigeria, has been bridged by reliance on consociational practices of one sort or another. Indeed, the primary reformulation of the notion of consociations has been traced to David Apter and his attempt to categorize the pre-independence sharing of federal power in Nigeria. Since a number of political scientists have referred to Nigerian experiences in their writings without being quite certain how extensive or genuine has been its consociational arrangements, the opportunity has been taken to comment as broadly as possible on this debate and its relevance to actual developments in Nigeria.

Democracy will therefore be shown in this study to be not as gratuitous a choice of a political system as might initially be assumed. What Crawford Young states about egalitarianism in Africa applies with the same force to democracy as a political creed:

4

In one way or another, the public doctrine of the modern state, in Africa as elsewhere, sanctifies the status of all citizens, and in recent years this doctrine has been extended beyond mere legal equality to include social and economic dimensions.[2]

It will be argued here that there is a certain ineluctability about democratic justifications of rulership. Moreover, such justifications cannot indefinitely be consigned to the realm of rhetoric. At some point, someone is going to demand democracy in political and economic fact, rather than merely in words. Furthermore, in the contemporary African context there is always a multitude of persons who are ready to step outside their frail life-situation and rise to battle for such a cause. So a key answer to the question of "Why Democracy?" rests, paradoxically, on the inadequacy of other available claims to the legitimate exercise of power in the contemporary world. And such a measure of legitimacy is not just an abstract notion that has been inherited from Western liberalism: it continues to make and break governments.

CLASS AND ETHNICITY

The dominant pattern of political behavior we find in Nigeria can be defined, on the one hand, in terms of the incessant pressures on the state and the consequent fragmentation, or what I have called prebendalizing, of state-power. On the other hand, such practices can also be shown to be related to a certain articulation of the factors of class and ethnicity. In order to come to grips with the essentials of Nigerian politics, it is necessary to develop a clearer formulation of the dynamic interaction between these two social categories. Moreover, the most problematic aspect of this discussion will be the delineation of ethnicity, since the ways in which class interests are pursued will be shown to involve, to an important degree, the emphasizing of ethnic symbols and boundaries in the struggle for wealth and power.

One of the major hurdles to be overcome in defining and addressing the phenomenon of ethnicity is attitudinal in nature. The notion has become deeply embedded in conflicting ideological frameworks, among both political scientists and political actors. An attempt will be made in this study to move beyond these opposed attitudes. On the one hand, there are those who contend that African politics (Nigeria being a particularly salient case) is primarily "ethnic politics" and that certain "primordial" identities inevitably determine political affiliations and intergroup relations. On the other hand, an approach which has been greatly influenced by Marxism considers ethnicity to be a dependent variable (the real motivating force being class formation), a form of "false consciousness" in which ethnic consciousness is superimposed over the interests of the masses and thus serves to camouflage the more fundamental and "objective" interests of competing classes.

In Part II of the book, a discussion of my perspective on ethnicity will be included. Subsequent to the completion of that exercise, the consultation of

5

works recommended by a colleague made it evident that political science and political anthropology have now converged in their understanding of ethnicity in contemporary Africa. The insights of Abner Cohen and David Parkin, in particular, are worth summarizing as they correspond in many ways to the arguments advanced in this book. Parkin acknowledges that there are often two perspectives regarding ethnic relations: those by outside analysts and those by the people we study who "make their own abstractions."[3] We need to be mindful of this second dimension, i.e. the self-definition of groups, because ethnicity is basically a "cultural system denoting group boundaries."[4] Moreover, the very fact of participating within such boundaries means sharing certain patterns of interaction using specific channels of communication.[5] Ethnicity is therefore "fundamentally a political phenomenon... It is a type of informal interest grouping" which is called into being as a result of the "intensive struggle between groups over new strategic positions within the structure of the new state."[6]

There is now precious little difference between the views of Cohen and Parkin as cited above and those of a noted student of African politics such as Crawford Young, who contends

> The rapid growth of cities creates social arenas where competition for survival is intense, and where the consciousness of other groups locked in combat for the same resources deepens.

> The importance of scarcity of resources and competition for status in the crystallization of contemporary identities can hardly be overstated.[7]

Abner Cohen identifies some of these resources which ethnic groups are mobilized to capture: "places of employment, taxation, funds for development, education, political positions."[8] On such a basis, we should therefore expect an intensification, and widening of the geographical range, of ethnically defined conflicts as more individuals are brought into situations of competitive interaction, especially in the absence of equally adaptable or attractive countervailing patterns of group identity and mobilization. By regarding ethnic groups as capable of functioning as informal interest groups, and as involving elements of rational goal-oriented behavior as well as affective attitudes, it becomes possible to analyze them as we do more structured and specific interest groups, bearing in mind, of course, their special advantages and attractiveness "in situations of political conflict or competition."[9]

What is particularly useful for our purposes about these congruent perspectives on ethnicity is that they connect directly with the most pressing questions regarding the state and politics in contemporary Africa. Ethnicity is regarded as "one type of political grouping within the framework of the modern state."[10] As an informal grouping, it cannot be expected to function in the same way as more formal organizations such as trade unions, farmer collectives, professional associations and chambers of commerce. Yet, it owes its continued vitality to the keen nature of the struggle for power and resources in a context of scarcity, insecurity and a lack of confidence in official norms and regulations. The widespread Nigerian view of the state as an entity composed of strategic offices which can be captured as the outcome of a competitive process – openly electoral or through the power of numbers and their collective influence – gives renewed purpose to the constantly evolving networks of region, ethnicity and religion. The special advantages of ethnicity in the communicating and insulating of political messages,[11] and in combining "an interest with an affective tie,"[12] suggest that we may now have the conceptual insights needed to lift our discussion of the politicization of ethnicity from the realm of competing ideologies.

An inquiry into the nature of the dynamic interaction of class and ethnicity takes us quickly beyond the normal purview of anthropologists. The study of the politics of African nations requires an examination of patterns of interaction which transcend any ethnic group, however loosely defined. Furthermore, such studies usually involve a concern with the horizontal ties established among individuals in the pursuit of influence over the national sources of economic power. What many scholars have discovered is that Africans today, in attending to their daily interests, are able to choose among a number of associational modes. If an individual can combine membership in a chamber of commerce with participation in a political organization which invests the pursuit of secular objectives with cultural meaning, such an individual is acting in a most rational and even "modern" fashion. To assert dogmatically that a choice should be made by a businessman or laborer between a class mode of behavior and a more vertically oriented pattern of relations is to ask such individuals to substitute an abstract rationality for an experiential one.

There is little disputing the fact that individuals at the top of the social hierarchy benefit disproportionately from the prevailing mode of interest-association. Yet, while making such an assertion, we should not overlook the fact that support for these arrangements is generated at *all* levels of the hierarchy. Crawford Young's use of the term "instrumentalities of survival"[13] is most appropriate and coincides with the arguments I shall advance regarding the pronounced tendency in Nigeria for individuals to seek support from their better-placed kinfolk in the pursuit of the most basic of economic and political goods. It is therefore necessary to correct the tendency to underemphasize the part played by non-elites in Africa in sustaining certain dominant patterns of socio-political behavior even though they seem to benefit so little from it. A different system might certainly be more to their advantage. The task of winning their support for such a change, however, requires the supplanting of attitudes and informal social networks which are *believed* to be as necessary to getting ahead in modern society as are the licences, scholarships and contracts which represent the most visible milestones of success and survival.

PREBENDAL POLITICS

The task of justifying the use of a new conceptual notion, or the revival of an old one, in the social sciences, should be squarely confronted by any scholar who advances it. In this case, the duty is rendered less daunting by the fact that anyone who understands and speaks perceptively about the struggle for economic and political power in Nigeria can be shown to be talking about prebendal politics. While the concept may be unfamiliar, the essence of political and social life in Nigeria to which it refers will be easily recognized by Nigerians and students of Nigeria. The historical association of the term "prebend" with the offices of certain feudal states which could be obtained through services rendered to a lord or monarch, or through outright purchase by supplicants, and then administered to generate income for their possessors, will be discussed in Part II. As used in this study, the adjective "prebendal" will refer to patterns of political behaviour which rest on the justifying principle that such offices should be competed for and then utilized for the personal benefit of office holders as well as of their reference or support group. The official public purpose of the office often becomes a secondary concern, however much that purpose might have been originally cited in its creation or during the periodic competition to fill it.

There are a number of questions which are immediately provoked by the use of the term "prebendal" to refer to Nigerian political practices. Where, it may be asked, does this prebendal pattern come from? How, and especially how extensively, does it operate? Finally, what are its consequences for the state, for the economy and for the future political and social progress of Nigeria? Any attempt to respond to the first question cannot perforce be conclusive. Just how far back one is prepared to go in history, how deeply one feels competent to examine social practices and even personal and group psychology, will determine how complex and elaborate are the answers that are produced. What might be profitably pursued by others is the important question of how the specific social practices of different cultural groups relate to the more general ones of prebendal politics. Comparative studies of various African states should also produce informative commentaries, since it will be readily seen by specialists of other regions of Africa how much the practices discussed correspond to those evident elsewhere. One specific aspect of Nigerian social life which will be explored more fully in this book is the way in which patron-client relations provide a sustaining framework for prebendal politics. Such a discussion will be presented within the general theoretical framework advanced, as it is crucial to understand how the factors of class and ethnicity have become linked together in a mutually reinforcing way by the widespread phenomenon of clientelism.

My response to the question of how extensively prebendal politics operates in Nigeria will include the provision of multiple examples throughout the text of instances of this practice in national and local life. An essay by Douglas Rimmer, which covers succinctly many of the points I shall explore in

Chapter 5, illustrates quite forcefully the argument earlier advanced that anyone who speaks knowledgeably and perceptively about Nigerian politics – or political economy – must at some point explain the prevalent nature of prebendal attitudes to government and the public power.[14] Rimmer contends that after 1945 the prime function of the Nigerian state became that of promoting improvements in the "material welfare" of the people and, as a consequence, "suasion of the state or its agencies was critical for all who had welfare to be promoted."[15] Such a consideration applied as much to the building of schools, the setting of wage-levels, as it did to the launching of private businesses: "political lobbying became a condition of commercial success ... the fortunes of a business community, or occupational group could depend heavily on political favor."[16]

The above statements can be regarded as succinct conclusions about which few will now disagree. The second stage of the exposition is that in explaining such occurrences the elements of an implicit theory of prebendal politics must be advanced. Here is Rimmer's version:

> the regional governments modeled their conduct on that of independent states. Each was concerned to cut what it could from the collective cake and to defend its own bakings from neighbouring depredations. This conduct was replicated at the local level and indeed was encouraged there by the political system in which parties and individual politicians represented themselves as the patrons of communities, both protectors and benefactors ...[17]

> Development policies became associated at almost every level with graft. For the most part the graft was "solidaristic". Either directly or through the medium of the parties, men in authority benefitted their supporters and home communities by provisions of amenities, misappropriation of funds, and nepotism in appointments. They received fealty and delivered largesse.[18]

> public economic power and patronage were valued mainly as instruments of distribution ... Appointments to public office (particularly ministerial and in the public corporations) were therefore decisive, and the dominant purpose of electoral activity was to control such preferment.[19]

What I intend to do in going beyond such statements is to develop a suitable conceptual approach and terminology. I shall try to build a model in which the interaction of the various relevant social processes will be delineated, thereby permitting us to achieve a fuller and deeper knowledge of these phenomena, as well as to highlight the possibilities and constraints they represent for Nigeria's future.

Nigeria's prolonged experience with military government, from 1966 to 1979, will be examined to see what attempts were made to transcend the prevailing system of representing group interests and distributing state-controlled resources. The nature of the political and constitutional reforms implemented by the three successive military regimes will be examined, as will the rapid expansion of the economy after the civil war. Special attention will be devoted in that survey to the drive for greater state direction and intervention in the economy, based on the leverage accrued to the state apparatus by the centralization of revenues from petroleum production. One further concept introduced at that point, because of the overwhelming role which the state assumed as a source of investment funds and even private income, is that of the "entrepôt state." My conceptualizing of the "entrepôt state" is a direct enlargement upon Terisa Turner's discussion of the *rentier* state in Nigeria, and of the state as a "market."[20]

DEMOCRACY AND PREBENDAL POLITICS

Popular support has remained an important factor in Nigerian politics, although subsets of the population – politicians, contractor/traders, soldiers, civil bureaucrats – may wrest a strategic role in mediating between the basic interests of the people (often manipulating and recasting them) and the instruments of the state, the national economy and foreign investors. The system of prebendal politics enables divergent groups and constituencies to seek to accommodate their interests. At the level of the individual, it is a pattern of social behavior that is quickly learned and accepted. It would be more comforting to say that it works because it is efficient, and that it is a rational and productive method of minimizing social costs and maximizing benefits. Unfortunately, such claims cannot be made: the system persists although it seldom satisfies such criteria. It is often wasteful, unproductive, and contributes to the increasing affluence of a relative few, paltry gains for a larger number, and misery for the great majority of the people. Since it is a self-justifying system which grants legitimacy to a pattern of persistent conflict, and since its *modus operandi* is to politicize ethnic, regional and linguistic differences, it serves to make the Nigerian polity a simmering cauldron of unresolvable tensions over which a lid must regularly be clamped, and just as regularly removed. Sisyphus would recognize a similar predicament to his own in Nigeria's political and social life.

During the first nine years of military rule (1966–75), civil servants came to play an increasingly central part in governing Nigeria. One of the aims of the 1975 *coup d'état* was indeed to reduce the predominance of the higher ranks of the bureaucracy and to check its abuses of power. Bureaucratic rule will be shown in Chapter 6 to be a consequence not only of the displacement of politicians by soldiers but also of the centralization of power in the federal capital, Lagos. Other contributing factors to the elevation of the bureaucracy were the vast increase in size of the public sector, the special circumstances of the civil war, and the increased commitment after that war to state-directed economic expansion. Of particular interest will be the ways in which the civil bureaucracy represented a temporary counter-force to prebendal politics but which inevitably succumbed to its resurgence.

Democratic politics and prebendal politics are two sides of the same coin in Nigeria: each can be turned over to reveal the other. At the beginning of Chinua Achebe's widely read novel, *A Man of the People*, the narrator Odili reflects ruefully while watching the crowd of dancers awaiting the arrival of the politician and Government minister, Chief M. A. Nanga:

> They were not only ignorant but cynical. Tell them that this man had used his position to enrich himself and they would ask you – as my father did – if you thought that a sensible man would spit out the juicy morsel that good fortune placed in his mouth.[21]

A little while later, Odili is himself subjected to the double-barrelled (individual/communal) justification for prebendalism by the Honourable Nanga:

> I think you are wasting your talent here. I want you to come to the capital and take up a strategic post in the civil service. We shouldn't leave everything to the highland tribes. My secretary is from there; our people must press for their fair share of the national cake.[22]

I shall explore what alternatives there appear to be to prebendal politics including those of "corrective" military government already attempted. During periods of civilian rule, as we shall see, there are no adequate countervailing mechanisms or processes to those of prebendalism. In the conclusion I shall return to the general theoretical discussion of Parts I and II with new and broader insights. The answer to Nigeria's dilemma, when it emerges, will involve a transcending of the system of social and political practices examined in these pages. An imposed resolution from the top will necessarily require considerable repression. Such a dénouement cannot easily be countenanced by anyone who admires the acquired freedoms of Nigerians in speech, the press, the judiciary, and political association, especially considering the striking absence of such freedoms in most other contemporary African states. If this exercise contributes in some way to a better understanding of Nigeria's political cauldron, then it will be only part of the vast effort needed to transcend the stultifying embrace of democracy and prebendal politics.

Part I

The problem of democracy

2

A democracy that works

There are regular attempts by scholars to devise a term that would be more precise than "democracy," or to forego its use altogether. Most participants in Nigerian politics, as most educated people the world over, would understand implicitly the core meaning of this sentence: "The gradual transfer of power from the military to elected citizens in Nigeria was meant to democratize the political system," although they might differ greatly if asked to identify the most fundamental element of this democratization. It obviously has something to do with the people, the greater mass of the people, the *demos*, but just what is that something is always open to a wide range of interpretation and emphasis. We have here a concept or notion that is general and fluid yet has a predictable emotive and judgmental impact.

ESSENTIALS OF DEMOCRATIC GOVERNMENT

During the period of transition from military rule in 1975–9, Nigerians who participated in that process chose a form of government which will be shown to qualify for the denomination "democratic" in several respects. Such a choice involves a further pattern of selection from among the available theories and practices of democratic government.

Robert A. Dahl, who has made numerous contributions to the study and theory of democratic politics, came to be dissatisfied with the term "democracy." He has attempted to have "polyarchy" adopted in its place.[1] Such a substitution has not taken full root, even among political scientists who share Dahl's general approach. It is interesting, therefore, that the definition of "democracy" suggested by Dahl is so reductive that if we accepted it we would then have little reason to retain it:

> I assume that a key characteristic of a democracy is the continuing responsiveness of the government to the preferences of its citizens, considered as political equals... I should like to reserve the term 'democracy' for a political system, one of the characteristics of which is the quality of being completely or almost completely responsive to all of its citizens.[2]

It is odd that democracy should be limited to a system "completely or almost

15

completely responsive" when the criterion of responsiveness is viewed by notable students of democracy as "vague and ambiguous."[3] It seems an overly convenient way to dispense with the term democracy, by pinning its fortunes to the more problematic notion of responsiveness: "It would be highly unrealistic to think that government acts simply in response to wants and demands. And it would be circular to contend that it *should* be responsive to demands that it may itself have engendered."[4]

This emphasis on "responsiveness" can also be seen to differ significantly from that of another school of political writing: "The immediate objective of classical democracy has always been to extend the opportunity for individuals to take an equal and an effective part in the management of public affairs."[5] The concern expressed here is for direct participation in government, not the responsiveness of the government to the governed. From the standpoint of Dahl and many American political scientists, the right to participate involves the freedom to express preferences, to make claims on government, and to have them taken equally into account. Dahl gives another criterion – public contestation – which he views as synonymous with such terms as liberalization, competitive politics and public opposition. Government responsiveness, according to his thinking, can really be seen as a probable outcome if the right to participate in making preferences, to compete, and to express opposition are guaranteed.

The liberal view of democracy usually embraces such notions as popular sovereignty, consent, equality and representative government. "Almost all Americans," it has been claimed, "accept these four elements: popular consent, political equality, majority rule, and popular consultation as the foundation of democracy."[6] The same authors do not attempt to settle a contradiction which they identify: the ultimate example of public participation – namely, direct democracy in small New England communities – proves on examination to be something of a "myth" when an analysis is made of the character of such procedures and their consequences for public policy.[7] Yet, they can also affirm from empirical studies that "Americans support, almost unthinkingly, reforms that enhance opportunities for citizens' participation in the policy making process... They believe the representative democracy of the large constituency to be an imperfect and unnatural version of true democracy."[8] I shall refer time and again to this fundamental tension between the participatory norm of democracy, even as popularly perceived, and the more "pragmatic" tendency to use the term solely to refer to "a process for making political decisions."[9]

Radical theorists often do not share this particular uncertainty about the fundamental meaning of democracy. For C. B. Macpherson, "democracy originally meant rule by the common people, the plebians. It was very much a class affair; it meant the sway of the lowest and largest class."[10] The notion of human equality implicit in this concept – namely, that no person should dominate another – took the form during the nineteenth century of the socialist ideal of a classless society. It is significant, therefore, that critics of the redefinition of democracy by modern Western social scientists should be particularly concerned with the latter's elimination of the need for, and desirability of, "popular political activity."[11] It can be suggested that the requirement of some method of direct participation cannot be evaded without evading the concept of democracy entirely. James Madison saw the democratic ideal (what he called a "pure democracy") as "a society consisting of a small number of citizens, who assemble and administer the government in person."[12] As a consequence, he viewed the emerging American system as a republic rather than a democracy, involving as it did "the delegation of the government... to a small number of citizens elected by the rest."[13]

With regard to Africa, Thomas Hodgkin has written of the greater influence on parties during the nationalist era of the "revolutionary-democratic tradition in Western political thought." According to Hodgkin,

the central concept of 'democracy' has normally been understood in its classic sense as meaning, essentially, the transfer of political and other forms of power from a small ruling European class to the mass of the African people... the African *demos*.[14]

From such a viewpoint, "the various institutions of government – cabinet, parliament, judiciary, civil service, local councils – may undergo relatively little modification in formal structure."[15] The democratizing of the state is to be found, instead, in the "new meaning" given to these institutions "once they become the organs through which the party, with its allied organizations, and thus the people, seek to realize their collectively agreed purposes."[16] The subsequent history of what became known as "single party democracy" in Africa fell considerably short of this expectation.

After independence, the insistence on real participation – not derivative or consequential – did fuel demands in Africa for new and appropriate structures for involving the *demos*. Both arch foes of the single party and arch proponents of the "democratic single party" staked their central claim on the need to facilitate the direct participation of all citizens. W. Arthur Lewis wanted the people of all segments of the population to be "represented in decision making," which convinced him of the necessity for coalition politics in Africa.[17] Julius Nyerere, in his attempt to debunk what he saw as the pretentious claims of Western democracies, argued that in a single party which was identified with the nation as a whole, all the people would have more of a say in directly selecting the individuals who would undertake the tasks of government, than if their energies were diverted into the ruinous game of party politics.[18] While it is not pertinent at this stage to evaluate such conflicting suggestions, it is important to indicate the continued relevance of the normative or prescriptive side of democracy – especially the pursuit of the most effective mode of popular participation – in debates about African government. Such a normative dimension will be shown in later chapters to be linked directly to the popular desire in Nigeria for social identification with individuals actually executing government policies.

17

Democracy and prebendal politics

REVISIONISM AND ITS CRITICS

It was inevitable that with the decisive shift in political science to an emphasis on how people actually behave politically, and how governments really perform, some basic ideas of democratic theory would either have to be abandoned or drastically revised. When a scholar of the traditional school of democratic thought is contrasted with a modern figure, the shift in emphasis and concern becomes starkly apparent:

> LORD BRYCE: [Democracy is] government in which the will of the majority of qualified citizens rules.
> JOHN PLAMENATZ: Democratic government means government by persons freely chosen by and responsible to the governed.[19]

In a categorical manner, J. A. Schumpeter tried to put to rest once and for all the seemingly metaphysical notions about how democracy serves the will and seeks the common good of the people, ideas which are subject to endless disputation. Democracy for him is an institutional process which is subject to verification as to whether it does or does not exist:

> The democratic method is that institutional arrangement for arriving at political decisions in which individuals acquire the power to decide by means of a competitive struggle for the people's vote.[20]

What was important for Schumpeter was the "vital fact of leadership," not paeans to the initiative of the people. The latter's primary function as an electorate was "to produce government." It was possible to deal frankly now with the question not just of leadership but, more strongly, of rulership in contemporary industrial societies. The trio of nineteenth-century demurrers from democratic, and especially democratic-socialist, optimism with regard to governing structures – i.e., Pareto, Mosca and Michels – were available to lend weight to the new concern with the behavior of elites and especially the new fundamental (and sufficient) requirement of open competition among them. What Schumpeter argued can be shown to have been earlier sketched by Max Weber:

> the term 'democratization' can be misleading. The *demos* itself, in the sense of an inarticulate mass, never 'governs' larger associations; rather, it is governed, and its existence only changes the way in which the executive leaders are selected and the measure of the influence which the *demos*, or better, which social circles from its midst are able to exert upon the content and direction of administrative activities.[21]

As was to be expected, the concept of democracy – indeed the *ideology of democracy* – has been too strong to be put so easily to rest. Critics have since charged that the revisionists sought to change democratic theory from its normative function of setting goals – and more practically, setting guidelines – to the more prosaic task of describing one particular form of government – that to which the revisionists subscribed.[22] If the facts of Western democracies with regard to the demonstrated role of the people – especially as they concern the degree of rationality of the voter, the level of

18

political participation of most citizens, and the actual decision-making process – could not be reconciled with democratic prescriptions, then those prescriptions had to be jettisoned. In their place elaborate models of democracy as corresponding to the prevailing competitive system among oligarchical elites, through the mechanism of periodic elections, could now be substituted.

WHY DEMOCRACY?

A significant proportion of national wealth was directly invested between 1975 and 1979 by the Nigerian Federal Government – or through a variety of avenues by private institutions – for the purpose of re-establishing a system of government that has failed far more often than it has succeeded in the developing world. What can justify that? Of the 29 countries that Dahl classified in 1970–1 as having progressed towards establishing "polyarchies," five can be identified as belonging to the "Third World."[23] Of these five – Chile, Uruguay, the Philippines, Costa Rica and India – only Costa Rica has not experienced since then a period of authoritarian rule. It is unnecessary to try and draw up such a list for Africa. Prior to the 1979 transitions from military to civilian rule in Ghana and Nigeria, only the relatively small states of Botswana, Mauritius and The Gambia could be called democratic without the necessity of affixing a list of qualifying adjectives.[24]

So why should Nigeria and Nigerians have bothered with returning to a political system which has such a poor endurance record in developing countries? Let us go back to Schumpeter. Since he was convinced that the classical tenets of democracy were inapplicable, and even in contradiction to the basic facts of political life, he tried his hand at enumerating the reasons for the survival of the doctrine. The four reasons he identified can be summarized as follows: the historical association of democracy with religious belief; the association of the forms and phrases of classical democracy with certain events and developments in a people's history; the fact that in some small and primitive societies the democratic doctrine actually fits the facts; and finally, that politicians appreciate democratic phraseology even while "crushing opponents in the name of the people."[25]

None of these four reasons can explain the most recent experiment with democratic practices in Nigeria. The one marginal exception is Schumpeter's second reason, since Nigerians do have "events and developments in their history which were enthusiastically approved by large majorities." Yet, since the outcome of such events in recent times includes the abuse of governmental power, corruption, falsification of voting results, political violence and finally civil war, it is difficult to pin an abiding faith in democracy on them.

A writer who has some interesting insights into this question is Juan Linz. His essay on the authoritarian regime in Brazil deals with a country for whom the question "Why Democracy?" has loomed as persistently as it has in Nigeria under military rule. Linz seems to place central importance on the ideological component – i.e., the expressed reasons, purposes and justifications for any existing political order.[26] What characterizes authoritarian regimes (a designation that would apply to most developing countries) is for Linz the absence of a "compelling ideology":

> Ultimately all authoritarian regimes face this legitimacy pull toward the polyarchical model, with political freedom for relatively full participation, or toward the committed, ideological single-party model.[27]

This explanation by Linz is a useful starting point because it shows a connection between the availability of a coherent ideology and the process of "institutionalization" – that is, only competitive party systems or "large-scale ideological mass parties" seem to have achieved a significant degree of institutionalization.[28] Linz adds, as a second-order explanation, the ideological impact that the most powerful countries – which typify one or another of the models – tend to have on the rest.[29] Such an argument is best left in abeyance, since the powerful countries often choose to foster regimes which do *not* look like them, especially when it comes to democratic practices.

One might, therefore, study the modern historical record of Nigeria very closely and not arrive at a better answer than that of Linz to a fundamental question: Why did the military regime appear to have only two long-term choices, and why did it opt for the more democratic of the two in 1975? Let us keep Linz's suggestion in mind, especially when the great "risk" represented by the deliberate relinquishing of authoritarian controls for competitive party politics in Nigeria is examined in subsequent chapters:

> the search for ultimate meaning, purpose, legitimacy and justice demands something beyond the adjustment of interest conflicts through bargaining. That is the ultimate difference between systems with and without political parties. Parties, while representing interests, also stand for a certain type of social order, or at least make that claim.[30]

An alternate explanation of "Why Democracy?" shifts the focus to the social and (especially) the economic realm. Liberal writers like Dahl might recognize some historical connection between competitive politics, a competitive economy and what he calls a "pluralistic social order," but such an observation is not made central to their analyses.[31] For Macpherson, however, the particular pattern of democratic government in Western societies results from the historical fact that it was preceded by the entrenchment of the competitive or market economy.[32] The process by which democracy was "liberalized" is a key one, for it ties together notions of capitalist development, class formation and class conflict, as well as such essentials of liberal democracy as competitive parties and majority rule. Macpherson identifies the essence of the liberal state as being

> the system of alternate or multiple parties whereby governments could be held responsible to different sections of the class or classes that had a political voice... The job of the competitive party system was to uphold the competitive market society by keeping the government responsive to the shifting majority interests of those who were running the market society.[33]

The choice by the leading elements in Nigerian society to re-establish a liberal democratic system, therefore, has specific implications for the structure of Nigeria's political economy. Such a decision also carries with it an implicit commitment – namely, that the claims of the poorer masses of the people will be accorded their "fully and fairly competitive place" within the institutions of the liberal state.[34] I will consider how such claims are capable of being manipulated, distorted and eventually incorporated into the strategies of members (or aspiring members) of the dominant class in Nigeria.

THE NON-DEMOCRATIC PATH

There is a wide body of theoretical writing in political science whose fundamental premise is that democracy is not a viable option, especially in the large and socially heterogeneous developing countries. Arend Lijphart, who has made a significant contribution to the study of democratic practices in "plural societies," began his important book with a needed understatement: "it is difficult to achieve and maintain stable democratic government."[35] Lijphart repeatedly emphasizes the need to challenge "the pervasively pessimistic mood of our times" regarding the prospects for democracy.[36] Before we get to the more contemporary dimensions of this "democratic pessimism," it is well to note that there is an established school of argument about the ways in which the segmentary nature of certain countries acts as an impediment to democratic politics. Lijphart cites one of the classic theorists of liberal government, as well as an influential modern social anthropologist, to demonstrate these assumptions about the cultural barriers to democracy:

> J. S. MILL: Free institutions are next to impossible in a country made up of different nationalities.
>
> M. G. SMITH: Cultural diversity or pluralism automatically imposes the structural necessity for domination by one of the cultural sections. It...necessitates nondemocratic regulation of group relationships.[37]

Despite these pitfalls or predispositions, countries which clearly share some of the least favorable conditions for democratic politics are still willing to take, and retake, "the gamble of democracy," to use Granville Austen's appropriate term for the Indian experience.[38] In so doing, their people are bucking the authoritarian current which has swept through Asia, Latin America, and now most of Africa, and are also failing to heed those political scientists who contend that they should not even undertake such a challenge. Anyone who is genuinely concerned with the deep and pervasive problem of authoritarianism and state terrorism in the developing world can understand Arthur Lewis's invective:

> As for our political scientists, they fall over themselves to demonstrate that democracy is suitable only for Europeans and North Americans, and in the sacred names of 'charisma' and 'modernization' and 'national unity', call upon us to admire any demagogue who, aided by a loud voice and a bunch of hooligans, captures the state and suppresses his rivals.[39]

21

One of the methods occasionally suggested for dealing with the political problems confronting any society is simply to eliminate politics and attend to public affairs by other means for as long as possible. Such a "solution" often suggests itself when the conflicts appear unmanageable: "The level of antagonism in political conflicts might decline if politics and government were to become less salient, less important as a source of advantages and disadvantages."[40] This perspective, as sketched by Dahl, has in fact constituted the central theme of the writings on political order and political change by Samuel Huntington. In place of the democratic norm of participation, "Depoliticization" becomes a more appropriate strategy. Nations can be categorized as civic polities or praetorian societies, the latter of which are "out-of-joint," where "all sorts of social forces and groups have become directly engaged in general politics."[41] While civic polities with "effective political institutions" can tolerate a high level of citizen and group participation, the same is not true of praetorian societies.[42] Participation in the latter must therefore be checked to enable institutionalization to proceed, often by military regimes which have intervened but which are often so hostile to politics that "with rare exceptions, they shrink from assuming the role of political organizer."[43]

It is clear that the Huntington model runs counter to any which positively emphasizes citizen and group participation. Indeed, he puts his conviction in the form of an axiom: "The stability of a praetorian society varies inversely with the scope of political participation."[44] This is reinforced by a perceived order of success in which "praetorian oligarchies may last centuries; middle-class systems, decades; mass praetorian systems usually only a few years."[45] There are a number of consequences which would follow if such verdicts were accepted – namely, an emphasis on the creation of an oligarchy or power elite, and a concern with the establishment of authoritative power structures (or "effective political institutions") enjoying a high degree of autonomy from the ebb and flow of popular demands.[46]

It is clearly no overstatement to contend that the democratic challenge in Nigeria runs directly counter to this influential pattern of thinking in Western political science. In a subsequent work, Huntington and Nelson affirm: "The liberal model of development . . . has turned out not to be a realistic or relevant choice for most modernizing countries."[47] Writing at a time in which Brazil has taken the first step towards democratization, and when Guatemala, El Salvador and Bolivia are at the forefront of concerns with state terrorism, it is pertinent to reflect on the normative inversion implicit in Huntington's remarks:

> The tragedy of a country like Brazil in the 1960s was that it was, in a sense, too developed to have either a Nasser or an Ataturk, its society too complex and varied to be susceptible to leadership by a military regime.[48]
>
> modernizing military regimes have come to power in Guatemala, El Salvador and Bolivia. But for Brazil it may be too late for military modernization and too late also for soldiers as institution-builders.[49]

22

Judging from the experiences of the countries Huntington commends, Brazilians as well as Nigerians might have good reason to seek alternatives to the reliance on soldiers as "institution-builders."

MAJORITY GOVERNMENT AND PARTY POLITICS

There are few procedural concepts that are as fundamental to liberal democratic thinking, yet which were so deeply troubling to early liberal thinkers and later democrats, as those related to the principle of majority rule. Along with the institutions and practices of liberal government, post-colonial societies have inherited the theoretical norm of majority government which they often find more difficult to exercise, and justify, than do Western democracies. It is significant, therefore, that it is in the very rethinking of the notion of majority rule that certain political scientists have rendered their analyses more pertinent to the concerns of developing societies.

The principle of majority rule was presented by John Locke as a rider to his social compact. By consenting to the establishment of a political community, the individual – according to Locke – implicitly consents to majority rule as a practical necessity:

> For when any number of men have, by the consent of every individual, made a community, they have thereby made that community one body, with a power to act as one body, which is only by the will and determination of the majority . . . It is necessary the body should move that way whither the greater force carries it, which is the consent of the majority.[50]

In the following century, the radical democrat Jean Jacques Rousseau found it necessary to move from his distinction between the general will and the aggregated will-of-all to an acknowledgement that if certain conditions are adhered to, such as full and free discussion and an absence of "partial societies," the general will can be arrived at by way of a majority vote.[51] Schumpeter, however, remained unconvinced and contends that the will of the majority is "the will of the majority and not the will of the people."[52]

A nineteenth-century liberal such as James Mill feared so much the abuse of power by those who controlled the weapon of majority rule that he portrayed even elected governments as consisting of potential predators who would govern in their own interest and contrary to that of the people, unless they could be kept in check by frequent replacement through elections.[53] In the United States, the doctrine of majority rule has similarly been treated with caution. James Madison was more concerned with the government's success in "balancing and adjusting sectional interests rather than responding automatically to a majority interest."[54] One of the great advantages in the United States was therefore the presence of "entrenched minorities" which would serve to check tyranny. In Madison's own words,

> Extend the sphere, and you take a greater variety of parties and interests; you make it less probable that a majority of the whole will have a common motive to invade the rights of other citizens.[55]

23

Prominent among subsequent American theorists who sought to discard the notion of majority rule, or what he called the "numerical majority," was John C. Calhoun. It is apparent that consociational democracy owes more to Calhoun than is usually made apparent. For Calhoun, it was not enough to rely on periodic elections, or institutional checks and balances "to counteract the tendency of government to oppression and abuse of power."[56] Instead, what was needed was "the adoption of some restriction or limitation which shall so effectively prevent any one interest or combination of interests from obtaining the exclusive control of the government."[57] Calhoun gave the name of "organism" or "concurrent majority" to such a system. "Concurrent minorities" might indeed be a more appropriate term, or even the concept of a "mutual veto" suggested by consociational theorists.

The challenge launched initially by some European political scientists to existing democratic theories, which they felt could not fully explain the practices in their smaller states, led them to the published series of lectures on West Africa by economist W. Arthur Lewis cited earlier. Lewis had launched in 1965 an incisive attack on the political parties and forms of political behavior that West African politicians had inherited from Europe, as well as on what he saw as the nefarious concept of majority rule. He called for a fundamental change in many aspects of the political process: the ways in which politicians thought and acted, the purposes of the parties they formed, the relationships established among contending political organizations during electoral competition, and the nature and practices of the post-independence governments.[58] He made a distinction between the kind of political behavior that was appropriate for Western "class societies," and that appropriate for African "plural societies."[59]

As quoted earlier, and regularly repeated by Lewis in his book, "the primary meaning of democracy... is the opportunity to be represented in decision-making."[60] A political system based on majority rule, in which the victorious party directs the government and the unsuccessful one opposes, violated for Lewis the fundamental rule of full participation for all. "Plural societies," he contended, cannot function peaceably if politics is regarded as a zero-sum game, which functions according to the "erroneous definition... that the majority is entitled to rule over the minority."[61] Lewis believed that "words like 'winning' and 'losing' have to be banished from the political vocabulary of a plural society."[62] While the system of competitive party politics should be retained, the main purpose of parties must no longer be "political warfare, which is tolerable in class but not in plural societies."[63]

Lewis called, finally, for "a fundamental change in political philosophy," according to which the aim of politicians will no longer be to "capture the government in order to benefit one group at the expense of another," but rather to represent the views of their sectional group of supporters and prepare to govern in coalition with the leaders of other parties and groups.[64] It has been necessary to present Lewis's views in some detail, despite their rather idealistic cast. If Nigeria, or any other African country, is to succeed in devising a democratic system that works, instead of simply reintroducing one of the systems which were rapidly collapsing as Lewis wrote in 1965, serious attention will have to be paid to the modification of those features of Western democracy which might exacerbate rather than attenuate conflicts of a sectional nature.

CONSOCIATIONAL DEMOCRACY: HOW RELEVANT TO AFRICA?

There is good reason to believe that major advances in democratic theory can be made by theorists working on the problems of developing societies. One of the major reformulations of democratic theory occurred when some Western political scientists, especially of the smaller European democracies, realized that their countries not only shared certain structural features of "Third World" societies, but that the most influential models of democratic government did not satisfactorily account for the ways in which their own systems of government had evolved. More specifically, some ideas expressed by David Apter about the Nigerian government of 1957–9 – namely, that authority was being exercised in ways that could be called "consociational" – served as a point of departure for the examination of such features (usually more entrenched and developed) in the smaller European democracies – in particular, Austria, Switzerland, the Netherlands and Belgium.[65]

One of the main elements of consociationalism is the recognition that the aims of democratic government sometimes require the modification of certain fundamental democratic practices. In a sense, consociationalism links up with the suggestions already noted in John Stuart Mill, M. G. Smith and of course Calhoun, that certain democratic objectives cannot be achieved via conventional routes in societies that are "deeply divided" or "segmented."[66] There was thus available to the consociationalists an existing body of reflections which they could elaborate and make the basis for their own analytical studies:

> ROBERT DAHL: [Intense conflicts] never seem to be handled for long by the normal political process employed in other kinds of issues. For this sort of conflict is too explosive to be managed by ordinary parliamentary opposition, bargaining, campaigning, and winning elections.[67]

> S. M. LIPSET: A stable democracy requires a situation in which the major political parties include supporters from many segments of the population. A system in which the support of different parties corresponds too closely to basic social divisions cannot continue to operate on a democratic basis, for it reflects a state of conflict so intense and clear-cut as to rule out compromise.[68]

For any government which operates on the basis of consociationalism, one persistent problem is inevitably that of being the easy target of criticism for its undemocratic features. Arend Lijphart indicates that this was obviously the case with the very effective grand coalition government in Austria

25

(1945–66).[69] Similarly, Nordlinger points not only to "the marriage of convenience" represented by this coalition, but to the fact that crucial decisions tended to be handled outside the cabinet altogether, among "a handful of top leaders."[70] In the case of Nigeria, such consociational practices are usually vehemently criticized as being "opportunist," the "ganging-up of parties," and "government by secret cabal." The consociational theorists, therefore, suggest ways of "making democracy work" in a country like Nigeria which are likely to be rejected there as being too blatantly undemocratic. Nordlinger frankly avows that his six proposed practices of conflict regulation "all negate, contradict, or modify the orthodox model of democratic decision-making."[71] And Lijphart addresses the specific philosophical dimension usually advanced to explain the compelling nature of democratic theory and ideals:

> The Anglo-American stable two-party system is... not only a particular empirical type of democracy, but also a *normative model* which may form an obstacle to alternative attempts to establish stable democracy.[72]

Can political actors in developing societies move away from the dominant "normative model" of democracy without simply replicating the "sham democracies" which have proliferated, with their paraphernalia of bogus parties, life-presidents and 98 per cent election results? That is a question always to be borne in mind as we examine the practices and principles put forward by the consociationalists. Central to these theories is the inadequacy of simple majoritarian systems for countries with sharp cultural divisions. For Nordlinger, each of the six conflict-regulating practices he identifies represents a departure from orthodox or pure majoritarianism. He believes that one or more of these "nonmajoritarian" formulas must be included in any democratic model devised for a "deeply divided society": (1) a stable governing coalition, (2) the principle of proportionality, (3) the mutual veto, (4) purposive depoliticization, (5) compromises on divisive issues, and (6) the practice of unilateral concessions.[73] Similarly, in language which recalls Arthur Lewis's arguments, Arend Lijphart contends that in these societies, "all decisions are perceived as entailing high stakes" for the different segments of the population, and so "strict majority rule places a strain on the unity and peace of the system."[74] The four characteristics of consociational democracy he identifies, therefore, also reflect a clear departure from majoritarianism: (1) government by grand coalition, (2) the exercise of mutual veto or "concurrent majority," (3) proportionality, and (4) "a high degree of autonomy for each segment to run its internal affairs."[75]

The link between the ideas of Arthur Lewis and those of the consociationalists can be found in the compelling need they identify of avoiding "winner takes all" politics, and the consequent danger of creating a permanent minority. Such a concern is also at the center of Nigerian politics. While there is no intention here to join the debate over consociationalism or to apply any of its existing models to Nigeria, there is still much to be gained from

26

contrasting the insights of these scholars with those which Nigerian political actors have arrived at independently in their search for appropriate democratic practices.

One of the first problems for Nigeria that can be recognized in consociationalism is reflected in its very definition. For Lijphart, it means "government by elite cartel designed to turn a democracy with a fragmented political culture into a stable democracy."[76] Indeed, most of the theorists of this school propose a highly oligarchical system, in which attention is focused primarily on the behavior of political elites and on their capacity to "establish a viable, pluralistic State by a process of mutual forebearance and accommodation."[77] In Part II, the issue of class formation and class action in Africa will be discussed. Here it can be asserted that it is partly because many political scientists do not examine the class implications of their thinking that categorical statements about "elite cartel" and elite predominance can be so bluntly suggested as fundamental to the achieving of a "stable democracy." In many parts of the world, questions would immediately be asked about who or what is to protect the masses of the people from these "elites" whose actions in the public domain are known to be often more rapacious than beneficial. There is a certain faith in the benevolent capacity of the dominant elements in segmented societies which many Nigerians, for example, would find difficult to accept:

> they alone can initiate, work out, and implement conflict regulating practices, therefore they alone can make direct and positive contributions to conflict regulating outcomes.

> A necessary condition is ... a form of structured relations between leaders and non-elites in which the leaders are clearly predominant and their demands regularly fulfilled.

> Leaders must enjoy extensive independent authority to take actions and make commitments without being accused of ignoring, dominating, or coercing their followers.[78]

The analyses undertaken by consociationalists of the European democracies have already undergone sharp modifications by other scholars. The historical dimension has been found troubling, with consociational practices often seen as the outcome of prior events which cannot easily be replicated.[79] Consociational arrangements have also been seen as largely transitional and even in three of the four most regularly cited cases to have already been largely dismantled.[80] Finally, Brian Barry has struck off from the list two of these four countries as having never really satisfied the consociational model – namely, Switzerland and Austria.[81] In regard to non-Western societies, the picture is even more discouraging. The experiment of Colombia with alternating party governments after 1958 is sometimes cited, as also is the case of Malaysia, the latter of which experienced severe communal violence between Chinese and Malays in 1969. And, despite all the attention that Lebanon has received for its complex consociational devices, that country is currently faced with the prospect of dismemberment by domestic and external political forces.

At one point Lijphart lists Cyprus, Nigeria and Uruguay as having tried and failed with consociational approaches;[82] and even with regard to Nigeria, he identifies only the federal system (pre-1966) as being a consociational – albeit badly constructed – arrangement.[83] Finally, Barry weighs in with the argument that consociational approaches are less applicable to ethnic divisions than to those of religion and class, which is worth noting, since it is the ethnic dimension that is most prominent in many African countries, including Nigeria.[84]

Why, it might be asked, should we not simply discard this mode of analysis in view of the many problems identified with its use? One answer that can be suggested here is that the evidence still seems to suggest that many countries have no choice but to adopt some pattern of consociationalism – if only for a transitional period – if they seek a democratic future. As Lijphart contended,

> Under the unfavourable circumstances of segmentary cleavages, consociational democracy, though far from the abstract ideal, is the best kind of democracy that can realistically be expected.[85]

Before we leave this topic, it would be well to identify the many shortcomings of consociationalism for a country like Nigeria, although the latter's choice must involve the acceptance of some or other of these imperfections:

1. Consociational government is largely a holding operation with an inherent tendency to maintain the socio-economic status quo.
2. It seeks not to dissolve the plural divisions in society, but to accept them as "the basic building blocks."[86]
3. The desire for mutual accommodation places an emphasis on "closed door negotiations" so that ideological concerns are de-emphasized in the process of arriving at agreed policy.
4. Piecemeal or "consociational" engineering can often lead to complete governmental immobilism, with the consequent growth of cynicism towards the political process.
5. "Grand" or "overwhelming" coalition governments are preferred; and the emphasis on proportionality in all public actions de-emphasizes the importance of merit, especially in the making of appointments.
6. The system can only work if the political leaders enjoy "mutual security" in the restricted competition permitted from their opposing leaders, as well as from challenges from their mass followers.[87] Consociationalism therefore accentuates the oligarchical predilection of revisionist democratic theory.

This list can be continued further – for example, to reflect Daalder's concern that it might be "too cumbersome for large countries,"[88] or Lijphart's that it is an expensive system because of the multiplication of government units.[89] Yet, these are some of the many costs which Nigerian political leaders have long recognized and accepted would have to be paid if their country is ever to emerge from the cycle of democratic collapse followed by military authoritarianism. One must keep in mind, therefore, not only the consociational features that might have to be incorporated into a Nigerian democratic system to enable it to "work," but also the significant cost – financial and otherwise – that each of these features would impose on the Nigerian treasury and the Nigerian people.

3

Dilemmas of Nigerian democracy

Despite the abrupt changes in regimes that Nigerians have witnessed since the Second World War, there is such a degree of continuity of ideas, problems, even of political personages throughout this period, that each new regime seems to mark a new phase in an ongoing experiment. It is well to emphasize a certain unwavering political preference of Nigerians throughout these rather turbulent decades. That preference has been for a system in which Nigerian citizens would openly compete for political power, and one in which the exercise of power would be limited by constitutional rules, an independent judiciary, and some degree of balance between competing political organizations. One can therefore accept the following statement as correct for developing countries, only if Nigeria must first be regarded as a notable exception:

> Changes in the level, forms, and basis of political participation are more likely to be the unintended consequences or by-products of development than the result of conscious choices made by elites, groups, or individuals as either goals or means.[1]

The opportunities enjoyed by the Nigerian political elite to choose the form of political association for the nation – and the practice of being quite consistent in that choice – does not alter the fact that this option is a highly conditioned one, conditioned by the problems of underdevelopment, by the effects of class formation and ethnic identities, and by the ways in which Nigerians often pursue their interests even when they seem to be acting wholly "outside" the political arena. Both Juan Linz and Robert Dahl identify one likely option for a state which does not settle on one of the numerous forms of tyranny, or participation via the corporatist model. In speaking of Brazil, Linz contends:

> it would seem that some kind of multiparty system with a hegemonic party would be the most realistic option. In a sense, the hesitant efforts of "constitutionalization" and "civilianization" have been moves in this direction.[2]

Neither Nigeria nor Brazil has inherited from its anti-colonial experience "an authoritarian hegemonic party system" such as we find in Mexico or, in a

30

somewhat less authoritarian but still hegemonic form, in India. And so, unless Nigerians adopt a consociational "no winners, no losers" system, the problem of ensuring significant competition while facilitating the emergence of a dominant party will be an unceasing concern. In countries whose social composition raises the danger of segmentation and polarization, Robert Dahl sees a likely option to be a "mixed regime," which he characterizes as having "a broad citizenship but limits on public contestation, particularly on the right to form opposition parties."[3] Such regimes he feels are "prone to oscillate between liberalization and repression."[4] These statements capture something of the essence of Nigerian government and politics, regardless of whether the regime is military or civilian. A viable Nigerian democracy has to allow considerable room for self-expression and the assertion of group interests, yet these activities must be confined to channels that are more narrowly defined and structured than would be acceptable in most Western liberal societies.[5]

One of the words which became closely associated with the regime of General Murtala Muhammed – after it supplanted the nine-year rule of General Gowon in July 1975 and set in train the transition to civilian rule – was "discipline." Nigerians, he contended to wide agreement, were undisciplined in many areas of public life. In a certain sense, the "ungovernability" of Nigerians, the seemingly anarchic pattern of daily intercourse, have both advantages and disadvantages for political life. With the outbreak of the first military coup in 1966, commentators were quick to point to the "illusion of democracy" of the previous five years.[6] The prevalent myth of "relative political stability," they argued, had done a disservice to Nigeria during those years.[7]

With the benefit of hindsight, one can see that Nigerians did experience numerous abuses of power that are common to many contemporary developing societies: fraudulent elections, oppression of political opponents, intimidation of journalists and bribery of government officials. Yet there is something unique about the general context in which these acts have been perpetrated. For one thing, the identity of oppressors and oppressed has depended in Nigeria on which region or seat of government one is speaking about. The former dominant parties in the Western and Eastern Regions, the Action Group and NCNC respectively, might vigorously bemoan the repressive tactics used by agents of the governing party in the North, the NPC, against them and their political allies, but these same parties treated with equal scorn similar complaints by the opposition parties in their own fiefdoms.[8] Whether one examines attitudes towards freedom of the press, the sanctity of the ballot box, or the separation between public and private funds, Nigerian political actors usually managed simultaneously to uphold these values and to dispense with them in practice.[9]

This delicate compromise between crime and innocence was upset because of the attempt by one of the three major actors, namely the NPC, to use its control of the federal center to try and alter the balance of power decisively in its favor. It employed that power in the following crucial events: producing a highly disputed census count favorable to itself in 1962–3; imposing a minority faction of the Action Group party on the Western Region in 1962–4; manipulating the results of the 1964 federal election, especially in the North; and, finally, supervising the perpetration of what a normally temperate student of Nigerian politics calls "the crooked Western election of October 1965."[10] This election, as Kirk-Greene further argued, represented "the ultimate debasement of the democratic process in the reimposition of an unpopular government through chicanery and thuggery."[11] The fruits of these labors would not be harvested, however, as the erosion of the regime's moral legitimacy after the 1965 Western election served to trigger off the military intervention of January 1966.

Yet, there are few angels in the universe of Nigerian politics. Consequently, Nigerians often seek to devise structures that will prevent the materialization of the state of affairs they fear most, namely, that presumed opponents will take a decisive and perhaps ruinous advantage over them. I shall examine later the pervasiveness of this pattern of societal mistrust. The capacity for democratic politics in Nigeria appears to be rooted in the subtle awareness of the danger represented by unchecked power, since that power – in common thinking – has to be used for someone's benefit and to another's disadvantage, and there is a reasonable and even probable chance that one will fall on the wrong side of that equation.[12]

CHIEF OBAFEMI AWOLOWO AND CONSOCIATIONALISM

As we saw in Chapter 2, the need for consociationalism derived from the absence of a critical minimum of national unity and cohesion in particular countries. It was asserted that a certain pattern of trust, especially among the political elite, should make possible the creation of a system of power-sharing. In the case of Nigeria, it has been apparent that some combination of consociational devices will have to be introduced if the country is ever to develop a recognizably democratic system of government and politics.

One common item of information about Nigeria that is widely shared today, apart from the fact that it is an exporter of petroleum, is that it is made up of large ethnic groups often in conflict with each other. Many will still remember the 30-month Biafran war of secession from July 1967 until January 1970, when the Igbo people were regularly portrayed overseas as the victims of systematic oppression in the Federation. As inexact as these general opinions might be, they still touch on what remains a crucial feature of Nigerian politics, namely, the extent to which conflicts tend to take on the character of a struggle among sectional groups, whether defined by language, ethnicity, region or religion.

There is now a substantial body of scholarly literature which deals with what can be considered an ideal type of society in which such conflicts appear fundamental. Later on I shall look more closely at some of the writings on these "plural societies." In the words of J. S. Furnivall, who, together with

M. G. Smith, is usually regarded as the main formulator of the model, the people of plural societies

> mix but do not combine. Each group holds by its own religion, its own culture and language, its own ideas and ways. As individuals they meet, but only in the market place, in buying and selling.[13]

For Furnivall, such peoples have been brought together by the accident of colonial rule. Although Furnivall and Smith part company when the former places emphasis on economic factors to explain the persisting structure of plural societies while the latter points to the fact of cultural pluralism itself, they still agree on the specific nature of political authority in such societies. These, they contend, are held together by regulation and not integration, and one of the cultural minorities usually assumes a position of dominance over the others.[14] In view of the concern in this study with the kind of features that might be needed for a democracy that would work in Nigeria, it is well to note the quite contrary arrangement that the "plural" theorists see as typical of segmented societies:

> Since the various sections are culturally differentiated consensus is a remote possibility. Further, the subordinate sections are unlikely to accord equal value and legitimacy to the preservation of the hierarchic pattern. Thus authority, power, and regulation are of crucial significance in maintaining, controlling, and coordinating the plural society.[15]

If one were to devise a typology of societies from the (idealized) fully integrated to the highly segmented, Nigeria would fall closer to the latter category than to the former. One of the foremost political leaders in Nigeria, Obafemi Awolowo – a central figure in many of the political developments to be discussed in this study – pointed out in his first book, published in 1947, that Nigeria was a mere "geographical expression."[16] He has devoted a significant amount of his writing during the following three decades to arguing the need for each linguistic group in Nigeria to have as high a degree of autonomy as possible in the conduct of its internal affairs.[17] It is, therefore, pertinent to look briefly at how Awolowo's political thinking and actions appear when examined through the prism of consociationalism.

Awolowo and his party, the Action Group, were able to win control gradually of the former Western Region of Nigeria during the 1950s.[18] During the pre-independence election of 1959, the party campaigned strenuously to try and win overall control of the Federation, and Awolowo was unabashed in expressing his wish to be Prime Minister of the Federation. His strategy, as well as that of Azikiwe at the head of the NCNC, was to gain maximum support in his home region while vigorously challenging the two other major parties in theirs.[19] When Awolowo failed in this task, he opted to be Leader of the Opposition in the federal House and relinquished his Premiership in the West to his deputy, S. L. Akintola. Within two years, Akintola and Awolowo had split on ideological grounds, as well as in their ideas regarding the best strategy and tactics for the party.[20]

Let us now return to the contention that consociationalism – even for persons who might be unaware of the term – has been on the agenda of Nigerian politics for quite some time, and will inevitably be so in the foreseeable future. As happened in most of colonial Africa during the 1950s, a gradual transfer of power took place in Nigeria from the colonial authorities to local politicians. Beginning in 1954, when the first really federal constitution was introduced, political power at the center has always been shared by two or more political organizations, which contrasts with the situation in countries like Ghana or Tanzania in which one nationalist party has been able to achieve clear predominance. In the 1954 cabinet, in which Nigerians were still very subordinate to colonial representatives, the NCNC held six of the nine positions and the NPC the remaining three. The portfolios had been allocated on the basis of the parties' performance in the federal elections conducted in the three regions that year. After the subsequent 1957 elections, the NPC became the dominant partner in the federal government, and Abubakar Tafawa Balewa the country's first Prime Minister. Moreover, this government was a real grand coalition faced with the task of preparing the country for independence three years later.[21]

Chief Awolowo strongly opposed his party responding to the invitation to join the Balewa cabinet. In fact, he has consistently opposed "playing second fiddle" to northern political leaders throughout his political career. Yet, he was defeated in the debate within the Action Group leadership, and two representatives of his party joined the federal cabinet, including Akintola.[22] When the split within the Action Group dominated proceedings at the Jos Conference in May 1962, one of the central issues between the two factions concerned Awolowo's determination to fight the NPC on a national basis. Akintola considered that struggle to be a ruinous one; and both he and Prime Minister Balewa, drawing on their experience in the all-party 1957–9 cabinet, called for a *modus vivendi* that would allow each of the major parties unimpeded control of its region of strength, with an "all-embracing" – or what Lijphart would term an "overwhelming " – coalition at the federal center.[23] An associate of Akintola in this dispute, Chief A. Rosiji, who had also served in the 1957–9 Balewa cabinet, had even called for one single Nigerian party the year before the Action Group crisis.[24]

I have already spoken briefly of the sequel to this split in the Action Group, which included collaboration between Balewa and Akintola to disrupt parliamentary processes in the West, the declaration of an Emergency and subsequent trial and imprisonment of Awolowo and some of his associates for treason, the imposition of an Akintola government, and the final extreme abuses in the 1965 regional election followed by the entry into the political arena a few months later of the military praetors. In 1979, Awolowo led his new party, the Unity Party of Nigeria (UPN), in a national campaign aimed once again at seizing control of the Federation. And once again the party with the greatest support in the states of the Northern Region, namely, the National Party of Nigeria (NPN), won control of the federal government and

34

invited the dominant party with overwhelming support from the Igbo people to join in a coalition. Finally, once again the party led by Awolowo was not a partner in the federal coalition and indeed constituted the most resolute opposition to that government in the National Assembly and in the country at large, based on its control of five of the nineteen state governments.[25]

Does this mean that Awolowo, and the other leaders of the party he has inspired, have been consistent non-consociational actors in Nigeria over three and perhaps four decades? (The Action Group was formed in 1951.) The documentary evidence appears overwhelming, albeit with one interesting break in the record. After the overthrow of Yakubu Gowon by some of his military colleagues in July 1975, Nigeria experienced a hiatus that lasted a mere two months, before the new Head of State, General Murtala Muhammed, presented his program for the transition to civilian rule on the occasion of the fifteenth anniversary of independence, 1 October 1975. Since the end of the civil war in January 1970, many ideas had been floated on how the future Nigerian government should be structured. In the case of Awolowo, he also had put forward his views, especially after resigning from the Gowon government in 1971. However, in October 1974, General Gowon abruptly announced that he was postponing plans to hand over power to civilians in 1976. Less than a year later, he was overthrown.

Among the prominent political personalities who seized the opportunity provided by Gowon's overthrow to try and influence the new military junta was Chief Awolowo. More specifically, Awolowo wrote in support of proposals earlier made by Aminu Kano, the former leader of NEPU.[26] What is striking in his suggestions, however, is the number of clearly consociational elements he advanced. For example, he strongly argued that plans to conduct another census should be postponed: "As a people we lose nothing, on the contrary, we gain immensely in concord by postponing another national population census indefinitely."[27] Secondly, directly citing Arthur Lewis's condemnation of "Winner takes all" politics in Africa, he called for a "politico-probationary period" during the first five years of civilian rule. While evincing the same distaste as Lewis for the one-party system (but not sharing the latter's preference for a National Government), he made a strong case for the introduction of the principle of proportionality which is itself the very core of the positions taken by Lewis and the consociationalists:

> during the first five years... all the political parties who have seats in the federal parliament or houses of assembly should be involved in the extra-cabinet activities of our governments.[28]

Awolowo then went on to list some of these activities and institutions in which participation should be made proportional to the number of votes a party had won at the preceding election. These include "all organs" of government bodies and state-owned companies, parliamentary committees, and even government-sponsored delegations. It is noteworthy that a Nigerian political leader who has never been a supporter of all-inclusive governments – except

35

during the secession crisis and civil war – should have found it desirable to suggest a transitional period in which Nigerian political groups would agree to avoid divisive issues, and would accept a proportionate share of government appointments (and therefore benefits), rather than return immediately to the "war of all against all" that so typifies Nigerian party politics. Yet, although most prominent Nigerian political figures can be shown, at some point in their careers, to have favored a less intensely competitive system (if only for a transitional or probationary period) such suggestions are usually soon trampled underfoot in the drive to achieve decisive political advantage. I shall try and explore the reasons for so regular, yet unwanted, an outcome.

NIGERIA AND CONSOCIATIONALISM

At this point one can set forward what appears to be a precarious balance between the consensual tendencies in Nigerian politics and those which militate against and usually undermine them. On the positive side, there is the fact that Nigerians have had a significant amount of experience with coalition governments dating back to the mid-1950s. Even the military governments between 1966 and 1979 were esentially national governments, especially in the composition of the Federal Executive Council (FEC) in which civilians were heavily represented.[29] Nigerian political leaders from all regions, and from many ethnic groups and political backgrounds, have enjoyed their most extended – and perhaps most peaceful – experience working conjointly as appointed members of military-supervised cabinets at the federal and state levels between 1967 and 1979.[30]

The second "positive" element from the standpoint of consociationalism is that ideology has played a quite subordinate role in Nigerian party politics. It is necessary to be careful in addressing this issue, since there is a high ideological *content* to the exchanges between party enthusiasts and in published party programs. In the actual recruitment of supporters, however, and in the forging of inter-party alliances, ideology has usually been displaced in Nigeria by other considerations. The following statement by John Mackintosh regarding the politics of the First Republic has also been made by most close observers of Nigerian politics in one form or another: "There was no basic difference of ideology – though the AG leadership tried to create one – and no dispute as to the incidence of taxation or the distribution of wealth."[31] A more careful statement would be that the ideological positions assumed by the major parties – or by persistent factions, e.g., the left-wingers in the NCNC – cannot fully explain their alliances and affiliations or their behavior once in power. There was certainly a quite basic ideological difference between the populist NEPU in the North and the establishment NPC, and this difference was reflected in actual political actions. Richard Sklar would also make a stronger case than Mackintosh for the direct practical consequences of the ideological shift in what became the Awolowo wing of the Action Group.[32]

36

Yet, familiarity with coalition governments and the mainly non-ideological character of political affiliations have not tempered the unusual acrimony of Nigerian politics. The slogan of one of the five presidential candidates in the 1979 elections was "Politics without Bitterness."[33] The fact is that political opposition, in Nigeria as much as in many developing countries, does not quite work the way it is supposed to in the literature on liberal democracy. Robert Dahl identified "contestation" – the right to oppose – as one of the fundamental ingredients of a democratic system. It is a commonplace that the whole corpus of democratic rights and freedoms – of assembly, of speech, of the press – are intimately bound up with the protected freedom to offer constructive opposition to the government of the day. How then do we cope with the following axiom proffered by Mackintosh: "the evidence suggests that the existence of a virile active second party positively reduces the amount of freedom and security enjoyed by the citizens"?[34] He cites the case of the Mid-West Region carved out of the West in 1963, where "there was a general relaxation and much of the apparatus devised to subjugate political opponents could be abandoned" once the NCNC won firm control of the new region.[35]

The point that should be retained is that there is more to these observations than the simple apology for one-party states as being the best way to ensure public peace.[36] Rather, there is a deeper question to be explored, namely, *whether the very basis of party formation, identity and affiliation in Nigeria is of such a nature as to preclude a relationship between government and opposition party that is anything but one step away from warfare.* Ken Post and Michael Vickers made a notable attempt to conceptualize the political system in Nigeria during the period 1960–6.[37] Although there was such a system which governed the pursuit and public distribution of benefits – which they call the "System of Rewards" – and although that system was general and indulged in by most political actors, it never became stabilized. Here is the reason given by Post and Vickers, which touches on a very crucial dimension of the consociational model:

> there is no real evidence to indicate that the leaders of the three major parties had even an unconscious intention of working the System by mutual agreement in the 1960s.
>
> they sought most diligently to change the *status quo* where it did not suit them and to grab as large a share of the fruits as possible. The inter- and intra-party competition ... prevented the System of Rewards from stabilizing and played a large part in bringing about the military *coup* of January 1966.[38]

Contrary to the requirement set forward by Nordlinger, moreover, the political leaders did not enjoy any security with respect to the activities of their opponents. If anything, there were increasing attempts made to erode the base of rival political leaders through supporting opponents in their regions. More directly, a range of inducements was employed to get opposition legislators to cross the carpet in State and Federal Houses. From the 75 representatives the

37

Action Group elected in 1959 to the Federal House, a mere 13 remained at the time the parliament was dissolved in 1964. Conversely, the NPC's support rose from 134 of a total 312 in 1959, to an absolute majority by the end of 1961.[39]

It was pointed out that great hopes have been placed by political scientists on the political elite to devise conflict-regulating mechanisms. How then are we to work with such a requirement in the Nigerian context where the major blame for the sharp conflicts that do emerge are usually laid at the very feet of members of that elite?

> one can see in the educated elite the long term source of the disequilibrating factors which have brought the Federation to the point of disintegration. Rather than act as conflict managers, a role which one would expect of them given their educational skills, they were in a strong sense conflict generators.[40]

And Billy Dudley has incorporated into his analysis of Nigerian politics the additional concern that I suggested must be kept well in view in any scheme intended to reform Nigerian politics through maximizing the autonomy of the political elite. One must first explain how this autonomy will not be used to misappropriate public resources, thereby undermining the legitimacy of the whole system:

> few, if any government contracts or loans were given out by the political class unless they were offered ten percent of the value of the contract or loan in return, a return which then went, in part, to the private pockets of coalition leaders, and, in part, provided the resources needed for side-payments.[41]

A CLOSED POLITICAL CYCLE?

It can be asked if a re-enactment of the myth of Sisyphus is always to be the case in Nigerian politics. By this I am referring to the periodic attempts to neutralize certain divisive practices which are then countered by the pull of much more deeply determined forms of political contestation, a process which eventually drags the political actors right back down where they can only be rescued from their turmoil by a military intervention which begins the long trek back up the hill. This cycle recommenced in Nigeria with the brief seven-month rule (July 1975 – February 1976) of General Murtala Muhammed, whose regime pointed the nation resolutely in the direction of a renewed experiment with constitutional civilian government. In the speech with which General Muhammed inaugurated the 50-member Constitution Drafting Committee (CDC) in October 1975, we find echoes of the very aspirations discussed earlier, together with a frank acknowledgement of the deep impediments to the realizing of those aspirations. Murtala expressed the wish that politics in Nigeria "be transformed from its previous scenario of bitter personal wrangles into a healthy game of political argument and discussion."[42] His reflections on Nigeria's experiences in party politics cover in a summary manner virtually all the major criticisms made of West African politics by Arthur Lewis and others:

> most of our politicians could not distinguish between the art and artifacts of politics... The main political parties were in fact little more than armies organized for fighting elections... Winning elections became a life and death struggle which justified all means – fair or foul. So vile was the abuse of the electoral process that this has raised the question as to whether we need continue to accept simple majorities as the basis of political selection, especially at the centre.[43]

While the military regime did not wish to dictate to Nigerians the details of the political system they should adopt in order to achieve Lijphart's "best kind of democracy that can realistically be expected," they did nevertheless have some clear idea of which practices had to be curtailed, and which ones fostered:

> any Constitution devised should seek to:
>
> – eliminate cut-throat political competition based on a system or rules of winner-takes-all...
> – it should also discourage institutionalized opposition to the Government in power and, instead, develop consensus politics and Government based on a community of all interests rather than the interest of sections of the country;
> – firmly establish the principle of public accountability for all holders of public office...
> – eliminate over-centralization of power in a few hands, and as a matter of principle, decentralize power wherever possible, as a means of diffusing tensions.[44]

As should be evident from these excerpts, from the very start of this vigorous period of political renewal in Nigeria the country's political participants were made directly aware of the central dilemma confronting the nation and its citizens. The Murtala regime was clearly concerned to avoid initiating another sisyphean trek and so it counseled the Drafting Committee, and through it the nation, that

> if during the course of your deliberations, and having regard to our disillusion with party politics in the past, you should discover some means by which Government can be formed without the involvement of Political Parties, you should feel free to recommend [them].[45]

The members of the CDC did not follow this suggestion that they explore ways of governing Nigeria in a democratic manner without political parties. They did, however, devise a large number of requirements which they hoped would facilitate the emergence of the "free, democratic and lawful" system desired by the military regime, as well as the Nigerian people; one which would not soon be supplanted by an opposite system that was hardly free, democratic, or lawful. Still, whether these stipulations are some day looked back upon as mere pious hopes will greatly depend on the substratum of Nigerian political life.[46] The major elements of this substratum are the class,

39

ethnic, military and economic structures of Nigerian society. In addition, and interwoven with these elements, are the particular and even refined ways of pursuing self and group interests in Nigeria which I have termed prebendal politics. The success or failure of any political system in Nigeria, however constitutional and intricately crafted, will depend on its capacity to control, harness and yet liberate the energies that flow through these channels.

Part II

Nigeria's social dynamics and military rule

4

Politics in a multi-ethnic society

One of the many hurdles that Nigeria had to overcome in the attempt to return to civilian rule, and then to have such a new system entrenched, was the fact that competitive politics encouraged recourse to sectional identities. In this chapter, the discussion will be conducted on two levels. On the one hand, there is need for a clear understanding of the nature of the dynamics of Nigerian society, especially with regard to the phenomenon of ethnicity. On the other hand, the theoretical formulations which already exist concerning the nature of politics in segmented societies must be confronted so that a closer approximation between such theories and the socio-political realities of Nigeria can be achieved.

One section of the *Report* of Nigeria's Constitution Drafting Committee (CDC), which met between 1975 and 1976, is entitled "Promotion of National Loyalty in a Multi-Ethnic Society."[1] It is a useful summary of the various strands of informed opinion within Nigeria on this issue. The *Report* begins with the observation that, "as a general rule, every Nigerian owes or is expected to owe some loyalty to his community and/or sub-community." The open acknowledgement of such a normative dimension to such "loyalties" is itself significant. The *Report* then goes on to explain the fundamental paradox which confronted members of the CDC: "We are all agreed that loyalty to one's community ought not to be allowed to inhibit or detract from national loyalty, that is to say, loyalty to the Nigerian State." A resolution was then approved unanimously which stipulated various ways in which the State should seek to promote "national integration." Moreover, the following declaration passed, and survived intact, after another two years of debate: "The State shall foster a feeling of belonging and of involvement among the various sections of the country, to the end that loyalty to the nation shall override sectional loyalties."[2]

The problem which confronts Nigeria in this domain is indeed more daunting than that of conflicting "loyalties," one of which must be made clearly superior to the other. The struggle often becomes one of individuals seeking to monopolize State power on behalf of particular sub-national communities, as was discussed in Chapter 2 in my review of Arthur Lewis's

43

arguments. What enables the members of nation-states to compete, often in a fierce manner, for political advantage, and then settle down to a period of governance by the victors, is one of the more intriguing issues in political science. From such a standpoint it can be seen that members of the consociational school have taken up, using a different framework of analysis, a number of the same issues which exercised students of political culture a decade or more earlier.[3]

Many observers were surprised at the familiar nature of political alignments which surfaced with the lifting of the twelve-year ban on political parties in Nigeria in September 1978.[4] Of the five parties which were granted legal status, four of them, the NPN, NPP, PRP and UPN, could be shown to have clear links with the former dominant parties of the independence era.[5] Moreover, the pattern of votes demonstrated that considerable ethnic consolidation had taken place in support of the second and third strongest parties, the NPP and UPN, involving two sections of the population whose inter-dynamics have constituted so much of the background to Nigerian political events since the 1940s, namely the Igbo and Yoruba peoples. Moreover, the party which won control of the federal government, the National Party of Nigeria led by Alhaji Shehu Shagari, represented a successful harmonization of the counterposed themes of national and sectional loyalties. Even before the first votes were cast in the elections, here is how I reported the NPN's strategy:

> the NPN, as the party seeking the most direct path to political power, has replicated within itself the fundamental structure and principles of the post-colonial Nigerian state. The architects of the NPN know just what it is that enables a social formation like Nigeria 'to work.'

> The NPN recognizes that a basic principle of Nigerian political and economic life is the equal division of social goods, or what Nigerians often refer to as the 'national cake.' This principle is not conceived in the traditional liberal sense of equality of individual opportunity. Rather, the basic social units of Nigeria are taken by the NPN leaders to be the ethnic, linguistic and regional blocs of the population.[6]

Yet the fact that the NPN was specifically constructed as a party of continuity from the former military and civilian regimes did not mean that the principles it implemented represented a basic consensus among the competing political formations. Indeed, the strategy of the party which came second in almost every phase of the elections, the Unity Party of Nigeria led by Chief Obafemi Awolowo, implemented a different approach in its campaigning and recruitment:

> The general strategy of the Unity Party of Nigeria was diametrically opposed to that of the NPN. Chief Obafemi Awolowo insisted that potential adherents must accept the party's clearly defined program. He stoutly rejected what he called 'horse trading,' i.e., individuals negotiating their entry into the party, and hence the adherence of their local supporters, on the basis of the governmental jobs or positions promised to them. Chief Awolowo felt that where such local

elites refused to accept his approach, he could go over their heads and make a direct appeal to their people. With regard to the Yoruba, Awolowo correctly assessed that he had now become their unchallenged leader. He therefore felt that he did not need to make specific appeals to Yoruba solidarity, although this attitude did not prevent his followers from doing so on their own initiative.

> The voting results proved most conclusively that the non-Yoruba electorate was not prepared to accept Chief Awolowo or his party in the way that he intended.[7]

As can be seen from this comment, Nigerian politicians were constrained in their capacity to act on a purely ideological or programmatic basis. There is a process of "call and response" which operates, in both directions, between political leaders and their supporters. As important, therefore, as the behavior pattern, interests and objectives of such leadership might be, the *demos* in Nigeria also imposes its imprint on the style and content of the political process.

THE "PLURAL SOCIETY" AND NIGERIA

What is the best way to conceptualize Nigerian political society? Some students of Nigeria are more taken up with the existence of a dominant class, and with its highly consumerist behavior patterns, and thus give that category the greatest prominence in their analyses. Others find the "loyalties" of Nigerians to linguistic, regional and ethnic groups so prevalent, and so demonstrably salient to political life, that they make such sentiments the main focus of their analysis. A third set of scholars prefers to look beyond the internal dynamics of Nigerian society and places emphasis on the dependent nature of the country's political economy, treating domestic politics as subordinate to the activities of external forces and agents.

While I have not exhausted all the possible theoretical orientations, or combinations thereof, that can be brought to an analysis of Nigeria, there remains a need to translate the implicit understanding apparent in much of my earlier discussion into a more explicit formulation. The first general analytical notion that should be addressed is that of "the plural society" which was briefly discussed in Chapter 3. Much of the writing on consociational democracy refers to the unique problem encountered in such societies. Yet the notion has sometimes been expressed in terms that leave little room for the fluidity and unevenness to be found in any empirical situation:

> The hallmark of the plural society, and the feature that distinguishes it from its pluralistic counterpart, is the practice of politics almost exclusively along ethnic lines.

> a society is plural if it is culturally diverse and if its cultural sections are organized into cohesive political sections.[8]

Jürg Steiner has emphasized a point regarding consociationalism also made by others, namely that it is important not to impose too rigid a theoretical framework on a range of different societies, and that it is also necessary to

45

specify the time period.[9] He makes the further pertinent comment that cultural diversity does not necessarily mean segmentation, i.e., that such diversity may not necessarily lead to political cleavages.[10] Certain anthropologists have been even more critical of the use of the notion of a plural society. Frederick Barth referred to it in his influential 1969 essay as "the increasingly vague label of 'plural' society ... "[11] echoed by Elliot Skinner in his contention that the model of plural society "had tended to obfuscate the political factors that determine how complex societies function."[12] One can go back, however, and consider some of the early writings on the nature of plural societies to see what elements might yet be of relevance to Nigeria. Moreover, it should be noted that while Barth and Skinner object to the term "plural society" to describe the nature of certain multi-ethnic societies, they have nonetheless found it necessary to propose their own substitutes of "polyethnic social system" and "ethnic system," respectively.

The quite specific and technical sense of "plural society" was established by J. S. Furnivall and M. G. Smith. For the former, such a society is characterized by "internally autonomous and inclusive political units ruled by institutionally distinct numerical minorities."[13] Smith took pains to outline the unique political arrangement in such societies. It embodies

> a politically autonomous unit ruled by a culturally distinct and politically privileged minority ... the state is the representative political organ organized as a corporate group ... the mass of the citizens are not citizens but subjects.[14]

While it is clearly not possible to apply such a definition in a general way to Nigeria, as was noted in my review of consociationalism, still there are aspects of the dynamics of a plural society, when viewed as an ideal type, which can assist in explaining recurrent tensions in that country. For example, in a plural society overall authority is manifested in the form of "domination by one of the cultural sections."[15] As a consequence, as Leo Kuper contends, "there is pressure on subordinate cultural sections to deny legitimacy to the imposed order and to reject not only specific laws and authority, but law, order and authority as such."[16]

In the case of Nigeria, it can be stated that the lineages of the plural society constitute the kind of society which is generally feared and which, it is implicitly believed, would take effect unless individuals and their constituent groups, were not ever cautious and resourceful.[17] Moreover, when individuals feel that they – and consequently their solidarity group – have not received their fair share of social goods or other equitable treatment in governmental affairs, they often portray themselves as subordinate members of a *de facto* plural society. The tendency for such feelings to lead to challenges to prevailing "law, order and authority" is therefore great. Such an understanding is crucial for any adequate explanation of the pattern of staunch and often violent resistance by sections of the Yoruba and Tiv people to the regional governments in the first half of the 1960s, and that of the Igbo in the second half of that decade (including the attempted Biafra secession). To avoid the possibility of its being misunderstood, the essential argument being advanced here will be reiterated: the element of domination of a culturally diverse society by one of its cultural sections, which is central to the theory of plural societies, cannot be applied without considerable qualification to Nigerian political life, yet it is a perspective which is highly relevant to the *fears* that often motivate political perceptions and behavior. Such an argument is clearly reflected in the following summaries from the earlier-cited report of the CDC of two different sets of opinions among CDC members, which are, however, identical in the following contention:

> once it is agreed or provided that the component states and all ethnic groups shall be accorded fair and equitable treatment, it follows logically that no few states or combination of a few ethnic groups shall be permitted to dominate the government to the exclusion of others.

> There had in the past been inter-ethnic rivalry to secure the domination of government by one ethnic group or combination of ethnic groups to the exclusion of others. It is therefore essential to have some provisions to ensure that the predominance of persons from a few states or from a few ethnic or other sectional groups is avoided in the composition of government or the appointment or elections of persons to high offices in the state.[18]

POLITICS AND ETHNICITY

Following hard on the heels of the introduction of mass electoral politics in many parts of Africa was the appearance of political alignments along sectional and especially ethnic lines. It is clearly not the case that such alignments always reflect ethnic identities, or that the presence of multi-ethnicity will necessarily lead to multi-ethnic politics.[19] Yet, the politicizing of ethnicity did not turn out to be a temporary phase in the process of "nation-building" as the most optimistic scholars had hoped.

Here, in summarized form, are the key elements of my understanding of the politics of ethnicity:

1. The widespread notion that ethnicity is linked to certain "primordial sentiments" or "primordial identities" is very misleading. Many of the major ethnic categories in Nigeria (e.g., Yoruba, Igbo) emerged *pari passu* with modern electoral politics.[20]

2. It is often possible to distinguish ethnic boundaries from the cultural material – symbols, art, language, status hierarchies – identified with these boundaries. Both boundaries and cultural materials change, sometimes rapidly, often slowly.[21]

3. The predominantly political nature of contemporary ethnicity can be traced to (a) the capacity of ethnic boundaries to expand to include culturally related peoples or contract to a more exclusive group, as political interests dictate;[22] (b) the suitability of cultural elements for the transmission of political signals (indeed, these often become politically laden signals in themselves); and (c) the accessibility of cultural assertions to all individuals in

47

society, from the highest to the lowest in socio-economic standing, thus bringing to situations of competitive interaction a powerful Us/Them dichotomy. One of the strongest and most comprehensive analyses of the political function of ethnicity in Nigeria was advanced by Richard Sklar. He contended, very much against the tide of scholarly and journalistic writing in the early 1960s, that "tribalism" was "a mask for class privilege."[23] The instigation of ethnic identities and animosities he saw as deriving from class formation, especially the emergence of what he called the "rising class" in business, politics and the professions.[24] Although Nigerian political parties of the First Republic had "become identified with the interests of particular nationality groups," Sklar argued that these parties were really instruments "used to promote class interests in the acquisition and retention of regional power."[25]

A systematic attempt to advance a revised approach to that of Sklar in the explanation of ethnicity in Nigeria was made by Robert Melson and Howard Wolpe. Of their general argument, some of which has already been covered in various ways in this study, the following three points could be highlighted. Melson and Wolpe advance the idea that it is "modernization" rather than class formation which is the active agency promoting "communalism" in Nigeria.[26] They point to the fast pace of social mobilization and the competition in the modern sector as being responsible for the emphasis placed on communal identities.[27] Secondly, they contend that individuals in Africa can be either communal or non-communal actors depending on the social context. Hence, Nigerian workers can act along class lines, as in the successful general strikes of 1945 and 1964, and then turn around and ally with competing parties in accordance with their ethnic identity.[28] Finally, Melson and Wolpe advance an important argument regarding the exacerbation of communal conflict commensurate with the introduction of competitive electoral politics. Unlike Sklar, they place emphasis not so much on the manipulations of the "rising class" as on the consequences of mass participation in the political process which, they claim, "encourages aspirant politicians to make appeals to the most easily mobilized communal loyalties, and to define themselves primarily as the representatives of communal interests."[29] In regard to this latter point, while Melson and Wolpe are making an important observation regarding the contribution of individuals *at all* levels of the social hierarchy to the generating and sustaining of ethnic identities, a fully satisfactory statement of this point would involve a rephrasing of their argument to avoid resurrecting the notion of "primordial sentiments" which they earlier strongly rejected.

Ethnicity remains a vital social force for several reasons: the borders and cultural content of ethnic groups can be fluid or rigid according to the circumstances; it is an emotionally satisfying mode of self- and group-assertion; and its salience increases rather than being "over-ridden" by division according to social class during the struggle for survival and material advantage in the modern sectors of the society and economy. Elliot Skinner speaks pertinently about the competition in contemporary African states "between their component ethnic and social groups for the resources of the state."[30] "Almost by definition," he contends, "ethnic groups are competitive for the strategic resources of their respective societies."[31] Instead, therefore, of the customary view that ethnicity rushes in and occupies the space created for political competition, I wish to emphasize the reverse direction in this process, i.e., how competition for material goods, and hence for control of the state which governs access to them, accelerates the "ethnicizing" of Nigerian society. The term "sectional" can often be used in place of "ethnicity" because region, religion and language sometimes loom larger in such confrontations. The question therefore becomes: How can competitive and open politics be encouraged and pursued in Nigeria in the full knowledge that it generates the very forces which represent such a threat to the stability of that same system?

Certain alternatives to this apparently self-undermining cycle of political advance can be sketched here. The first of these is that horizontal alignments, namely those of class, might come to take precedence over ethnic, linguistic or religious identities. Such an option often rests on a specific expectation dear to Western social science, namely that instrumental modes of social organization would, in an increasingly modern and materialistic society, prevail over identities based on ascription and affective ties.[32] Indeed, what weakens such a prognosis is not only the fact that there is a strong cultural dimension to social classes, but also that the "rational" pursuit of economic interests can serve to stimulate as much vertical as horizontal modes of identity and social organization.[33]

A second option is that another less divisive mode of political association might take the place of ethnicity in the Nigerian context. One can consider, for example, whether the creation of new states in Nigeria will reach a point at which the potentially neutral category of statism (on the sub-federal level) can take over much of the emotional space now assumed by sectional identities.

A third option, not wholly distinct from the two above, is that multi-ethnicity, instead of being "over-ridden" as the drafters of the 1979 Constitution desired, might become a positive, albeit depoliticized, force in Nigeria. There has always taken place a deliberate borrowing, or unconscious adoption, of cultural elements by one set of people from another, even in recent Nigerian history. Today, the wearing of the garments of other cultural sections is deliberately pursued by governmental and some social leaders. At a more substantive level, however, it is clear that the breaking of the link between political action and sectional mobilization will require either a much longer time-frame than earlier scholars had been willing to allow, or the emergence of socio-economic changes which are not apparent at this juncture.

SEGMENTATION AND SOCIAL DISTRUST

Of the many attempts by other scholars to characterize certain general aspects of Nigeria's political sociology, a few will be considered in the final two

49

sections of this chapter. The process of self- and group-definition is an inherently complex – some might say dialectical – one. Part of the paradox derives from the fact that the sense of "we-ness" is not necessarily auto-determined. Often it is a definition imposed by others before it becomes solidified in terms of one's kin. Sometimes it begins from encounters with others whose self-definition is exclusive of oneself, which initiates a process culminating in the assumption of a new group definition by those excluded. What Crawford Young says about the north of Nigeria could be repeated for other regions and their constituent groups: "As for political identity Hausa-Fulani defined themselves by opposition to the cultural threat posed by southern Nigeria."[34] In short, the individual Nigerian, especially in a context of competitive group interaction, enters into a system of sectional oppositions from which it is usually impossible to opt out.[35] Barth has captured this very Durkheimian sense of the constraining nature of ethnicity in such contexts: "ethnic identity implies a series of constraints on the kinds of roles an individual is allowed to play, and the partners he can choose for different kinds of transactions."[36]

Once such an "ethnic system" has become a dynamic feature of a particular society, it comes to affect not only behavior but consciousness. In discussing the steps which led to the collapse of the Nigerian First Republic, and then the disastrous events of 1966, including the massacre of Igbos in parts of northern Nigeria, Kirk-Greene refers quite appropriately to the "background of *believed* oppositions, of dissent and distrust."[37] It is no surprise that much of the penetrating analysis we have of this phenomenon of social distrust concerns the academic community itself. Universities in Nigeria are state institutions in which individuals compete on a seemingly continuous basis for preferment. It is the special arena in which aspirant elites from different parts of the country are brought together, often for the first time, to be prepared for leading roles in the society. There is an obvious contrast between the academic ideals of enlightenment and the often grim realities of inter-ethnic antagonisms; and, finally, all academic personnel, whether indigenous or of foreign nationality, are inevitably drawn into the prevailing matrix of imposed identities and "believed oppositions."

In his study of the University of Ibadan, Pierre L. van den Berghe used the expression "competitive mistrust." Some of his arguments are unlikely to be challenged by persons who have worked for any length of time in that university or other comparable institutions of a "federal character" in Nigeria:

> By and large, people expect members of ethnic groups other than their own to be 'tribalists,' i.e., to be biased in favor of their fellow ethnics and against 'strangers.'... Most people assume that all others except those in the same circle of intimates (fellow kinsmen, fellow townsmen, or persons linked by patron-client ties) will behave in ways which further the other person's interests at the expense of oneself.[38]

While it is possible to trace historically the emergence of this phenomenon of

50

"believed oppositions" or "competitive mistrust" to developments within urban centers, the error should not be made of assuming that the spread of these sentiments takes place uniquely from urban to rural areas, and from the modern-educated to those with little or no formal education. Crawford Young adopted from the work of David Abernethy the interesting term of "ethnic missionary" to describe the urban migrant who becomes "concerned lest his ethnic group fall behind others in the struggle for wealth power and status."[39] There was a seemingly ineluctable process in which the way forward for individuals became that of encouraging communal solidarity and then mobilizing "their people" against those who appeared to be gaining an advantage, whether this involved access to modern education, jobs in the administrative sector, or seats on legislative councils.

Although the above statements undeniably reflect the original trajectory in the development of an ethnic system based on competitive mistrust, such a system eventually became more widespread, and its motivations, signals and perceptions have become the cultural stock of both elites and non-elites alike. Skinner refers to this process of diffusion using the language of strategies and tactics:

> The nature of ethnic groupings in each society and the competitive short-term tactics and long-term strategies they employ are functions of history and of the resources they seek to control. Groups with more effective tactics and strategies normally gain competitive advantages over the other groups within their societies.[40]

There is an understandable tendency for such tactics and strategies to be adopted by "outsiders" who now perceive themselves as "disadvantaged groups" within a competitive system. Common to the members of different ethnic groups, in the language of Barth, there emerges "a congruence of codes and values – in other words, a similarity or community of culture."[41] It is important to recognize that social system formation takes place simultaneously on various levels, which can be represented as sets of concentric circles:

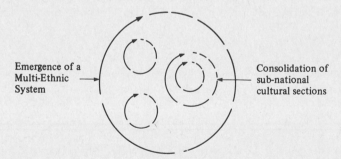

Emergence of a Multi-Ethnic System — Consolidation of sub-national cultural sections

A question which must be left for further discussion is whether the similarity in tactics and strategies adopted across the spectrum of Nigerian society can eventually facilitate mutual accommodation and even cohesion, or whether the parallel process of emphasizing group boundaries and cultural dissimilarities will serve as a fully countervailing factor. The second concern that can also be deferred at this stage is the recognition that however much the process of group solidarity and competitive mistrust might have become generalized along vertical axes within Nigerian society, the environments of elite interaction will continue to serve a unique role in facilitating the persistence of this mode of social behavior. Billy Dudley, a Nigerian political scientist, was more categorical in his presentation of this argument:

> what has been called 'tribalism' is seen to be part of the mechanism through which the political elite maintains itself in power and exercises its influence. It is therefore an attribute of elite behavior ... the educated elite became the chief proponents and purveyors of parochialism and particularistic values.[42]

The same point was expressed in harsher terms by Dr Kenneth Dike, a former Igbo Vice-Chancellor of the University of Ibadan: "It must be said to our shame that the Nigerian intellectual, far from being an influence for national integration, is the greatest exploiter of parochial and clannish sentiment."[43] In the discussion in Part III of the transition to civilian rule in 1978–9, it will be shown how his self-criticism by Nigerian academics must be considered within a broader framework which recognizes the contribution to the maintenance of this system of opposition and distrust by individuals and groups from all sectors and strata of the society.

SEGMENTATION AND MATERIAL REWARDS

Most students of Nigerian politics have had to grapple not only with the phenomenon of vertically segmented groups but also with the even more daunting realization that such identities become highly salient to political affairs and to the activities of governmental bodies. Robin Cohen, in a study primarily concerned with trade union issues in Nigeria, felt it necessary to make the following succinct observation about the politics of the First Republic:

> behind the liberal facade of formal political institutions and debate lay a series of vicious struggles over the allocation and distribution of political offices, the award of contracts, positions in the corporations and state boards, and the distribution of social and economic benefits.[44]

The special tactic that came to predominate in these "vicious struggles" was the articulation of the conflict in terms of culturally defined groups.

A notable attempt to create a model of these interlinked processes was made by Ken Post and Michael Vickers in their 1973 study. Post and Vickers recognized that the key factor in Nigerian politics had become the mutually reinforcing interplay between cultural identities and the pursuit of material benefits within the arenas of competitive politics. The term "Conglomerate Society" (which was their adaptation of the "plural society"), as well as that of

52

"System of Rewards," was used to capture the essence of the Nigerian political and social order:

> In the case of the Conglomerate Society, the basic conflict was the mobilization of people, not towards some transcending national loyalty but rather towards identification with an intermediate cultural section. The System [of Rewards] structures political life in such a way as to make it a constant struggle for rewards of various kinds, and much of this struggle was between sections...

> Thus we may sum up our discussion of the System of Rewards by saying that in general its basic capacity to produce conflict was rooted in the 'style' of politics which it inevitably produced, its effect upon political behavior and values.[45]

There is much that is insightful and useful in Post and Vickers' attempt to grapple with the nexus between the key elements of Nigeria's political life. One way in which their model is not fully satisfactory, however, is in the resort to a tautologous argument: what they call the "System of Rewards" is seen as structuring political life so as "to make it a constant struggle for rewards." They have compressed several strands of their argument too tightly, thereby losing any sense of causality. The struggle for rewards is a basic factor in all social life. The peculiar manner in which that struggle has become routinized in Nigeria involves to an important degree the mobilizing of what Post and Vickers call "cultural sections." The "System" which then emerges includes the ways in which such "sectionalism" becomes a resource (a) for members of the "rising class" in struggling for a disproportionate share of social benefits and for control and ownership over units of the economy (usually mediated through the monopolizing of strategic state offices), and (b) which simultaneously enables a non-elite member of the society to feel, as I have written elsewhere, that "the real hope of socio-economic betterment lies in the success of his relative, or other son of the soil, in getting a lien on the public purse and trickling a few coins down to him."[46]

In addition to carrying the above analysis a step further with my discussion of prebendalism, the importance in Nigeria of individual and group participation, and of the need for political activists to appear responsive to the wishes of wider sets of people, will be linked to my discussion of the deep-seated, or socially intrinsic, nature of the problematic of democratic government in that country. The reader of an earlier draft of these chapters recognized the importance of "relating notions of democracy to the private appropriation of publicly defined economic advantages." He therefore acknowledged the relevance to Nigeria of "democracy as a crucial defense by small groups to protect their access to the public till."[47]

In his influential critique of group theory, Mancur Olson stated: "If the individuals in any large group are interested in their own welfare, they will not voluntarily make any sacrifices to help their group attain its political (public or collective) objectives."[48] A comparable statement for the Nigerian case, however, must acknowledge that the very *perception* of the welfare and interests of individuals becomes intricately connected with those of his or her

53

group. Indeed, the fundamental social process in Nigeria is one in which these two propositions – (a) I want to get ahead and prosper, and (b) my group (ethnic, regional, linguistic) must get ahead and prosper – cannot logically be separated, whether in the context of behavior, action or consciousness.

Now I have expounded in these pages the various dimensions of politics as it relates to the multi-ethnic nature of Nigerian society, the final area that remains to be explored, on a theoretical level, is the basic mechanisms that connect political entrepreneurs with political brokers and general supporters, and all of these with the arena of public offices. The factors of clan, ethnicity and public offices in Nigeria will be shown to be brought into a dynamic relationship which is upheld by patron-client ties and by prebendal attitudes to the pursuit and exploitation of state-power.

5

Clientelism and prebendal politics

Two fundamental elements of the socio-political system which affect and often determine the allocation of public goods in Nigeria are the phenomena of clientelism and prebendalism. Clientelism is as essential to a satisfactory analysis of Nigerian politics and society as are the features of ethnicity and class. It is clientelism, often referred to as patron-client ties, which is the common thread underlying ethnic, regional and religious identities. Clientelism is not seen here as an alternative framework of analysis to that of class or ethnicity, as some writers maintain. An individual seeks out patrons as he or she moves upward socially and materially; such individuals also come to accept ties of solidarity from their own clients which they view as fundamental to the latter's security and continued advancement as well as their own. Clientelism therefore is the very channel through which one joins the dominant class and a practice which is then seen as fundamental to the continued enjoyment of the perquisites of that class. Ethnicity, as I have discussed at length, comprises sets of easily mobilized identities which can be invoked to add greater strength to patron-client ties and can mask the more materialistic motivation of patrons and clients alike.

The state in Nigeria is essentially comparable to the state in most developing countries which are minimally industrialized and in which the majority of the population is tied to agrarian pursuits often of marginal or precarious profitability. The state enjoys a pre-eminent position because the nation was created by foreign conquest and domination and not through a gradual process of aggregation or expansion of indigenous societies. The colonial power, and the economic processes it fostered, defined the essential elements of the future for the subjugated peoples. Continued foreign penetration and domination of the economy after political independence, together with the constraints to peripheral capitalist industrialization in the world economy, meant that access to the state remained disproportionately important in the struggle for resources for upward mobility.

Nigeria, in the decades following independence, has never had a stable state-power, and the form of politics which operated at all levels – irrespective of the regime in power – can be termed "prebendal politics." A "prebend" is

55

an office of state, typical of feudal Europe and China, which an individual procures either through examinations or as a reward for loyal service to a lord or ruler. According to Max Weber,

> We wish to speak of '*prebends*' and of a 'prebendal' organization of office, wherever the lord assigns to the official rent payments for life, payments which are somehow fixed to objects or which are essentially *economic* usufruct from lands or other sources. They must be compensations for the fulfilment of actual or fictitious office duties; they are goods permanently set aside for the economic assurance of the office.[1]

The peculiar political and economic conditions of the post-colonial world have contributed to the entrenchment of a form of state organization, and of attitudes regarding the uses of state office, which are pre-modern. Instead of the constitutional and legal systems, as well as the stated impersonal norms, determining the form of this state organization, such legal-rational features largely serve to camouflage extensive prebendal practices.

I shall contend that clientelism and prebendalism are two of the fundamental principles of political organization and behavior in Nigeria. An individual seeks the support and protection of an *oga* or a "godfather," while trying to acquire the basic social and material goods – loans, scholarships, licenses, plots of urban land, employment, promotion – and the main resource of the patron in meeting these requests is quite literally a piece of the state.[2] Such an argument can easily be made in the case of ministerial appointments, or positions on government boards. It also applies, however, to individuals within the nominally private sector, since the business world is hemmed in by bureaucratic regulations which derive from the nationalistic and developmental concerns of post-independence governments. To do business one must be able to procure import and export licenses, building and other permits; and then there is the welter of development grants and loans that can reduce the burden of initial capital investment.[3] In the case of Nigeria and some other African countries, there are the special phenomena of marketing boards (or other renamed agricultural agencies) which became the depositories of large sums taxed from peasant agricultural production. The access of individuals to the use of these funds was secured via the capture of regional governments by political parties during the terminal colonial period. More recently, the expansion of petroleum production in Nigeria, which amounts in years of high output to 85–90 per cent of state revenues, heightens the centrality of the state as the locus of the struggle for resources for personal advancement and group security. One way of seeing the extensive corruption in Nigeria is as const tuting part of "the economic assurance of office," which in the quotation above from Max Weber is presented as a fundamental component of a prebendal system.

The existence of a prebendalized state, and the easy adaptation of traditional patron-client relationships to the pursuit of modern material goods, means that these two features of the system – prebendalism and clientelism – are mutually reinforcing. To obtain and keep clients, one must gain a prebendal office; and to be sure that in the distribution of prebendal offices an individual or his kin have a reasonable chance of procuring one, clients must be gathered together to make their collective claims as well as to prove that the aspirant patron (or potential holder of prebendal office) is a person of consequence whose co-optation would be rewarding to the "political entrepreneurs." The reintroduction of electoral politics, therefore, revitalizes and promotes clientelistic networks. The widespread desire for prebendal office can also be seen as an ever-present stimulus for the maintenance of, or return to, electoral politics. Administrative appointments under a military system also involve the distribution of prebends, since there is seldom any real change in the socio-economic system with the intervention of soldiers in politics. Yet a competitive electoral system, with its vast array of ministerial and sub-ministerial appointments, with legislative offices and their private staff positions to be filled, is a veritable boon to prebendal politics. Opportunities are multiplied as political parties compete for votes, and minor patrons (or brokers) enjoy new leverage to procure preferential treatment, since it is the aggregating of votes which determines success, and the only route to such votes is via the recruitment of presumed influential mediators.

Having sketched in this free-handed manner the basic ingredients and parameters of Nigerian politics, I can now examine some of the theoretical literature to see what further insights can be added, and what adjustments or refinements must be made to these theories to enhance their relevance to Nigeria. One special advantage of the prebendal/clientelistic mode of analysis is that it opens up to the study of Nigerian politics more direct lines of comparison with other African as well as non-African experiences.

THE CLIENTELISTIC MODE OF ANALYSIS

"Clientelism," "patronage systems," "patron-client clusters," are terms that are used interchangeably to refer to the same phenomenon. The basic theory derives from anthropology, and among the many available formulations, the following by James C. Scott is clear and explicit:

> The patron-client relationship – an exchange relationship between roles – may be defined as a special case of dyadic (two-person) ties involving a largely instrumental friendship in which an individual of higher socio-economic status (patron) uses his own influence and resources to provide protection or benefits or both, for a person of lower status (client) who, for his part, reciprocates by offering general support and assistance, including personal services to the patron.[4]

The study of clientelism as a crucial "mechanism of power,"[5] especially in developing societies, proliferated very rapidly during the 1970s. Some authors, such as Alex Weingrod, saw a difference in the use of the notion of "patronage" by anthropologists and by political scientists. For the former, it is "a type of social relationship," while for the latter it is "a feature of government."[6] In the case of Nigeria, it will be argued that this distinction is

57

not a meaningful one: patron-client ties reflect a social relationship which has also become a crucial element of the governmental process.

René Lemarchand, in his influential essay, refers to the "spillover of clientelistic reciprocities."[7] Most individuals are bearers of a range of possible identities and ties, a point that was made in my earlier discussion of ethnicity. It is the special task of the political entrepreneur in a country like Nigeria to manage, or facilitate, the spillover of these reciprocities so that the force of moral sentiment is added to the pursuit of state office and material benefits. With regard to the ways in which clientelistic modes can flow into and reinforce each other, Lemarchand cites the intriguing example of Senegal, in which "the transformation of feudal into saintly patron-client ties has occurred via the Muslim brotherhoods and then these same ties have become operative in the contemporary context of clan politics."[8] In the case of Nigeria, many relevant insights can be gleaned from the examination of this complex process by C. S. Whitaker in his general study of Northern Nigeria.[9] It is quite likely that this process explains to an important degree the dominant role that individuals from the former Northern Region have been able to play in Nigerian politics from 1950 to the present. Finally, the very manner in which the dominant party in the 1979 elections, the National Party of Nigeria, was constructed, can be shown to be based on the creation of a "pyramid" of patron-client clusters, to use Lemarchand's idea,[10] which brings to party politics the "transcending through incorporation" of sectional identities.

CLASS, CLIENTELISM AND ETHNICITY

Part of the attractiveness of the clientelistic mode of analysis to scholars is that it suggests a way of overcoming what they see as the inadequacy of class analysis and the self-fulfilling nature of ethnic models of politics. I shall deal briefly with the first concern, and at greater length with the intractable problem of escaping what can be termed "ethnic determinism." James C. Scott, for example, sees the "overall values" of "the class model of conflict" as being "dubious in the typical nonindustrial situation where most political groupings cut vertically across class lines."[11]

Scott's attempt to portray the clientelistic model as an alternative to what he sees as the less suitable one of class has been ably contested by other scholars. Thus Peter Flynn not only shows how the phenomenon of clientelism helps us to understand the mechanisms of class control, but also demonstrates how such a perception is implicit in Scott's own writings on Southeast Asia.[12] Lemarchand, in a more recent essay, similarly argues in support of the compatibility between class and clientelistic models of analysis.[13]

Yet, the emergence of a pervasive patron-client system does affect in important ways the articulation of class action. Indeed, it can be contended that such networks serve to legitimize the unfair share of goods and services enjoyed by individuals of high socio-economic status. Sydel Silverman has pointed out quite cogently how much of a myth the assumed flow of goods and services downward in such systems usually is.[14] Hence the importance of what Judith Chubb has called the "element of hope" in her study of clientelism in Palermo in southern Italy.[15] Her study parallels in many respects my contention that the pervasive phenomenon of clientelism as a strategy of both survival and upward mobility in Nigeria is not diminished by the persistence of affluence for a relative few and penury for the many.

As has been the case in class analysis, so also is ethnicity often regarded as a social phenomenon which is at variance with that of clientelism. Lemarchand, for example, advanced in his early essay the following analytical distinction:

> Although clientelism and ethnicity are in many ways interrelated, they refer to basically different levels of solidarity; whereas clientelism describes a personalized relationship, ethnicity is fundamentally a group phenomenon.[16]

Lemarchand presented an unnecessary contrast between these two phenomena, although his formulation is consonant with much of the anthropological literature. Although ethnicity is a "group phenomenon," it is also one which is usually manifested through the behavior of individuals. The individual strategies that Judith Chubb discusses, which involve attachment to a patron,[17] can become generalized into the attachment of a kinship group, depending upon the composition and structure of the society in question.

Richard Sandbrook perceives this possibility clearly when he writes of the ways in which ethnic groups and sub-groups can become the basic clusters in patron-client relationships.[18] The operative clientelistic ties in such situations are established between leaders and sub-leaders of such groups. (All the while, I would emphasize, individual clientelistic strategies *within* ethnic sections also continue.) While suggesting the instrumental nature (i.e., exchanges of political support for material benefits and services) of clientelistic ties, scholars are often obliged to recognize the "non-monetary" affective nature of such relationships, which often enable them to persist over time.[19] James Scott, for example, concedes that "there is no contradiction ... in holding that a patron-client link originates in a power relationship and also holding that genuine affective ties reinforce that link."[20]

In the case of Nigeria and many other parts of Africa, we do not need to engage in what amounts to "back-pedalling" because there is no point in beginning with Scott's initial assertion that patron-client clusters are associations of people who "are not close kin."[21] Sandbrook is more direct in arguing that although "mutual self-interest" or "mercenary ties" motivate the establishment of such clusters, they can derive added strength by being combined with a "moral tie" such as that of kinship.[22] What clientelism can bring to an ethnically structured political system is a mechanism which, over time, can potentially shift the focus away from relations based on cultural identity. Indeed, clientelism might prove as effective a mechanism in engendering this transformation as growing class consciousness. Such a suggestion has been made by Lemarchand:

In the case of ethnicity, perceptions of mutual interest are dependent upon, and limited by, perceptions of cultural affinities; clientelism, on the other hand ... may cause a redefinition of one's original tribal identity by reference to a wider cultural focus.[23]

The basic mechanism of linking up with a patron can therefore operate among individuals with "shared" cultural characteristics, as it can among those who belong to different ethnic groups or who are not ethnically differentiated. From such a standpoint, ethnicity is largely an added variable which will affect the pattern of factionalism or patron-client clustering in a society. What the distinctive case of northern Nigeria demonstrates is that "a wider cultural focus" – in this case "Northern identity – can serve to link together a complex aggregation of different peoples over several decades through multi-layered clientelistic ties. It may well be that a challenge not yet met in Nigerian national politics is the need to "generate and maintain consensus among distinct client groups," as Judith Chubb states,[24] using both monetary and non-monetary patronage resources.

It is important not to lose sight of the still evolving nature of clientelistic practices in Nigeria. The approach of the NPN in the campaign and elections of 1978–9 was very much to use a clientelistic strategy which would incorporate different ethnic sections of the population into one party through the affiliation of individuals acknowledged to be patrons of their particular communities. It is possible to posit as a possible culmination of this process a system based on what Lemarchand calls "mass clientelism" – i.e., with large blocs of the population linked in such a manner to the public power.[25] In Nigeria, before the overthrow of the first civilian government in January 1966, clientelistic ties sometimes existed between minority communities in one region and the dominant party in another.[26] What was often regarded by scholars at the time as a conflict-generating pattern of alliances can now be seen as a forerunner of the more comprehensive and pragmatic links achieved by the NPN organizers in 1978–9. By way of a diagrammatic presentation, political clientelism in the Nigerian context can be further clarified.

Clientelism and Party Formation: A Diagrammatic Sequence

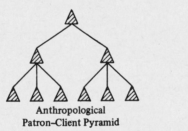 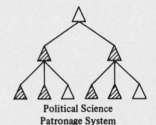

Anthropological
Patron–Client Pyramid

Political Science
Patronage System

The simple model on the left depicts a hierarchical cluster of dyadic ties between individuals of superior and inferior status. The usually shared characteristics of language, ethnicity or religion among individuals belonging to such a pyramid is suggested by the uniform shading. On the right is a model of the basic patronage network in which a political boss is linked to subordinate brokers who can guarantee the political support (usually electoral) of a set of individuals who are materially rewarded for their loyalty. Shared ethnic or other characteristics may or may not be relevant in such networks. In many cases political ties are reinforced by a "social relationship," using Weingrod's expression, while in others the link is strictly instrumental and therefore more easily shifted to other patrons.

Nigeria A
Ethnic and Regional Clientelistic Clusters

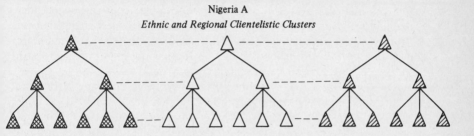

Each of these clusters represents a different ethno-linguistic or regional group in Nigeria. The creation of these links, which I have discussed in the sections on the politics of ethnicity, have been evolving throughout the modern (i.e., colonial and post-colonial) periods. Individuals seek to advance materially and socially by establishing ties of a dependent nature with well-placed members of their ethnic or regional group. Horizontal links between individuals of different clusters (indicated by the broken lines), but of comparable economic status, do exist, but they are usually weaker than the vertical ties of solidarity. These horizontal ties are often stronger among members of a higher socio-economic category than among those of a lower one, reflecting not only the level of consciousness of class interests but also the capacity effectively to pursue those interests.

Nigeria B
Rival Party Structures

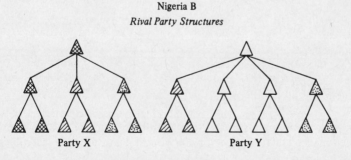

Party X   Party Y

61

Democracy and prebendal politics

Nigerian political parties, whether of the pre-1966 or post-1978 periods, are basically similar in structure. Individuals do not belong to parties in any random fashion. Clientage networks, either of a traditional nature or those created in preparation for electoral competition, link individuals who usually share or can claim to share an ethno-linguistic identity. In the diagram on the left in "Nigeria B," the closer similarity of shading between two of the three component clusters is meant to indicate the process of ethnic consolidation among ethnic or regional sub-groups as a consequence of national electoral competition. In both parties, the predominance of a particular "nationality group" among the supporting elements, as indicated, is responsible for such parties being designated as "belonging" to the Igbo, Hausa-Fulani or Yoruba, despite the presence of other – but usually more dependent – ethnic clientage groupings.

The party structure outlined in "Nigeria B" can remain the basic model as long as there is party politics in Nigeria. A party such as the NPN, which prides itself on its success in embracing a wide array of ethnic groups from numerous states of the Nigerian Federation, is really a successful aggregation of many vertical ethnic clusters as indicated in the diagram on the right in "Nigeria B."

Nigeria C
Alternative Party Structures

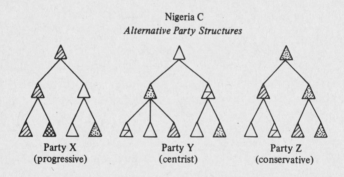

Party X
(progressive)

Party Y
(centrist)

Party Z
(conservative)

The critical question is whether the "Nigeria B" pattern could become stabilized under civilian rule, thereby requiring some consociational arrangement either in the composition of the federal government or within the apparatus of the dominant party itself; or whether a pronounced shift can take place away from such a pattern. If the latter occurs, one would envision a new network of party supporters as indicated in "Nigeria C." Residues of ethno-linguistic clusters would persist, as is shown in the far left and right diagrams. However, these would now co-exist with various patterns of vertical linkages among individuals with different ethno-linguistic identities. If such a development ever took place, Nigerian politics could also become more overtly ideological, and the ideological tendencies earlier evident among Nigerian parties can increasingly become an important indicator of political affiliations. The polity is still shown to be highly clientelistic in its socio-political linkages, but these can be as much trans-ethnic as ethnic in nature. It almost goes without saying that these diagrams represent, at the time of writing, an ideal case for a country like Nigeria. The question remains, therefore, how much the pattern in "Nigeria B" will continue to prevail and prevent the realization of pattern "Nigeria C."

An even more "futuristic" option is one in which both clientelism and ethnicity are no longer the main determinants of political affiliation. In such a scenario, parties would aggregate individuals from various socio-economic strata, and the relative proportion of these strata as represented among party supporters and within the party leadership would vary according to the distribution frequently associated with parties in the mature liberal democracies. Such an option represents quite an abstraction when compared with the dynamics of social identity and political mobilization in contemporary Nigeria. It is my concern to analyze these actual dynamics, and to see what paths can conceivably lead from them to a more stable, efficient and democratic polity.

THE BASIS AND EXTENT OF PREBENDAL POLITICS

My discussion of prebendalism so far has been based on certain crucial observations regarding the treatment of state power as a congeries of offices which can be competed for, appropriated and then administered for the benefit of individual occupants and their support groups. One can also distinguish here clientelism from prebendalism, although for some scholars the term "political clientelism" will cover both the nature of social relationships and the ways in which the public power is utilized to maintain them. For me, the two notions constitute complementary aspects of a general phenomenon. Clientelism defines the nature of individual and group relationships within the wider socio-political sphere, while prebendalism is primarily a function of the competition for, and appropriation of, the offices of the state.

Although my perception of this phenomenon can be traced back most pertinently to the writings of Max Weber, the German sociologist did not arrive at the exact formulation I am using. A wholly separate category of political authority is being considered here which consists, in part, of elements of what Weber saw as patrimonial, and especially decentralized patrimonial, authority. For me, prebendalism is not necessarily a subset, or consequence of, patrimonialism, although that can sometimes be the case, as northern Nigeria demonstrates with its traditional (patrimonial) emirates which have evolved in the contemporary context to embrace a prebendal use of state offices. To clarify these points, let us first look at a central dichotomy in Weber's typology of authority systems:[27]

Traditional patrimonial administration	Western bureaucratic administration
1. Staffing on the basis of personal loyalty to a Chief, either of a traditional nature or freely entered into.	1. A regular system of appointment and promotion on the basis of free contract.
2. No well-defined areas of competence – shifting of tasks and powers.	2. Clearly defined spheres of competence, subject to impersonal rules.
3. Hierarchy of authority based on traditional legal norms and precedents, yet subordinate to the arbitrary decisions of the Chief.	3. A rational ordering of relations of superiority and inferiority.
4. Technical training not a basic qualification for office.	4. Technical training as a regular requirement.
5. No regular salaries. Upkeep provided by Chief's household, or stores, or through the creation of benefices.	5. Fixed salaries, typically paid in money.

Weber's conception of patrimonial authority was not an inflexible one: it shaded into sub-types at its margins. Recruitment could be on either a patrimonial or "extra-patrimonial basis," the latter involving individuals who were not previously kinsmen or dependents of the Chief. The most important shading which yields the sub-type of decentralized patrimonial authority is that in which an individual becomes the holder of a benefice or prebend. Unlike "pure patrimonialism," in which "there is complete separation of the functionary from the means of carrying out his function," in the decentralized case, both the governing powers "and the corresponding economic advantages have been appropriated."[28] A number of other consequences flow from such an altered system, including the possibility that promotion can be made "on a basis of seniority or of particular objectively determined achievements."[29] Let us contrast a typology of Weber's decentralized patrimonial administration with one based on my conception of a prebendal system (see table on page 65).

We have moved on from the insights Weber had at the turn of the century to a more distinct formulation which applies not only to Nigeria and other postcolonial countries, but also to dependent sections of some Western industrialized nations. A prebendal system is one in which "legal/rational" and other societal norms of authority merge, producing a hybrid that cannot be conveniently subsumed under any specific heading. On the one hand, there are

Decentralized patrimonial administration	Post-colonial African prebendal system
1. Overarching traditional authority system with loyalty (strong or attenuated) to a Chief or Ruler.	1. Varying mix of authority systems including personalistic, legal-rational, military-corporatist, and sub-national traditional authorities.
2. Offices of state as prebends granted by the Chief.	2. Offices of state as prebends acquired through appointment by superior office-holders or won through popular election.
3. Appropriation of economic advantages of state office.	3. Exploitation of economic advantages of state office while pretending to uphold stipulated public duties.
4. National patrimonial ideology extended to decentralized units.	4. Clientelistic responsibilities used to justify extra-legal use of offices.
5. Integrated state order with centrifugal tendencies.	5. Fissiparous state order, often unstable and conflictual.

legal rules stipulating the purview of offices, how they are to be staffed, the required technical training and the material entitlements for office-holders. On the other hand, however, personal loyalties and communal identities, the private appropriation of the means of administration and, finally, the transformation of offices from their stipulated administrative purpose into a direct or indirect economic resource, are factors which have equal weight in determining the nature and exercise of public power.

The office-holders in Weber's decentralized patrimonial administration – feudal knights, Indian *jagirdars*, Egyptian Mamelukes – were able to exercise many of the powers which accrued to the patrimonial order as a whole.[30] In the case of a prebendal order, however, its fundamental instability is in part attributable to the absence of a continuous authoritative force and a legitimizing ideology. Offices can be won and exploited, but they can also be snatched away, not so much by a dissatisfied Chief as by rival contestants with their opposed army of supporters. Office-holders in a prebendalized state affect a patrimonial stance – "Whether you vote for us or not, we will remain in power."[31] Yet they lack the plenary power to sustain their claims. There is a "tug" towards patrimonialism in the Nigerian system. It can be seen in the political hegemony over the nation that politicians from the north have been able to exercise largely as a consequence, as has been mentioned, of the more extensive patrimonial basis of authority in that part of the country. It can also be seen in the survival of traditional systems of chieftaincy in many parts of Nigeria, or their adoption where they did not formerly exist. A correlative of this second point is the pursuit of chieftaincy titles by aspirant politicians, largely for honorific purposes, but also because of the attitudes of deference and respect such titles often still command. Finally, and perhaps most significantly, the "patrimonial tug" can be seen in the necessity of having "grand patrons" for Nigerian political parties.

The last point above will be demonstrated when I discuss aspects of the transition to civilian rule in Part III. It can be stated briefly here that a great deal of the maneuvering during the period of party formation in 1978 involved the attempt to obtain for emerging political coalitions the adherence of individuals regarded as capable of serving as Grand Patrons. In the case of Dr Nnamdi Azikiwe, two of the parties, the NPN and NPP, waged a keen battle to have him declare his affiliation to their organization. His decision to join the latter precipitated a further realignment and the emergence of a third party, the GNPP. In the case of the UPN, Chief Awolowo was both party leader and Grand Patron, while in the NPN the actual position of Grand Patron was bestowed on Alhaji A. Makaman Bida, although it would have been ceded to Azikiwe had he accepted it. Similar observations can be made in regard to lesser patrons – e.g., Joseph Tarka of the Tiv people – and the patrimonial role they fulfill, ensuring the political affiliation of sectional groups.

This "tug" towards patrimonialism in Nigerian politics should not be regarded as the basis for the construction of a political system: it is a factor, a sentiment, but neither a direction nor a goal. The country's constitutional, legal and political systems are too determinedly "Western-oriented" to permit such a change. The position of Grand Patron or Chief serves more as an instrument for the consolidation of a particular group and their monopolization of a subsection of the national patrimony than as an actual office from which power and authority can flow through the system. My attempts to devise a formal conceptualization of prebendalism, and then to contrast it with patrimonialism, may also be seen as a necessary corrective to the over-use of the latter concept in contemporary analyses of the state in developing countries.

In a highly pertinent essay, Robin Theobald has criticized the decreasing analytical utility of the term "patrimonialism" because of the quite different socio-political systems to which it has been applied. Wherever reliance on an exchange of favors or resources between "strategically located individuals" frequently occurs, or where the granting of "fiefs and benefices" to elites by a ruler to complement his coercive authority takes place, "patrimonialism" is applied as a "catch-all concept."[32] Without engaging in a full discussion of Theobald's critique, it will be suggested here that "prebendalism" would more appropriately fit some of the cases he reviews which fail to meet such important requirements of a patrimonial order as the presence and ultimate authority of a ruler and the general legitimating role of a traditional ideology.

Yet, the mere existence of a patronage system, even one based on clientelistic ties of significant duration, should not warrant the application of the term "prebendalism." To preserve the analytical sharpness of this formulation, a prebendal system will be seen not only as one in which the offices of state are allocated and then exploited as benefices by the office-holders, but also as one where such a practice is legitimated by a set of political norms according to which the appropriation of such offices is not just an act of individual greed or ambition but concurrently the satisfaction of the short-term objectives of a subset of the general population.

Let us conclude this discussion by reflecting on a clear evocation of the "universe of understanding" in Nigeria which sustains prebendal attitudes to politics.[33] It is part of the report of a Nigerian political scientist and sometime political correspondent, Dr Haroun Adamu, of a tour he made in the south-east and north-east areas of the country:

In a specific case, at Ngo town, in Andoni, Rivers State the people there through their leaders requested the governor, Zamani Lekwot, to appoint one of their sons to his cabinet. This is a normal request. For, it is strongly believed in this country that if you do not have one of your kind in the local, state and/or national decision-making bodies, nobody would care to table your troubles before the decision-makers, much less find solutions to them. Therefore, having someone in one of these bodies makes a community feel a part of the system since that community is vicariously participating in the government, be it local, state, or federal.

Governor Lekwot's answer seems to me rather inadequate. He told the people of Ngo that Executive Councils are not houses of representatives where all communities have equal representation. It may well be that if Governor Lekwot were to appoint his commissioners from all the various communities in the state then his cabinet would be most unruly. However, appointments to such a high office must be based on a very important criterion – that of representation, be it on the basis of community or administrative zone. This issue of representation and thus participation ... gives a feeling of belonging to a group of people who feel neglected ...

One other place where this view is prevalent is Bauchi State ... A young businessman whose contact with various groups in the state is tops, would like to know from me whether those in authority over there in Lagos are aware that they in Bauchi have no representation in the Federal government.

'What do you mean?' I asked.

'It is that simple,' he said, 'we have no one in the Supreme Military Council; we have no one in the National Council of State and we have no one in the Federal Executive Council.'

'Would the state have fared any better if you had anyone in those bodies?' I countered.

'Sure. When I come to Lagos on business, I do not have anyone to go to with my problems to help me solve them. That's the difference. I am not blaming anybody,' he continued. 'This country is rather massive. It could be an oversight and not by design. But it is left for those of us who suffer as a result of this oversight to scream so that the government could hear us and rectify the situation.'[34]

The positive aspects of prebendal politics can be discerned in this report. Ideas of representation and participation, of identity with the government and especially the bridging between center and periphery in a geographically extensive country, are well reflected. So also is my contention that a critical dimension of democracy in Nigeria involves this perception of the degree of access of individuals, defined very often in terms of a communal group, to the economic advantages that pertain to government offices, whatever their specific function. Such prevalent attitudes, however, render it difficult to achieve the full "institutionalization" of the state, the delegation of precise functions to office-holders who can be expected to conduct public business on the basis of regular and predictable procedures.

Several aspects of my notion of prebendal politics are foreshadowed in the work of contemporary scholars. René Lemarchand refers to the practice of "patrimonial clientelism" as involving "the doling out of offices in return for administrative and political benefits."[35] A statement of his which comes quite close to my formulation is the following:

> What is involved ... is the creation of new solidarities based on expectations of concrete, short-run benefits. Although the men in charge of running the machine may occasionally bolster their authority by charisma or coercion, they can best be thought of as political entrepreneurs. Their job is to weld together disparate ethnic segments through the allocation of prebends.[36]

With regard to the basic motivation which sustains such a system, Richard Sandbrook rightly points to the general element of insecurity: "Legal guarantees of physical security, status, and wealth are relatively weak or non-existent." As a consequence, individuals seek attachment to "'big men' capable of providing protection and even advancement."[37] The study of clientelism points us in the direction of relationships of power and attachment, that of prebendalism towards the material resources needed to cultivate or maintain such relationships and the consequences of such pressures on the nature of the state. It is a full circle: "a public post could be a client-creating resource," as James Scott contends;[38] it should also be seen that the support of a set of clients can be used to give legitimacy to the pursuit and appropriation of such posts.

Both strong and weak are united in the basic outlook which sustains such a system. John Waterbury writes tellingly about the effect of "real or perceived vulnerability," which is experienced even by those who appear politically powerful but are as a consequence "exposed."[39] The many "vulnerabilities of 'modernisation'" forge a pact between patron and clients, leaders and supporters.[40] The apparent gap between the struggle to maintain and increase power, on the one hand, and that of coping and survival, on the other, is reduced in daily life. Everyone recognizes that they are "playing the same game," a remark Frederick Barth applied to ethnicity but which applies doubly to a prebendal system in which the manipulation of state-power is added to the manipulation of cultural identities. As should be anticipated, the factors of clientelism and prebendalism emerged with greater force when the lid was gradually lifted towards the end of the 1970s on open political mobilizing and party formation.

6

Military rule and economic statism

In Part I, I explored the ideals of democratic theory and discussed how these are realized or modified in practice. It was also indicated how democracy has remained on the Nigerian political agenda despite the many upheavals. Any governmental system which seeks to be democratic must be responsive to the ways in which its constituent groups and communities pursue their fundamental interests, while providing a framework for transcending some of these traditions over time. In the case of Nigeria, the social context in which its citizens pursue their material and other interests, and combine politically to defend them, has created a difficult terrain for all governmental systems. This social context and its political manifestations have tended to be particularly antithetical to the entrenching of constitutional government. As a consequence, rule by the military has served as a means of suspending, if not resolving, the contradictions between democracy and prebendalism. Moreover, during its long stint in power, from 1966 to 1979, the effect of rule by the military government was to accentuate the centrality of the state in the nation's economic system and thus, in a circular fashion, to fuel the various features of prebendalism.

After the first military *coup d'état* of 15 January 1966, political parties were disbanded by governmental decree. A similar fate befell all legislative bodies. The political vacuum created by these actions was eventually filled in various ways. One consequence of these developments is that the military and civil bureaucracies had to undergo what Amos Perlmutter, following Moshe Lissak, calls "role expansion."[1] Furthermore, such an expansion of these corporate and bureaucratic forces also had certain implications for the relative balance of influence of the various constitutive groups of Nigerian society. Quite specifically, it meant that the "minorities" in Nigeria – usually understood to refer to the *majority* of the population belonging to the numerous ethno-linguistic groups that are not Yoruba, Igbo or Hausa-Fulani – were able to play a much greater role in governing Nigeria because of (a) their numerical predominance in the military, (b) their significant representation in the federal civil service and especially their monopolization of many top positions, and (c) their greater commitment to the Nigerian

69

Federation, in contrast to the centrifugal pull of the three large sectional blocs of the population.[2]

The impact of regional and ethnic minorities on the political evolution of Nigeria, especially since 1966, cannot be given the full attention deserved by such a subject here. However, an attempt will still be made to indicate its relevance at various points in the ensuing discussion. Of equal importance is the fact that the established Nigerian way of pursuing basic, and especially material, interests could not be abolished by mere pronouncements or decrees of a military government. The process of clientelism and prebendalism continued without abating, despite the abolition of politics *per se*; and none of Nigeria's military governments between 1967 and 1979 was able – whatever their verbal commitments – to substitute a differently structured means of allocating and acquiring public goods.

After eleven continuous years of military rule, as the quotation from Haroun Adamu (p. 67) demonstrated, the attitudes which underlie prebendal politics were strongly in evidence. And it was not the military governor of just one particular state in the Federation, or the Federal Military Government itself, which constantly had to explain why an indigene from state X, or ethnic group or clan Y, had not been appointed to particular governing bodies. Such pressures were continuous, and they were exerted at all levels of the governmental system. In short, the boundary between the military and civil society, once the former intervened in the political arena, became a permeable one in both directions. Here is an example of the kind of representations (in this case, to former Brigadier Jemibewon, Governor of Oyo State) to which any member of the military government who enjoyed patronage powers was constantly subjected:

> we believe that because of your apparent dislike for the excise of Ogun State from Oyo State you could not care less for what arrangements are made for a successful take-off of the State. This attitude appears more vividly in the appointments of staff and the distribution of the necessary infrastructures for the take-off. The appointments are heavily weighted on the side of the Ijebus to the exclusion of the Egbados and the frustration of the Egbas. For example seven permanent secretaries were appointed from Ijebu division alone when it was possible for serving officers in other States of the Federation of very senior or higher grade to be considered for such appointments. Recently in the judiciary we understood that a senior Magistrate with no administrative experience was preferred to the experienced officer recommended by the Chief Justice as a Chief Registrar for Ogun State. We understand that most of the heads of divisions have to be Ijebus even though there might have been a possibility of upgrading the officers from other divisions to effect a working balance.[3]

Jemibewon refers to this letter as reflecting "the tragedy of our times" – if so, it was a tragedy that the military could contain but neither uproot nor transcend.

The political options which confronted Nigeria's military rulers were as follows:

1. They could hand power quickly back to civilian politicians so the latter could devise and operate a system which more directly reflected the widespread desire of Nigerians to have one of "their kind" in all possible prebendal posts so that their people would have "someone to go to with their problems."[4]
2. They could attempt to create a system which would not be fully responsive or respectful of such demands, but which went some distance in being so, while introducing elements and structures aimed at transcending this "communalized" prebendal view of the state.[5]
3. They could postpone indefinitely any attempt to accommodate the state to the existing social order and behavior patterns, and seek instead to use the state-power at their command to reshape completely both governmental structures as well as the social forces which impinged upon them.

Nigeria's military governments, and especially the Muhammed/Obasanjo regime (1975–9), eventually settled for the second of these three alternatives: a middle way of seeking to induce significant changes in socio-political behavior but without making the commitment (especially in planned duration of the regime) to ensure that such changes actually occurred. The consequence of such a compromise, or resignation, was that the first option was likely to reassert itself under civilian rule because of the increased tempo of demands by members of the public on government officials and the lack of self-restraint by the politicians in acceding to or even abetting these demands. Finally, the ways in which Nigeria's military has evolved in its recruitment and promotion methods has narrowed the gap between itself and civil society. In 1962, the dominant politicians from the far North pushed through a law calling for a quota system of recruitment into the army identical to that of popular electoral representation. From that point onwards, the Nigerian military has itself been "prebendalized," not, of course, to the same extent as the civil bureaucracy, but enough to limit its capacity to disregard such processes in the political sphere:

> Whereas before the system was introduced, recruitment and mobility were thought to be dependent on the individual's ability, with the [new] system the suspicion soon grew that this mattered less than who were one's 'patrons.' The 'unintended consequence' of the political decision to introduce a quota system was the politicization of the military.[6]

MILITARY RULE AND PREBENDAL POLITICS

One statement made by Major Kaduna Nzeogwu after he seized power in northern Nigeria in January 1966 will be echoed during many subsequent governments, and especially governmental changes, in Nigeria:

> Our enemies are the political profiteers, the swindlers, the men in high and low places that seek bribes and demand 10 per cent; those that seek to keep the country divided permanently so that they can remain in office as Ministers or

71

VIPs at least; the tribalists, the nepotists, those that make the country look big for nothing before international circles; those that have corrupted our society and put the Nigerian political calendar back by their words and deeds.[7]

Even though Nigeria was gradually broken into warring parts as a direct consequence of this coup, on both sides of the divide there was an agreement about the "terrible malady" of public corruption identified by "major Nzeogwu and his colleagues."[8] In a letter to Gowon and the military governors of the three other regions in October 1966, Colonel Ojukwu reminded them that the army at the time of the first coup in January 1966 "was held as the saving Messiah for the country," and that its programs

included that of purging the country of corruption, of making sure that ill-gotten goods were disgorged, of making the public and those who abused their positions of trust to feel that such actions do not pay.[9]

Ojukwu went on to refer to the need to continue with the commissions of inquiry into public institutions and private wealth "in order to sweep clean the public life of the country." Similarly, on the federal side, as Gowon first met with the civilians invited to join his government in June 1967, he cautioned them:

we will have to prepare a code of conduct which will ensure the good behaviour of all Commissioners and other public officers. As far as the Military Administration is concerned, the so-called 'ten percent' is dead for good.[10]

The commitment to rid the nation of corrupt use of public office gave way – even while the civil war was in progress, but especially after peace was restored – to corruption on a grand scale in Nigeria. Gowon is directly implicated in this collapse in standards, not because of his own misdoings, but because of his unwillingness to discipline his subordinates, to shuffle his cabinet (largely composed, after June 1967, of civilian commissioners, mainly former politicians), and to respond positively to the charges and information with which he was inundated concerning the malfeasance and arbitrary conduct of his chief subalterns, the military governors in the twelve states.

The governors in the states were under no obligation to account to the citizenry for their actions, since the Supreme Commander himself did not exact such accountability. Moreover, they enjoyed a monopoly of the legitimate use of force and the capacity to silence any protests about the ways in which they appropriated, or allowed others to misappropriate, state property. If the military governors during Gowon's administration "carried corruption to an unparalleled degree in the history of Nigeria," as Jemibewon asserts, it is not merely because a bunch of rogues happened to occupy those positions of responsibility at a particular time.[11] The factors which enabled the governors in Gowon's post-war regime to act as if they were provincial chiefs in a decentralized patrimonial order were the Head of State's weak leadership, the great flow of capital funds to the state coffers from petroleum export, the large post-war construction projects which required the awarding of contracts to local and foreign businesses, and finally, the limited accountability of any military administration.

There was little except force and the selective distribution of largesse to sustain such behavior in the absence of a supreme patrimonial ruler and an appropriate state ideology. As Kasfir aptly put it: "Government seemed to have lapsed into the private business ventures of its officials."[12] Any dividing line between public and private had disappeared: the very basis of prebendalism was stretched by the excesses, since they obliterated the notion of a "public office" subject to personal and communal manipulation by office-holders. According to Gowon's successor, Murtala Muhammed, "the military governors were running their fiefs like 'personal estates'."[13]

While it is necessary to recognize the weak leadership of Gowon and the limited political accountability of military officers for the constantly mounting abuses of the post civil war period, it is also important to recognize that a shift of major proportions had taken place in the nature and extent of the state during the post-war decade. Such a shift correlated directly with the magnitude of the increase in the state's financial resources:

The Federal Budget[14] *(in 'naira' millions)*

	1970–1	1973–4	1976–7
Revenue	756	2,172	7,070
Current expenditure	774	1,120	3,574
Capital expenditure	99	529	4,913

Since income from petroleum came to constitute over 80 per cent of federal revenue, the importance of the federal center – to which these revenues were paid directly – increased proportionately. As a consequence of this major shift in the relative importance of the public sector in Nigeria, the state assumed the capacity to determine not only Who gets What, When and How, but the very nature of the What around which the scramble would ensue. When the state itself becomes the key distributor of financial resources – and this in the absence of any socialist ideology – all governmental projects, whether the construction of all-weather roads, the staging of an Arts Festival, the building of a new capital, etc., become submerged by the intense pressures for the conversion of these projects into means of individual and group appropriation.

After the civil war ended in January 1970, the Gowon government had established a nine-point program which can be summarized as follows: (1) the reorganization of the armed forces; (2) the implementation of the Second National Development Plan and repair of the damage and neglect from the war; (3) the eradication of corruption in Nigerian life; (4) settlement of the question of the creation of more states; (5) the preparation and adoption of a

73

new Constitution; (6) the introduction of a new Revenue Allocation Formula; (7) the conducting of a national population census; (8) the organization of genuine national political parties; and (9) the organizing of elections and the installing of popularly elected governments in the states and the center. To these nine could be added the establishment of a new federal capital, which was also a major goal of the Gowon regime, but about which little was done before his overthrow.

All the major elements of Gowon's program, adopted by his successors Murtala Muhammed and Olusegun Obasanjo after his overthrow in July 1975, involved increased financial outlays by the federal government, as well as the taking over by the government of areas of activity in which state or local governments – as well as private individuals and community groups – had formerly played a significant if not dominant role. The implementation of a Universal Primary Education scheme meant that huge sums would thenceforth be provided by the federal government for the building of classrooms (with set minimum standards) all over the nation; it also meant that private contractors would now be drawn even more into lobbying state and federal officials for the lucrative contracts.[15] On the political/ideological side it meant that the state was assuming new responsibilities in ensuring the education of all Nigerian children. The massive construction projects involved in building the many new bridges and express highways, of housing units and pavilions for the 1977 Festival of Black and African Performing Arts (FESTAC) and the Trade Fair, for providing barracks to house tens of thousands of soldiers, all contributed to multiplying the impact, as well as the centrality, of the state in Nigeria.

The general consequence of the increase in the number of areas in which the central state apparatus now felt authorized and capable of making a direct impact, and the fact that the military regime simultaneously began the process of returning political authority to the people and their direct representatives, was that Nigeria was being bequeathed a statist political order which accentuated rather than attenuated prebendal attitudes to politics.

Richard Sklar demonstrated in his early writings how the regional governments in Nigeria had become engines for the generating of a "rising class' during the 1950s and post-independence years. As part of this generalizing process, not only was the location of the "cake" to be subdivided shifted from the regions to the center, but that "cake" became more of a material entity, even more something "out there," distinct from the daily productive energies of the people. The national purse to be distributed became increasingly filled with funds gained from the pumping of crude oil from the Nigerian subsoil and offshore areas and its transshipment abroad, a process which involved minimal input of Nigerian labor. Compounding the apparent absence of any limits to the state's financial capacity was the fact that the military government throughout the post civil war decade had no operative theory of the limits to government action.[16] Whatever seemed a sensible idea for the "development" of Nigeria after 1975 was undertaken, whether in

74

education, land use, agricultural policy, company ownership, national culture, local government reform or trade union organization.

The second decisive feature of the military government, especially after Gowon, was that, although it became more politically sensitive and sophisticated, it was still accountable to no one but the collective will within the Supreme Military Council (SMC). Following the assassination of Muhammed and the increasing assertiveness of Obasanjo, a strong commitment against the emergence of any lines of division within the SMC further minimized the Council's limited conciliar and controlling function.[17]

The combination of these factors – the seemingly unlimited capital funds, the absence of any boundaries to government intervention, and the limited accountability of the regime – meant that the process by which the energies of Nigerians have become highly focused on the actions, and identity, of state officials, was decisively enhanced by the experience of military government. The actual effects of military rule went contrary, therefore, to the expressed commitment to alter the dominant pattern of socio-political behavior, especially the intensity of partisan political competition, the sharpening of ethnic and regional identities and the abuse of office through corruption.[18]

In a typically incisive discussion of the problems of Nigeria's post-military civilian government, Claude Ake made the following relevant comment:

> the crux of the problem of Nigeria today is the overpoliticisation of social life.
>
> We are intoxicated with politics; the premium on political power is so high that we are prone to take the most extreme measures to win and to maintain political power ...
>
> As things stand now, the Nigerian state appears to intervene everywhere and to own virtually everything including access to status and wealth. Inevitably a desperate struggle to win control of state power ensues since this control means for all practical purposes being all powerful and owning everything. Politics became warfare, a matter of life or death.[19]

A clear gap can be seen to exist between the above observation by a leading Nigerian political scientist and the hope expressed six years earlier by General Murtala Muhammed. When Murtala inaugurated the Constitution Drafting Committee on 18 October 1975, he cautioned the delegates: "Politics must be transformed from its previous scenario of bitter personal wrangles into a healthy game of political argument and discussion."[20] One can suggest at this point that the transitional military regime of Muhammed and Obasanjo, while seeking to lay down "the basic infrastructure of a stable political order,"[21] also by dint of enhancing the state's omnipresence and omnicompetence in the devising and implementing of national projects, added even more fuel to prebendal politics in Nigeria, as I have defined it – that is, politics as an unremitting and unconstrained struggle for possession and access to state offices, with the chief aim of procuring direct material benefits to oneself and one's acknowledged communal or other sectional group.

MILITARY RULE AND THE STATE BUREAUCRACY

Concomitant with the struggle for decolonization in the 1950s was another conflict between the desire to retain a civil service that was above the tug-of-war of particularist groups and the demand for a civil service that would precisely reflect the balance in numbers and weight of these same groups. As the state evolved during the post-independence era so also did its corps of officers: at one moment an instrument to be broken up and made to serve competing social groups; at another, a more unified force fighting to stay above the fierce struggle for marginal advantage in civil society.

Nigeria's top civil servants were recipients of a heritage of corporate unity from the colonial era, even though the vast majority of them only tasted real power after that period was over.[22] Certain aspects of this heritage had a greater capacity to survive in the new independent polity than others. The first of these was that the civil servants were servants – i.e., that it was their special duty to serve their political masters in a self-effacing manner. Another tradition, which Britain was itself struggling to abandon at home, was the superiority of the generalist over the specialist, of the liberal arts graduate over the technician. This second tradition was wedded to a third phenomenon which has generated considerable controversy in Nigeria, namely, the practice of appointing one person to supervise and represent the civil servants in each government department, and ultimately one officer at the top of the entire civil service who enjoys the additional power of being Chief Secretary to the Government.[23] These hierarchical principles – predominance of the administrative over the professional branch, a chief officer in each department or ministry, and a supreme head of the entire service with a specific advisory role to the government of the day – were taken without alteration from British metropolitan and colonial practice.[24] The pronounced political role that the Nigerian higher civil service has been able to play since independence can be attributed, paradoxically, to the greater capacity of the service for adhering to these principles when compared with the military. The latter decimated its own leadership at the point of seizing political power; and the main group of political actors, the civilian politicians, never found a way to generate the minimal mutual security considered necessary by consociational theorists for the governing of sectionally divided societies in a system of representative rule.

The tendency for the political activities of the state bureaucracy to expand following the seizure of power by the military is now widely recognized by many scholars. In the case of Nigeria, this "role expansion" seemed to increase commensurate with the military's retention of power, reaching such a peak in the final years of Gowon's government that his overthrow was followed by a massive purge of the public service. After he assumed power in January 1966, General Ironsi relied to an increasing extent on a small group of higher civil servants, some of whom he appointed to head task forces to examine various aspects of governmental structure and policy.[25] Their advice was not always politically timely. The act which spelled the rapid demise of Ironsi's regime – i.e., the Unification Decree of May 1966 – included among its chief provisions the elimination of the regional centers of government and the regional civil services. There was now to be one national service, which meant that the writ of the central military government would be applied by administrators throughout the land without interference from local and regional communities.[26]

The overthrow of Ironsi – and the repeal by his successors of the Unification Decree which had met with fierce opposition from Northern bureaucratic elites – did not block the process his government had been over-eager to consummate. The gradual shift to a more national form of government was enhanced, and entrenched, by the very fact of military rule, by the predominance of oil income in the federal budget and the arrogating by the central government to itself of the lion's share of this new national wealth. Finally, this process was decisively advanced by the break-up of the powerful regions into a multiplicity of states after 1967, and by the *de facto* and then formal acknowledgement of the superiority of the federal public service over that of the country's constituent governments.[27]

With the dismissal of the federal government and the four regional civil governments in January 1966, the Secretaries to each of these governments (and simultaneously Heads of their respective Civil Services), together with the permanent secretaries of federal and state ministries, assumed by default the political as well as administrative control of the state apparatus. There was no attempt by the soldiers simply to step into the shoes of the many dismissed government ministers and deputy ministers. According to the civil servants themselves, they successfully resisted the plan of the military leaders to appoint members of the higher civil service, and especially the permanent secretaries, as political heads of their ministries.[28] But what's in a name? Between the January 1966 coup and June 1967, at which time the first civilian commissioners were appointed, these civil servants directed the work of their ministries.[29] The habit of having to undertake detailed policy work for the politician-ministers during the previous civilian regimes, and then of ensuring continuity in the governing of Nigeria when the attention of the military leadership was consumed by the impending danger of civil war, served to facilitate a system of bureaucratic dominance which would not end with the mere appointment of civilians as federal commissioners by the military.[30] Indeed, there were a number of specific factors that were to render Nigeria between 1966 and 1975 a military regime in name and a more general bureaucratic polity as far as the real actors and agencies of policy formulation were concerned.

Nigeria's first military ruler, J. Aguiyi Ironsi, attempted during his six and a half months in power to set in place a governing apparatus from the shambles created by the January 1966 military coup. He never succeeded. At the time of his overthrow, the military, which was then theoretically sovereign, had splintered into mutually hostile segments corresponding to the place of origin of the soldiers. When the coup plotters struck again on 29 July

1966, Nigeria was even more shorn of a governing center. The following day, a group of Nigerian permanent secretaries and other civil servants made a pilgrimage to the army barracks at Ikeja in Lagos to argue the case that Nigeria should be kept together as one entity. In the rather telling words of Ayida, when their driver was asked in Hausa by soldiers on guard to which tribe his passengers belonged, he answered, "They are civil servants."[31] At that point, and throughout the years of crisis until January 1970, Nigeria's higher civil servants repeatedly demonstrated that they, more than any other corporate or social group in the country, could lay claim to being guardians of the splintered Nigerian nation.[32]

Three of the areas in which Nigeria's higher civil servants demonstrated that they were effectively the major governing force of the nation during the civil war years were the formulating of constitutional policy regarding the desired structure of the Federation, the conduct of negotiations with Biafrans and other intermediaries outside Nigeria, and the devising of plans and programs for economic development and reconstruction following the war. With regard to the federal structure, an "Ad Hoc Constitutional Conference" consisting of delegates representing the four regions of Nigeria convened in September and October 1966. The region which was most resolutely in favor of maintaining the Federation in its existing form was that of the Mid-West which, it should be noted, provided a disproportionately high number of federal civil servants.[33] Yet it was at the talks held in Aburi, Ghana, in January 1967 – which brought together Gowon, Ojukwu, and the entire SMC for the first and only time since the overthrow of Ironsi – that the role of Nigeria's civil servants was felt in a decisive way regarding the constitutional structure of the nation. Their role became apparent, ironically and symbolically, because of the weak performance of the federal side as a consequence of the exclusion of these state officials from the Conference.[34]

When Gowon returned from Aburi and his top civil service advisers saw the concessions he had made in their absence, they realized that Ojukwu had maneuvered Gowon and the rest of the Supreme Military Council into agreeing to the virtual gutting of the powers of Nigeria's central government, and to the creation of a loose confederation which would have little chance of surviving as one polity.[35] Gowon subsequently reversed his positions and glossed over the concessions made.[36] The battle was thus effectively joined between the Federation and the Eastern Region.

At each of the major conferences which took place after the outbreak of hostilities – in various African and European capitals – there was usually a strong representation of federal permanent secretaries in the Nigerian delegations. At times, one of them would be left in charge of the delegation when diplomatic protocol permitted it.[37] On one significant occasion, when Arnold Smith, the Commonwealth Secretary, decided to hold secret preliminary talks between Nigerian and Biafran representatives, it was Allison Ayida, Philip Asiodu and Ahmed Joda – three federal permanent secretaries who also belonged to the kitchen cabinet along with a few top military officers – that Gowon chose to send to London for the talks.[38]

The moment when these senior bureaucrats appeared threatened in their predominant role in the military government was when Gowon finally disregarded Ojukwu's fierce opposition to involving civilians in Nigeria's government and appointed civilian commissioners – mainly former prominent politicians – to the Federal Executive Council on 12 June 1966. Instead of the higher civil servants once again receding, however, to the position of subordinates to these political figures, the consensus of informed opinion is that relations between permanent secretaries and civilian commissioners were conducted on a much more equal plane. Indeed, in some respects the bureaucrats enjoyed certain advantages over their commissioners. Both sets of officers were appointees and indeed "servants" of the military, a designation which did not inconvenience the civil servants as much as it did the politician-commissioners.[39] As members of parallel corporate groups, with similar principles of hierarchy and a commitment to efficient organization, the civil servants found it easier to relate to the soldiers in power than did their former political "masters," the politicians. The latter found themselves in the awkward position of being associates-in-government as well as rivals of the military officers, since they had to keep their ties to their constituencies in readiness for the struggle for power in post-military Nigeria.[40]

In the crucial area of determining policy, the civil servants continued even more than before to be the chief architects of the government's programs. In place of the political party caucuses and legislative bargaining sessions which produced government policies, the decision-making process was now telescoped into meetings of the federal cabinet, with permanent secretaries attending and arguing their briefs on an equal footing with their commissioners. Moreover, the informal pattern of consultation preferred by Gowon with his kitchen cabinet, or in bilateral negotiations with the government officers specifically concerned with a particular matter, continued unabated:

> Under the Gowon regime a personalized system of control had evolved over the bureaucratic machine, in which the Head of State tended to deal directly with selected Federal Permanent Secretaries (popularly termed 'super-permsecs'), particularly Mines and Power, Finance and Economic Development and Reconstruction, by-passing on many important issues the formal machinery – the Federal Executive Council comprising the Federal Commissioners.[41]

There was, consequently, much more than name-calling to the designation "super-permsecs" conferred on the handful of top civil servants in Nigeria, whose powers of securing patronage, of drafting major government projects, and of privately advising the Head of State on political matters reached the highest pinnacle during Gowon's post-war rule.

The real essence of the Nigerian polity during the years of military government, therefore, is that it was a civil-military diarchy on two levels: (1) an overt political one with power-sharing between soldiers and civilian politicians (past or prospective), and (2) a more structured and perhaps significant one in which the pre-existing civil bureaucracy became enmeshed at its highest level with the military bureaucracy, both of which jealously guarded their corporate identities while making the most of this temporary marriage of convenience.[42] When, after July 1975, the military leadership erupted from within to try and propel itself out of the political arena, an intrinsic part of that process was the expulsion of the higher civil administration from its super-ordinate position in the federal and state governments.

THE STRATEGIC ELITE AND ECONOMIC POLICY[43]

We can now shift to a more abstract level of discussion in considering the political role of Nigeria's civil bureaucracy under military rule. It is possible to identify three models of the relationship between state and civil society which are relevant to the Nigerian experience. The first model is the conventional liberal one:

I.

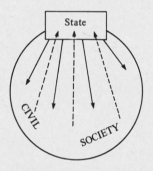

This diagram shows the state occupying a position "above society" yet with individuals and communities having the opportunity to gain entry to its councils and to participate directly in this exercise of power. The bold arrows indicate that the state can act authoritatively, despite this reverse process of participation, in the issuance of commands and the allocation, control and regulation of social goods.

II.

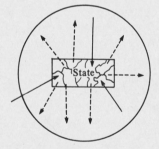

This second diagram depicts the effects of prebendalism on the state in a country such as Nigeria. The bold arrows indicate both the major flow of resources into the coffers of the state itself and the direction of societal energies and attention – i.e., to achieve control of *a piece* of the state, in the form of prebends, that can be used to channel resources for the use of specific individuals and their communal groups. The Nigerian state is in theory cohesive and authoritative; yet, since in practice it is invariably "prebendalized," its capacity to act in a unitary and coherent manner is always susceptible to being undermined by the sum of competing particularisms.

III.

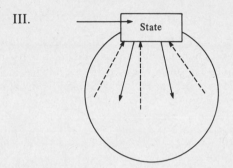

This third diagram depicts the model of the relationship between state and civil society that was implicit in the thinking and actions of certain key individuals who shared authoritative power in Nigeria during the civil war and the immediate post-war years. To an increasing extent, the state was the recipient of the major consolidated block of national income – i.e., revenues from petroleum export. When necessary, the state had the capacity to keep societal inputs, of delegated participants and class and communal demands, at its boundaries (as indicated by the broken arrows). The fact of military rule also meant that the state had the capacity to make authoritative commands in the allocation of social goods. Diagram III, it must be emphasized, reflects the thinking and goals of Nigeria's military rulers and higher civil servants. The reality is that such potential was not coherently or conclusively realized because prebendalism, depicted in Diagram II, was relentless; and the military and its co-opted allies lacked the determination, or confidence, to impose for any significant length of time their preferred political arrangement on society.

The inheritors of state power in Nigeria in July 1966 – the surviving rump of the military command after two violent coups, and the more intact civil service, despite the departure of many of its Easterners – saw their duty as being that of rescuing the Nigerian Federation from dismemberment and achieving the rapid return of power to civilians. The longer these groups remained in power because of the failure to achieve the reintegration of the Eastern Region through diplomatic efforts, the more their perception of their duty broadened. What they dimly perceived, but never confidently asserted, was that the prolonged Nigerian crisis provided them with the opportunity to try to be "revolutionaries from above."

81

Contemporary political sociology has moved towards greater recognition of the importance of changes within the structure and composition of state-power in explaining the consequent revolutionizing of the society at large. This shift in emphasis among the main elements of the Marxian scheme has been ably expressed by Theda Skocpol:

> Social revolutions do, of course, accomplish major changes of class relations; and they affect the basic areas of social and cultural life such as the family, religion, and education. Equally if not more striking, however, are the changes that social revolutions make in the structure and function of states, in the political and administrative processes by which government leaders relate to groups in society, and in the tasks that states can successfully undertake at home and abroad. Nor are such changes in the 'state order' at all mere by-products of the changes in the social order. Indeed to a significant degree, it is the other way around: The changes in state structures that occur during social revolutions typically both consolidate, and themselves entail, socio-economic changes... An emphasis on state building is warranted... because of the clear importance not only of political but also of state structures in determining revolutionary outcomes.[44]

Theda Skocpol quite rightly wanted to raise to a higher level of importance the middle term in the process: social revolution → new state order → new social order. Her analysis parallels that of Ellen Trimberger, who examines instances of "revolution from above" – e.g., Turkey under Ataturk and Peru under Velasco – in which military bureaucrats become revolutionaries despite their more limited objectives when they first seized power. In the case of Nigeria, the seizure of power was not a consequence of a social revolution, nor did the military bureaucrats ever adopt a revolutionary program. What they settled for was a reformist "revolution from above" based on the following elements: a strategic elite consisting of civil servants, military officers and certain prominent academics;[45] a commitment to economic nationalism which coincided with the military's concern for national security;[46] the inheritance of a large public sector which expanded even further as a consequence of the war effort and mounting oil revenues; a commitment to public sector economic leadership which hovered undecidedly between socialism, state capitalism, and state-assisted private capitalism (or mixed economy); and the plenary and autocratic powers conferred on the state by military rule which could then be used to impose new structures, programs and a sense of "national purpose" on society.

There occurred a "revolutionary" expansion of the public sector under the aegis of an active civil bureaucracy, a supportive military and an enthusiastic set of advisers from the universities. By 1974, the public sector alone accounted for 39 per cent of the Gross Domestic Product, compared with 9.2 per cent in 1962.[47] As the state assumed greater responsibility for controlling, directing and investing in economic expansion, the number of parastatal agencies soared. By 1975, according to Terisa Turner, half of the people working in the federal and state civil services – 160,000 – were employed in statutory corporations.[48] Such an expansion is directly related to the post-war commitment to expanding the public sector, coupled with the ease of doing so because of the great increase in oil income (as a consequence of OPEC action) from $160 million (US) per month in September 1973 to $77.0 million in May of the following year.[49] By 1980, the total public expenditure of $18.7 billion in Nigeria represented 1.5 times the entire GDP of 1964.[50]

At no time during the military era was the commitment and capacity to expand the state economic sector matched by an equal determination to limit the growth of the indigenous and foreign private sectors. So although the state bureaucracy had the financial capacity to restructure economic relations and to alter radically the allocation of capital investment, it never utilized that power to such ends. Moreover, the public sector was woefully inefficient and susceptible to being manipulated for corrupt purposes. From being expert managers of the state apparatus during the secessionist crisis, higher civil servants became superintendents of an "overloaded state" which had expanded without a concurrent ideological justification for its enhanced role. These bureaucrats were increasingly subject to corrupt inducements from home and abroad (facilitated by their own diminishing moral constraints). In sum, they came to reflect in their behavior the ideological weakness of a military regime which had never risen to the challenge of using its autonomous power to make radical changes in the economic realm.

BUREAUCRACY, PREBENDAL POLITICS AND THE INTREPÔT STATE

The bureaucratic polity of 1966–79 did not produce an adequate response to prebendalism. In the struggle between a state order seeking to be authoritative and a social context whose abiding political process involves the penetration of the state's boundaries and the capture of its offices for individual-cum-communal ends, it is the pursuit of autonomous state power which has been blunted in Nigeria. An unanswered question concerns the mechanisms or strategies that could insulate the state from the full flow of the currents of prebendal politics. In Nigeria the resistance to these currents is largely verbal. However extensive and authoritative the Nigerian state might have become, the process of expansion rested on an increasingly soft base. There were two main aspects to this "soft underbelly" of the state order. The first was the process of staffing state offices itself and the second was the emergence of an entrepôt state which pretended to be *dirigiste*.

Advancement by merit and appointments on the basis of academic and technical qualifications are elements of the rational-legal bureaucracy conceptualized by Max Weber. However, the desire for a meritocratic service in Nigeria, and the pressures for direct and equitable representation of the country's component groups within the state administration, could not be fully harmonized. One or the other of these values had to give way and, to an increasing extent, it turned out to be the former. Habibu Sani, a former bureaucrat in the administration of Kwara state, who subsequently served for a period as researcher and management consultant, has provided one of the most explicit statements of the prebendalizing of the Nigerian civil bureaucracy:

> The component units of the federation ... [after 1954] saw themselves as competing for the key posts of permanent secretaries and other chief executives of the federal Boards and Corporations at the centre. Every Regional Government saw to it that it was given a fair share in the distribution of these important posts in very much the same way as it saw to it that the national political cake was equally shared.[51]

Sani goes on to argue that this pattern of struggle for the appropriation of state offices prevailed under the successive civilian and military regimes. At the regional and state levels,

> the concept of 'ethnic balancing' in the appointment and promotion of officers to intermediate and senior posts has been accorded a greater dimension. The various ethnic groups forming the state ... clamour for all manner of posts for their respective sons of the soil in the various arms of the public services. Any appointment, promotion, or even dismissal to a new post is seen and judged from the narrow perspective of the effect it has on the unofficial quota of the ethnic group concerned.[52]

The individuals responsible for the development of an effective civil bureaucracy which was committed to national purposes could not overcome this entrenched attitude that the very offices of the bureaucracy were highly desired spoils of the system. Indeed, the constant pressure in Nigeria for the creation of more states is fueled to a significant extent by the unrelenting pursuit of prebendal offices. At one of the chief annual gatherings of Nigerian higher civil servants, politicians and academics, one participant was able to provoke derisive laughter within the group by pointing out that "the civil service even within the period of our history was itself part of the cake which was being shared by the political leaders."[53]

Now, how could that which was "being shared" achieve enough autonomy to enable it to control and then alter the sharing process itself? No adequate answer to this question was found during the pre-1979 period of military rule. Such a failure has meant that, after the return to partisan politics in the Second Republic, the bureaucratic apparatus of the state at both federal and state levels was even less able to execute its recruitment, assignment and promotion activities on the basis of non-partisan criteria. To return once again to Sani's insightful remarks, the state order in Nigeria – under military or civilian rule – has yet to find a way of transcending and dissolving – even within its ranks – the fundamentally debilitating process I have analyzed:

> In a plural society such as ours, people have the tendency to measure justice, equity and fair play from an enlightened self-interest point of view. This is to say that their primary consideration in any bargaining process is the extent to which the members of their ethnic or cultural group stand to gain or lose in the societal allocation of scarce resources.[54]

What renders the prebendalizing of the Nigerian state an issue of considerable theoretical importance and complexity is the peculiar economic role and character assumed by the state order. It was suggested above that the Nigerian civil bureaucracy often laid claim to a *dirigiste* role which was undermined by the state's entrepôt character. This apparent paradox can now be clarified. The desire for greater state direction, which emerged during the period of military rule and the secessionist crisis, has been discussed. An ebullient advocation of a *dirigiste* role for the bureaucracy was made in the aftermath of the war by a permanent secretary in a Northern state government who, five years later, would be called to higher duties in the federal government:

> Unlike the western societies where many more efficient political institutions exist, the bureaucracy here is the major instrument of social change. It is the main if not the only engine of directed growth... The bureaucracy as a whole must have, as a primary role, the function of aggregating and regulating political institutions, and implicit in its own privileged position it has also the role of deciding or influencing the course of development.[55]

Older and wiser heads in the civil service did not share Yaya Abubakar's enthusiasm for the "political primacy" of the bureaucracy. Yet, such an ideal was even further from the reality of the essential nature of the Nigerian state when considered from the perspective of political economy.

Terisa Turner has been as insightful about this aspect of the state's character as Sani has been about the constraints to its internal staffing. Turner recognized that one of the factors which lends a peculiar character to Nigeria's political economy is the central role of the state in determining the distribution of financial resources, whether these involve loans or contracts from state agencies or the "gatekeeper" role of the state in mediating relations with foreign capital.[56] The ability to gain access to the individuals who make such decisions has become central to the system. Moreover, since there are fewer high state officials than businessmen, the competition for preferment is especially keen and easily redounds to the benefit of those officials willing to exploit their advantageous positions. I now wish to enlarge on Turner's specific suggestion that the state itself in Nigeria has developed as a "major market" by substituting the term, "the entrepôt state."

The term "entrepôt" is frequently used in studies of Africa's colonial and pre-colonial economies to refer to trading centers which combined the features of a domestic market with those of an exchange point for long-distance trade – e.g., those on the southern margins of the Sahara. When looked at from the standpoint of contemporary political economy, Nigeria has experienced the advanced development of what we may call an "entrepôt state" because of several general as well as specific factors:

1. the export of primary agricultural products has been succeeded not by that of manufactured goods, but of mineral (petroleum) products;
2. the state has become the most important source of investible capital, whether for its own ventures or those of individual Nigerian capitalists;
3. foreign capital remains the most *effectively* utilized investment capital in the economy, especially for large-scale undertakings;

85

4. the post-secessionist ideology of public sector leadership has not led to a collectivist economy or state monopoly capitalism, but rather to a system embracing three diverse components: a large but unprofitable state capitalist sector, a trading-oriented indigenous private entrepreneurial sector, and a politically subordinate but highly profitable foreign-owned or foreign-dominated sector.

In such an entrepôt state, the functions of managing access to state capital, links to foreign capital, and appointments to corporate state offices are major, and perhaps pre-eminent, ones. In the absence of a full retinue of civilian politicians in the government, and with a relatively small military contingent in political posts, the top stratum of civil servants was able to dominate these functions. As we shall see when I briefly discuss the anti-corruption purge which began in August 1975, state officials became, to an increasing extent, major beneficiaries of the very system they were in principle committed to supplanting.

There is much available literature and ongoing research (in addition to that of Terisa Turner) to fill in the details of the emergence of the entrepôt state in Nigeria. Sayre Schatz, for example, has provided substantial information on how the granting of government loans, as well as contracts for supplies and construction work, became increasingly governed by "non-economic criteria" during the pre-military period.[57] The high proportion of the development budgets which was committed to construction projects (which, in turn, favored the issuance of contracts), the political manipulation of the classification of eligible contractors, the increasing shift to negotiated contracts from open bidding practices, the deleterious impact of the reliance on contractor-finance, the process of channeling projects to particular areas and the indigenes thereof, these and many other practices came to serve as effective instruments for privatizing public wealth more than they contributed to achieving balanced socio-economic development.[58] Ayida's comment with regard to the 1962–8 Development Plan is therefore particularly apt:

> The point is that the Six-Year Plan was so large that one could always get a Plan project for any deal contemplated. Besides, the National Plan was not phased, and since there was no programmed annual capital expenditures, the planners left the politicians with a package deal, a paradise for smart operators.[59]

Expectations regarding public sector leadership after the civil war were dashed as the state fell back to a mediating role between indigenous aspirant businessmen and foreign capital. Of particular importance in this regard was the sizable indigenization program, launched in 1972, in which aspirant entrepreneurs and *rentier* capitalists were able to purchase blocks of shares and outright ownership of foreign businesses. Many of them were able to do so with loans obtained from state-owned development banks, or from the larger private banks in which the state was assuming an increasing share of the equity. As Akeredolu-Ale put it, such undertakings demonstrated that private individuals had succeeded in "cornering the public purse."[60] Indeed, given the high level in Nigeria of the defaulting on "development loans" from state agencies, such loan programs can more appropriately be seen as instruments of private capital accumulation.[61]

An entrepôt state is therefore *sui generis* in the contemporary world, since it possesses the interventionist powers of the liberal welfare state, enjoys the centralization of financial resources more appropriate to state collectivist systems, and yet fails to make effective use of the potential autonomy conferred by these powers and resources.[62] Moreover, such a state order draws *within itself* the actual struggle for financial resources which normally obtains within civil society. We can now see, taking into consideration the entrepôt nature of the Nigerian state, why its own internal dynamic has rendered those who command its apparatus so profoundly incapable of resisting the process of prebendalism.

ECONOMIC STATISM AND CORRUPTION

The removal of Yakubu Gowon as Head of State in Nigeria on 29 July 1975 was succeeded by a more disciplined conduct of government business and a firmer commitment by the new military regime to begin the delayed process of transferring power to civilians. One of the most decisive actions of the Muhammed government was its anti-corruption drive, which resulted in the dismissal and summary retirement of over 11,000 public officials throughout the Federation.[63] This action had both political and economic implications, as the revelations about the unfair financial advantages secured by state employees were combined with harsh criticism of the political role higher civil servants had usurped during the Gowon era.

As mentioned above, the purge – despite its apparent extensiveness – could not be anything but superficial. For one thing, at a time in which the new regime was seeking to improve the machinery of the government, these actions had a debilitating effect on the state apparatus, since many of the individuals dismissed often possessed needed technical and administrative skills. Moreover, it had to be a superficial operation because the gains made by certain state officials had been achieved through direct collaboration with private and foreign capitalist elements who would soon be free to function much as before. Finally, it was superficial because Nigeria is not a vindictive political society: the speed with which individuals, whose misdoings have been thoroughly exposed publicly, are able to bounce back to positions of prominence, would amaze most foreign observers.[64]

It can be argued that the changing of the guard in July 1975 had a more severe initial effect on the public service than it did on the military command, a development which reflects the fact of the relatively small number of military officers in Nigeria's military governments, as well as the real powers enjoyed by senior public servants in that regime.[65] Permanent secretaries in both the federal and state governments suffered the highest proportion of dismissals of any stratum. Most of the secretaries to the state military governments were quickly removed.[66] Yet, the man at the very top of the administrative system, Allison Ayida – who had been appointed Secretary to the Federal Military Government by Gowon just three months before his overthrow – was retained in his post until he decided to leave government service the following year. Ayida had thus spent a decade at the summit of Nigeria's governmental bureaucracy as a permanent secretary in the three central economic ministries and left it with his reputation untarnished. With great fanfare, the announcement was made by the Muhammed government that permanent secretaries would no longer be permitted to attend meetings of the federal cabinet (the FEC). Yet this announcement, like several others made during those heady days, was soon overlooked in practice.

The purge also had the character of a settling of accounts, not only among rival groups and individuals in the society, but also among the constituent elements of the strategic elite that had ruled Nigeria since the secessionist crisis. A remark by one of the planners of the July 1975 coup, Lt. Colonel Yar'Adua – "civil servants have influenced major decisions in the last twelve years. They have enjoyed virtually unchallenged the exercise of powers all these years" – reflects the general sentiment regarding the past abuses of power.[67] It can also be interpreted, as was suggested, in the light of intra-elite considerations of how the Gowon regime had become a shell or screen for the exercise of political power by civil bureaucrats.

The new regime sought to institutionalize the anticorruption drive through the establishment of a Corrupt Practices Investigation Bureau, as well as a Public Complaints Commission (PCC), the latter with branches in all nineteen states. The breadth of the PCC's area of responsibility can be said to reflect the absence of general representative institutions in Nigeria as much as it did the scope of the problems of corruption and abuse of power:

> to inquire into complaints lodged before it by members of the public concerning any administrative actions taken by any Minister or Department of the Federation or any State Government, statutory corporation, local government authorities and other public institutions and of companies whether in the public or private sector and of any officials of any of the aforementioned bodies.[68]

Assets panels were set up to conduct investigations of governors and higher civil servants who were believed to have made the most corrupt use of their offices. The comments of the government and its actions with regard to the reports of these panels make instructive reading. In the case of Philip Asiodu, one of the "super-permsecs" of the Gowon era, the panel stated,

> between 1974 and 1975 Mr. Asiodu was able to raise loans amounting to ₦345,000 in his personal capacity. In addition, he was connected with loans amounting to ₦1,105,000 raised by companies of which members of his immediate family or with himself as partner were the sole owners.[69]

The panel concluded that the ease with which these loans were raised suggested that Asiodu "had taken advantage of his position in Government."

88

Yet he was given "the benefit of the doubt" by the panel except in those cases of specific proven irregularities in the loan documents he submitted.[70]

Another permanent secretary, Alhaji I.M. Damcida, who was asked to explain a list of loans he had procured while in office from private individuals, banks and government sources, was only forced to forfeit the shares which he admitted having received as a gift, despite the more damning conclusion reached by the panel: "The officer is unquestionably guilty of professional misconduct by accepting loans from people associated with his work – to wit Ministry of Defense contractors while he was heading the Ministry."[71] In the case of Alhaji Femi O. Okunnu, the Federal Commissioner in charge of the contracts-disbursing Ministry of Works, the fact that the Government accepted the panel's timid conclusion reflects the absence of any real standard of acceptable behavior for senior government officials. The panel reported that Okunnu

> obtained two loans of ₦40,000.00 and ₦35,000.00 from the U.B.A. and Standard Bank respectively in 1973 and 1974. The U.B.A. loan was to help finance the purchase of Siemens (Nig.) Ltd. [which] was very much involved with the Federal Ministry of Works in which Alhaji Okunnu was the Commissioner. The Panel also had information that Siemens (Nig.) Ltd. was actually brought to Nigeria by Alhaji Okunnu and Dr. Seriki, the former Lagos State Commissioner for Works and Planning.

The comment of the government on this report was that Okunnu's actions in this matter were "indiscreet and showed bad judgment for a high government official," yet it concluded, in a seemingly contradictory vein, that the bank loan "was obtained in the ordinary course of business" and so it recommended "no action."[72] The "ordinary course of business" in an entrepôt state clearly allows for "extraordinary" business dealings by many government officials.

More generally, the reformist military regime of July 1975 tried to draw a distinction between the corrupt use of office, in the way of bribes or kickbacks, and the utilization of state authority to enable the official, or his family, to become owners of residential property, company shares and business concerns:

> Massive borrowings from banks by senior Government officers though they were not illegal, certainly . . . were not to be encouraged. But massive borrowings by public officers from persons who may have official dealings with the public officers in any manner which places such officers under financial obligation to an extent that it could lead to public scandal or be construed as an abuse of office is absolutely irregular.[73]

Since most persons dismissed from the service were retired with full benefits, Paul Collins contends that one effect of the purge was to create a "privileged class of pensioners."[74] Since most retired individuals went into the business world, using their knowledge and contacts to develop their enterprises quickly, they can be said to have been forced to operate more completely as private businessmen and women than was possible before they left the service.

89

It can be contended, finally, that the effects of the 1975 purge might be as much negative as positive. Corrupt public officials will certainly learn from the 1975 experience to be more careful in their illicit dealings and avoid placing the bulk of their surplus income in such easily identifiable assets as bank accounts, real estate and personal shares. It also means, moreover, that greater attention will be paid to careful timing – it is better to make one's fortune quickly and leave the service well before the regime collapses and another investigation of assets is conducted. The harmful effects such "strategies" might have on the stability of the state and the cost-effectiveness of government programs can easily be imagined.[75] The moral of the 1975 purge, therefore, is that public servants are as much bound by the informal rules of the prebendal system as are lay-citizens: it is more legitimate to use public authority to share in what is general (e.g., government or bank loans) than to rely on that same authority to obtain direct benefits from private individuals.

The "gatekeepers" in the entrepôt state had the good luck or skill to obtain the positions desired by many. The immense facilities the Nigerian state offers in assisting private primary accumulation renders its capacity to promote the general interest a secondary and derivative one. The members of Nigeria's dominant class – whose activities are so focused on the state – have a great interest in ethno-clientelism as part of their own self-promotion. The attitudes that underlie prebendalism enable them to function simultaneously along the axes of self, class and communal interests. Such a system has been made to work, albeit at the cost of political stability, economic development and social justice. It is from the working-out of the succeeding political cycles, therefore, that we will learn if gains can be made in any or all of these three dimensions via the path of constitutional change bequeathed by the democratizing military regime of 1975–9.

Part III

The return to tripartism in the Second Republic

7

Personality and alignment in Igbo politics

On Thursday, 21 September 1978, the Head of Nigeria's Military Government, General Olusegun Obasanjo, gave an address on the occasion of the promulgation of the country's new constitution. He also announced the lifting of the ban on politics, thereby initiating the final stage in the transition to civilian rule. The three years that had been devoted previously to the making of the constitution, and to establishing an institutional apparatus for the new polity, clearly reflect the priorities and assumptions of the Military Government. As long as the established and aspirant politicians could be excluded from the transitional process, or kept on a tight leash, the better were the chances that the new system would survive their machinations. At the moment of political rebirth, Obasanjo's address was strikingly replete with fears about the motives and practices of those individuals who would now be returning to center-stage in the Nigerian polity:

> Political recruitment and subsequent political support which are based on tribal, religious and linguistic sentiments contributed largely to our past misfortune. They must not be allowed to spring up again. Those negative political attitudes like hatred, falsehood, intolerance and acrimony also contributed to our national tragedy in the past: they must not be continued. These negative attitudes must not be allowed to enter into the practice of the new political system.[1]

The fears expressed at the time of the lifting of the ban on politics, that such practices as "horse-trading, shifting alliances, sectional interests, and petty loyalty" would sabotage the new Republic, were certainly real. What is also real, however, as has been argued in this study, is the existence of an underlying logic to the pattern of politics in Nigeria which is upheld by widespread norms regarding the appropriate behavior of individuals, their class affiliates and communal supporters. Nigerian politics at the local, state or national levels often appears to be a free-for-all struggle for advantage which generates unrestrained verbal attacks among political opponents. The variety, range and multiplicity of these conflicts, however, stand in marked contrast to the precise nature of the outcome of the process of party formation and especially the alignment of sectional groups as reflected in the election results of July/August 1979. Five parties were registered for the elections, each led by a senior politician from the days of the First Republic. There reappeared a modified yet clearly tripartite system of power-sharing with the dominant party in the Federation being strongest in the northern states, the second-placed strongest among the Yoruba and the third-placed predominant among the Igbo. Though the outcome appeared straightforward and familiar, the routes followed by individual political actors to reach this consummation turned out to be tortuous ones. This process indeed reflects a notable duality in Nigerian political life involving a contrast between a complex series of events and actions and the simplified pattern of alliances which determine the final arrangement.

WAITING FOR AZIKIWE

In each of the three corners of the Nigerian triangle, there was great variation in the rapidity with which the final pattern of political alignments was reached. The strongest party in the West, the UPN, was fashioned from the outset around the candidacy of one man, Chief Obafemi Awolowo. In the North, the leading party, the NPN, a few months after its launching in September 1978, eventually settled on one of its founding members, Alhaji Shehu Shagari, as its presidential candidate. I shall discuss those two cases in Chapters 8 and 9. In the third corner of the Nigerian triangle, the subject of this chapter, the situation was ambiguous and unsettled until just before the final days of 1978. No party was clearly predominant, although the political formation which became the NPN seemed more successful in winning the affiliation of well-known Igbo politicians. Moreover, the major political figure, Dr Nnamdi Azikiwe, gave the appearance of keeping alive several conflicting options regarding his own involvement in the forthcoming party contests. One individual captured the essence of this process by referring to the fact that the nation seemed to be kept "in waiting for one man."[2] While the major political figures moved around the country in search of adherents to their cause, Dr Azikiwe remained at his Nsukka retreat, receiving delegations, dispatching lieutenants, and waiting for the political card game to deal him a decisive hand.

What were the factors responsible for this initially indirect and even indecisive politics of the leading figures in the Igbo states of Imo and Anambra, and of Dr Nnamdi Azikiwe in particular? The first reason relates to the legacy of the civil war. Less than a decade after the ending of that bitter conflict, it was genuinely believed by many Igbos that no Igbo could possibly win the election for first President of the Second Republic. One major aspirant for the governorship of Anambra State, C. C. Onoh of the NPN, bluntly expressed this widely held view, exclaiming to his fellow Igbos that those who "conquered them" in the civil war could not now be expected to be "ruled" by them.[3] Politically ambitious Igbos, who saw it as axiomatic that no serious presidential candidate would be an Igbo, rushed to secure second place (as a communal group) in the political formation emerging under the leadership of northern elites. One theme that Igbo "leaders of thought" could all agree upon is that their people had to take full advantage of the new political process to return fully to "the Nigerian family."[4] This desire to be part of the political mainstream was coupled with a sharp sense of grievance about the failure of Igbos to obtain a fair share in the distribution of national largesse in the form of roads, schools, public appointments, and government contracts during the oil-boom decade of the seventies.

The unique personal prestige of Azikiwe complicated such assessments about the best approach to what can be called "Igbo redemption." He saw himself as Nigeria's first citizen, as the "Father of the Nation," and as an individual of unequalled national pre-eminence whose name had been written into the 1963 Constitution as the country's first President. A young and assertive northern radical even cautioned Azikiwe not to re-enter partisan politics and thereby risk tarnishing his status as "the most respected person" in Nigeria.[5] Azikiwe's delayed decision about his preferred role in the campaign and elections became a matter of overriding interest to all, both hopeful allies and likely opponents. For that reason, he was urgently encouraged by some to get involved in partisan politics and equally strongly by others to remain above the fray. Even those who argued the latter course often added a qualifier: if Azikiwe did decide to become involved in the contest, he should be certain to join their side. The analogy of an extended card game is quite appropriate. Dr Azikiwe had the option of pulling a chair up to the table, or walking around to see who had the strongest hand (and thus was worthy of his support), or withdrawing after admonishing everyone to play fairly. Being an astute and highly calculating politician, the 73-year-old Azikiwe encouraged many of the players to feel that he might choose any of these options until finally, and dramatically, he made his choice known during the third week of November 1978.

The final general point that should be mentioned at this stage is that the very person of Azikiwe called into question all well-laid plans for a "new Nigerian politics." Individuals who were Azikiwe's lieutenants in the struggle for independence and during the First Republic – men such as Dr Jaja Wachuku, Chief R. B. K. Okafor, Dr K. O. Mbadiwe, and Chief Nwafor Orizu – were now substantial individuals in their own right, wealthy and of wide experience. The states of Imo and Anambra were composed of a multiplicity of communities, each with its "favorite sons," many of whom had diligently created a reputation for philanthropic commitment to their people through contributions to the building of schools, churches, and scholarship funds. A further matter of speculation was whether Azikiwe's decision to break with the Biafran leader around the midway point in the civil war in 1968, and to urge a negotiated settlement of the hostilities, had fatefully wounded him in the eyes of his people. Such a hope on the part of his opponents had never been put to the test.

Those who gambled on Azikiwe's continued charismatic control drew on a deeper understanding of Nigerian politics, and on the expected behavior of the Igbo people when confronted with the overriding issue of national representation. Political power in Nigeria depended in a fundamental way on the capacity to achieve group consolidation. The capacity of people who are organized in dispersed lineage systems to undertake cohesive political action is well known to anthropologists and well demonstrated in the case of the Tiv and Igbo in recent Nigerian history.[6] "Igbo kwenu" – "Igbos unite" – was a cry made famous during the civil war. Such a sentiment was long implanted and remembered. The question was whether it could be made politically salient again and to what effect. It was also widely believed in 1978–9 that there were four prominent Igbo individuals who could regenerate and also symbolize that cohesion: one was a former governor of the Eastern Region and a medical doctor with no vocation for party politics, Dr Akanu Ibiam; the second was the still-exiled leader of the secession, Emeka Ojukwu; the third was the former Premier of the Eastern Region, Dr Michael Okpara, who returned from voluntary exile in October 1978; and the fourth and most senior was Dr Nnamdi Azikiwe. When Azikiwe finally made his decision, the preferences of a community of several million moved with him. Indeed, at that moment, he symbolized the community as an operative unity. A metaphysical Hegelian vocabulary is difficult to avoid here. An individual such as Azikiwe provides the element of subjectivity, of concerted action, to a collectivity which would otherwise reflect potentiality. Those who had guessed rightly could now prepare to complete the operation of winning state-power; those who had bet wrongly would seek to limit their losses by winning at the center what Azikiwe's reconsolidated ethnic clientele was going to monopolize in their home states.

THE GUBERNATORIAL ELECTIONS: BY ONE FOR THE MANY

One of the principal alterations in the Nigerian political system between 1966 and 1976 was the creation of a multi-state federation in place of the pre-1966 system of regions. During the military era, the implications of these changes had not been fully realized because of the centralized military command structure. On 1 October 1979, however, ample executive power would thenceforth be exercised by the individuals and parties which won control of the nineteen state governorships. Second only in importance to the issue of securing a strategic position in whatever government took control of the federal capital were gubernatorial contests. Before discussing these unfolding contests, there are certain dimensions of the state-issue in Nigeria which should be briefly reviewed.

Nigeria emerged from the civil war in January 1970 with a twelve-state structure which had been declared by Gowon in 1967 to undermine support for Biafra among the non-Igbo groups in the former Eastern Region. The tactical thinking behind this decision was that a victory of the federal forces would mean an end to the minority status of these peoples in the East. In

February 1976, in response to the report of an investigatory commission, General Obasanjo declared the creation of seven more states. Despite these changes, considerable energies are constantly exerted to mobilize support for new states in Nigeria. More specifically, a careful account is kept regarding the putative gains and losses of various sections of the population with the creation or rejection of new state boundaries. Thus, it is frequently stated in Nigeria that the "former North" now has ten states, giving it a slight numerical edge over the "former South." Similarly, after the 1976 reform, the Yoruba were portrayed as having acquired "four states" – Oyo, Ondo, Ogun and Lagos – with a strong representation in a fifth, Kwara, in contrast to the Igbo who were "given" only the two states of Imo and Anambra. This disparity was seen as a tangible reflection of the loss of Igbo parity with the Yoruba as a consequence of their defeat in the civil war.

The demand for the creation of additional "Igbo" states was therefore a strong one, and it took the form of vigorous representations by political figures to various governmental commissions. Indeed, an attempt was made in the final days of the Constituent Assembly of 1977–8 to write the creation of new states into the 1979 Constitution. Prominent among the leaders of this effort were several Igbo representatives such as Dr Chuba Okadigbo. For my purposes here, it is interesting to note the deliberate creation of a new communal identity among the people of one area of Anambra State (the most prominent of the two "Igbo" states) for the purpose of mobilizing support for a new state and concurrently facilitating the election of individuals associated with this demand.

Let us consider for a moment the efforts of one such individual. Christian Onoh had played a minor part in pre-1966 regional politics. In 1972, however, he achieved sudden prominence by claiming that the people of "Anambra North" were discriminated against in various ways to the advantage of those in "Anambra South."[7] Many of the political elites, including Dr Azikiwe, originated in Onitsha in Anambra South, an area of the state which had achieved an early spurt in development, especially in the areas of education and commerce, compared with the more fertile agricultural region of the state designated as Anambra North.

Onoh hoped to capitalize on his strenuous personal efforts since the early 1970s on behalf of the "Wawa" people. The term "Wawa" was formerly a derogatory one used to designate the accents and dialects of the people of that area. Adopting the classic role of the "ethnic missionary" which I discussed in Chapter 4, Onoh helped arouse a communal identity among the people of a new constituency he hoped would someday become a separate state. With the return to civilian rule, the basis of Onoh's special claim to office, in addition to his acquired wealth, particularly in landed property, was his personal identification with the idea of a separate communal and geographical identity of a large subsection of the citizens of Anambra State.

Onoh's calculations were realistic enough: the 1963 census showed that the designated Wawa area had a million more people than the 1.7 million located

97

in Anambra South (referred to as the Ijekebe). The difference in land area was even more significant, with the former area being three times the size of the latter.[8] As a person who had acquired vast personal land holdings, and who had used the elements of geography, dialect differences, and a feeling of relative disadvantage to generate a new sense of community among a significant section of the Anambra population, Onoh felt himself well positioned to capture the state governorship in 1979. Should he succeed, he would then be one of the foremost Igbo political figures in Nigeria since, as Onoh repeatedly affirmed in public, an Igbo could not be elected to the position of President of the Second Republic. Onoh, therefore, seemed poised to achieve a commanding position in state and national politics.

C. C. Onoh has a well-earned reputation for being a determined fighter, equally good at the open and what is referred to as the "underground campaign." He had demonstrated his determination in several other disputes, such as the pressuring of the Federal Commissioner from Anambra in the Obasanjo government, Professor Godwin Odenigwe, into resigning over his use of his office to create a favorable apportionment of the local government areas in the state as well as his intercession on behalf of those he favored in chieftaincy disputes.[9] Of course, a C. C. Onoh in Odenigwe's position is unlikely to have acted differently. Onoh easily defeated all other contestants for the gubernatorial nomination in Anambra state, who included Odenigwe, Chuba Okadigbo (University Senior Lecturer and later NPN political broker) and Alex Ekwueme, director of Nigeria's most successful architectural firm and subsequently Shehu Shagari's running-mate for Vice President of Nigeria. Odenigwe from Anambra North had already been weakened by Onoh's earlier campaigns against him, while the two viable candidates for the nomination were both from Anambra South and thus ideal foils for Onoh's campaign.

Ethnic consolidation, as I discussed earlier, can take place at various levels and even at some of these simultaneously. In the 1978–9 campaign and elections, the struggle for effective control of state-power sometimes pitted individuals who promoted a broad definition of the operative community against advocates of more restricted or parochial definitions. Onoh's gambit was a bold one and seemed destined to succeed. The National Party of Nigeria to which he belonged was outperforming the other parties in its recruitment of prominent Igbos. Yet Onoh did not have the support of Dr Azikiwe. Indeed, the latter was the pre-eminent son of Onitsha (his ceremonial title being the Owelle of Onitsha), and Onoh had built his political career on the alleged domination of Anambra's political and economic life by the people of Anambra South and Onitsha in particular. The greater the sense of division a politician such as Onoh could generate among the people of Anambra State, the less effective Azikiwe's appeal to universal Igbo identity would be. Here we see the crux of political entrepreneurship in Nigeria: the pitting of one level of communal identity against another, of a more exclusive definition of the community against a more inclusive one and vice versa.

Sam Mbakwe of Etiti in Imo State owed his political prominence to his vigorous support for a variety of issues related to the disadvantages and discrimination Igbos believed they suffered after the end of the civil war. Mbakwe was a lawyer by profession and had served in the former Eastern House of Representatives during the First Republic. As the chairman of a construction company, he had achieved the financial independence which enabled him to play an active part in the unfolding post-military politics and to provide his fledgling party, the Nigerian People's Party, with the resources needed for its campaign in his state. Yet Mbakwe's personal authority was not narrowly based. His strenuous efforts on behalf of Igbos were matters of public knowledge. He had campaigned for the creation of a separate Imo state from part of the territory of the pre-1976 East Central State, and for the return to their rightful owners of properties abandoned by fleeing Igbos before and during the civil war. Indeed, Mbakwe was the leading critic of the very notion of "abandoned property." During the 1978–9 political campaigns, he added to this record by stressing the representations he had privately made to get Igbos absorbed into the army and civil service after the war.[10]

Yet, Sam Mbakwe, a genial and unassuming man, was astute and determined in the line he followed – the very opposite of Onoh's in Anambra – and which took him to victory as the first civilian governor of Imo State. To begin with, Mbakwe saw the need for Igbos to "consummate the general amnesty" and achieve reintegration into the Nigerian "body politic" on an equal basis with other Nigerian communities. Hence he rejected the idea that Igbos should confine their ambitions to the vice-presidency of the Federation and its many lesser offices. "What makes him [the Igboman] avoid the Presidency?" Mbakwe rhetorically inquired.[11] As will be discussed later, Mbakwe successfully combined his individual participation in the NPP, before it took on an Igbo coloration, with his involvement in parallel negotiations on behalf of Azikiwe with leaders of other political formations including the NPN. In contrast to those of Onoh, one of Mbakwe's clear objectives was to bring Azikiwe into partisan party politics on the best possible terms for the latter and, by implication, for the Igbo people.

In general, party activities were less intense in Imo State than in the more developed Anambra. One of its prominent politicians from the First Republic, Dr K. O. Mbadiwe, had lost credibility over the years among his own people by being implicated in the misuse of government funds. And the still highly respected Dr Michael Okpara adopted a position of public silence after his return from many years of exile in 1978. Sam Mbakwe won the NPP nomination for governor without great difficulty and then triumphed over his opponents from the other parties in the elections, including the strong Dr Nwakamma Okoro, a former president of the Nigerian Bar. The affiliation of Dr Azikiwe to the NPP in late December 1978, and his subsequent nomination as the party's presidential candidate, was a complete ratification of Mbakwe's line. While touring Imo State, Azikiwe could freely extol Mbakwe's consistent efforts on behalf of the Igbo people since the civil war. The combined reputations of the two men could hardly be surpassed in the effort to generate a mobilized ethnic vote.

A third gubernatorial candidate who merits a brief discussion is Dr A. A. O. Ezenwa, perhaps the most individually impressive of all such candidates in Anambra and Imo States. Ezenwa hailed from Abagana in "Anambra South." He had achieved a distinguished reputation as an educator, having served as principal of a leading secondary school, Christ the King College in Onitsha, and as president of both the Nigerian Union of Teachers and the Federation of African Teachers. Ezenwa was adopted as the standard bearer for a splinter group of prominent Igbo nationalists who could not reconcile themselves to anything less than an untrammeled Igbo voice in national politics and the formation of an "Igbo-oriented" political party for the transitional elections. Notable among this group – known for a brief period as the People's Progressive Party – were the wealthy director of a construction company and publishing entrepreneur, Arthur Nwankwo, and the noted Nigerian novelist, Chinua Achebe. They differed from the line of Sam Mbakwe discussed above in three ways: they refused to acknowledge and depend upon the grand patronage of Dr Azikiwe; they were little inclined to subordinate their Igbo nationalism to a new coalition of "minorities"; and they refused to enter into tacit alliances or understandings with the northern political elite. Mbakwe's pointed response to the maneuvers of this group was that they should "read the Constitution."[12] In short, he saw their approach as having little hope of satisfying the basic constitutional prohibition of avowedly ethnic parties. Moreover, it soon became apparent that the Igbo masses were not prepared to entrust their fate to a gathering of "new Turks" however passionately they spoke the language of Igbo redemption, pride and self-reliance.

Yet, this "rump" of the Igbo "Progressives" consisted of highly adept and accomplished individuals in the world of Nigerian affairs, who nonetheless refused to let pragmatic considerations dictate the essence of their political strategy. The more opportunistic of their peers, who rushed to support parties which drew their leading figures from other parts of the country, were castigated by them as "political prostitutes" who run "from pillar to post ... from one party to the other for selfish ends."[13] They hoped that Azikiwe could be discouraged from entering the fray, which would permit them to have a straight fight with candidates who could not match Ezenwa either in personal charisma or in his established probity in organizational matters. When Azikiwe did enter the arena, they sought to play down his influence by contending that under the new federal system the competition for President of the Republic and that for governors of the states were distinct.[14] In other words, the voters should understand that they were not running against Azikiwe. Finally, fearing that they would be denied registration as a party, they first attempted to merge their People's Progressive Party in a wider Progressive National Congress which included other party fragments that had failed to achieve a broad-based strength. Then, a more promising solution was offered to them and they readily seized upon it. This option was to merge their group with the People's Redemption Party (PRP) led by Alhaji Aminu Kano and S. G. Ikoku, the latter a long-standing Nigerian radical originally from Imo State. The PRP leaders saw definite advantages to themselves in this merger, since their previous attempts to organize an Anambra branch of their party had had little success. Moreover, the popularity of Aminu Kano among Igbos had been severely tarnished by his involvement in the pro-Shari'a movement in the Constituent Assembly.[15] The PRP therefore allowed the PPP to supplant the existing PRP organization in Anambra, and even to substitute Ezenwa as the PRP's gubernatorial candidate in place of Engineer Egbunike who had provisionally received that designation. For Ezenwa and his colleagues, the PRP tie had much to recommend it: it gave them the national cachet they needed to secure official registration; the PRP was financially and organizationally weak and so the Anambra branch could conduct its activities with very little fear of being dominated by the national office; and Aminu Kano's ideology of "democratic humanism" was sufficiently nebulous to enable them to continue to espouse their political ideas and proposals with little need for alteration.

On a practical level, Ezenwa hoped to benefit from the backlash to Onoh's attempt to polarize Anambra politics, since he turned out to be the only candidate from Anambra South of the five nominated for governor. To further the fragmentation of "Anambra North" votes among his four opponents, Ezenwa even called for the creation of an "Abakaliki State" which would include the extensive agricultural eastern portion of "Anambra North." Ezenwa and the new Anambra PRP were very innovative in analyzing the problems of the state in the areas of education, economic development and physical amenities and in the variety of programs they proposed for alleviating them. Yet, all of this effort was to no avail. As the leading political columnist at the time in Anambra State reported, the fate of Ezenwa and the PRP was sealed when Azikiwe, with the NPP's gubernatorial candidate in tow, visited Ezenwa's home of Abagana and the entire town turned out to hail them.[16] The strongest reputations for personal achievement seemed to be eclipsed whenever the Grand Patron made his appearance. Success in the gubernatorial and senate races was determined primarily on the basis of a candidate's affiliation or non-affiliation with Azikiwe. Ezenwa therefore went down to defeat, although universally regarded as the most capable person in the race for governor of Anambra State. Ability, personality and inventiveness did matter, but not when it had to withstand the force of ethnic consolidation.

The final two gubernatorial contenders I wish to discuss, Mbazulike Amechi and Jim Nwobodo, could be treated together, so much were they at the center of the drama of personalities and alignment in Anambra State politics. Among the score of people who criss-crossed Nigeria during the second half of 1978 claiming to seek the best arrangement for bringing Igbos back into the "Nigerian family" and, conjointly, the most fitting political role for Dr

Azikiwe, Mbazulike Amechi commanded a careful hearing. During the First Republic, as a principal organizing secretary for the NCNC, Amechi had gained the reputation of being a faithful lieutenant of Dr Azikiwe, a reputation he did little to modify during the long military interregnum.[17] He was an early and active member of Club 19, the association of members of the Constituent Assembly seeking to create a new political force that would represent Nigeria's disparate communities. Yet, like another Club 19 member, Sam Mbakwe, Amechi's "minority" position was that Club 19 should be a means, a stepping-stone, to achieving the more pressing issue of the return to national political life of the Igbo people. As Amechi frankly admitted after his gambit failed, "we decided that we must not lead them into opposition or minority come October 1979."[18] To achieve his goal of returning his people to "the mainstream of politics and government" in Nigeria, Amechi came to adopt a two-fold strategy: an alliance would be forged among three (or fractions of three) parties – namely, the NPP, NPN and PRP – and Dr Azikiwe would be designated as the first presidential candidate of this grand party.

While Amechi busied himself with the various aspects of this scenario, another individual was moving more quietly to create a dominant role for himself via a different strategy whose centerpiece would also be Dr Azikiwe. Jim Nwobodo was a newcomer to high-level political maneuvering among Anambra State politicians. Unlike Amechi, whose home district was Nnewi-Ukpor of Anambra South, Nwobodo came from the Enugu local government area. Indeed, his brother, John Nwobodo, had defeated C. C. Onoh in the election to the local government council in 1976 and was subsequently chosen as the council's chairman. Jim Nwobodo had made his mark as the proprietor of a rapidly growing chain of companies dealing mainly in insurance and medical supplies, and as the owner of the Enugu Rangers Football Club. His campaign advertisements projected an image of youthfulness and drive. His only previous political achievement, however, was his election during his undergraduate days as secretary of the Student Union of the University of Ibadan. Yet, despite these apparent shortcomings as a potential candidate for the governorship of Anambra State, Jim Nwobodo was able at every stage to outmaneuver his strong rivals.

It took Jim Nwobodo some time to decide in which political camp he should exert his efforts, a fact subsequently emphasized by Amechi in referring to Nwobodo as a "bird of passage."[19] After attending the planning meetings of several party formations, Nwobodo finally decided on the NPP.[20] In October 1978 he was designated as pro-tem chairman of the Anambra State NPP, while his chief rival, Amechi, had to settle for the position of secretary. Amechi was embittered by this decision and especially the nefarious means he publicly hinted were used by Nwobodo to upstage him. Jim Nwobodo, in his newspaper advertisements, openly promoted his willingness to secure financial rewards for those who supported him. He was described as "a generous Nigerian" whose "generosity of heart is as bulky as his wallet."[21] Nwobodo had apparently amassed a vast war-chest in preparation for the electoral campaigns and, in dealing liberally from it, he constantly challenged his less affluent rivals to dare and match him. Nwobodo's biggest coup was his participation in the delivery of Dr Azikiwe to the NPP, an historic achievement about which future commentators should seek to enlighten us further.[22]

Amechi had hopes of trumping Nwobodo with an even grander strategy, and from mid-November 1978 his plans were set for implementation. At a meeting held in Lagos, three of Azikiwe's former close associates, Dennis Osadebay, the former premier of the Mid-Western State, R. B. K. Okafor of Imo State, and Amechi, met with three leading members of the NPN, Shehu Shagari, Shettima Ali Monguno and Adamu Ciroma. Amechi felt that there was enough interest expressed in his general strategy, whose crowning moment would be a party held on 19 November 1978, in Enugu, to celebrate Azikiwe's seventy-fourth birthday. Amechi believed that the formation of a combined party consisting of major fractions of the NPN, NPP and PRP could be announced at that time. Moreover, his script called for distinguished political figures from all parts of the country to propose Dr Azikiwe as the most fitting presidential candidate of the new party, a proposal the latter would then gracefully accept.

At the final moment, however, Azikiwe cancelled his plans to attend the celebration and the entire gambit collapsed, taking with it, unfortunately, one political leader from Ibadan, Chief Mojeed Agbaje, who died in a road accident during his return from Enugu. Agbaje had not learned in time of the cancellation of the Amechi-Azikiwe event. Jim Nwobodo, along with other like-minded persons, had succeeded in getting Azikiwe to stay his hand a while longer. Instead, a different last-minute coup was pulled off. Just before the NPP held its meeting scheduled for 16–18 November 1978, to choose its presidential candidate in Lagos, Jim Nwobodo arrived with a delegation from Azikiwe bearing a handwritten letter from the latter offering to accept whatever position the party chose to bestow upon him.[23] There was no question that the only appropriate position would be that of presidential candidate of their party. Amechi was incensed by the train of events, which he condemned as his "betrayal by Azikiwe."[24] He took the unusual step of venting his bitterness in personal statements or paid advertisements in the press, contending that the strategy Azikiwe had adopted would ruin whatever chances he had of winning the presidency. Amechi saw Azikiwe headed for an "anti-climax" in his political career, a "humiliating defeat," a disaster from which he should save "himself, his admirers, his people and his country" by withdrawing from the election.[25] "For reasons very difficult to believe," Amechi wrote, Azikiwe "was bent on projecting Mr. Nwobodo to the governorship of Anambra by all means and at all cost." Amechi, after firing these salvos and giving the clear threat of revealing "certain facts and specific incidents which may be embarrassing to our respected elder statesman," departed in a huff to take up a ceremonial position in the NPN.[26]

That Jim Nwobodo, a politically unknown figure before the last months of

103

1978, would wrest the governorship of Anambra State from several distinguished and "politically seasoned" individuals in that state, reflects an important dimension of Nigerian politics. Despite the wide range of ideological and tactical positions, despite the variety of sub-national and sub-regional communal identities, the process of winning power was reduced to a calculus based on certain criteria which eventually eclipsed all other mechanisms and factors in determining who would be accorded the decisive nomination. Here are the elements which took Jim Nwobodo to the NPP nomination and, as a consequence of Azikiwe's affiliation to that party, to the governorship of Anambra State. It is a formula which reflects my earlier analysis of the fundamental determinants of socio-political behavior in Nigeria:

1. A firm public rejection of the notion that "people from some areas" (i.e., Igbos) "cannot vie for the Nigerian presidency."[27] When decoded, this statement meant that Azikiwe was as much entitled as the leader of any other major section of the population to exercise executive leadership of the Federation. Nwobodo combined this affirmation with a restatement of the goal of Igbo redemption: "Our people must be helped out of the psychological degradation of being regarded as second (or even third) class citizens in their fatherland."[28]

2. A willingness to be perceived as an effective agent in the process of acquiring material resources for redistribution among his electors. As his campaign advertisement put it, the NPP in Anambra had already received "nutrients for its growth from Mr. Nwobodo's generosity and material contributions."[29] With the NPP and Nwobodo in power in Anambra, it was made unambiguous that others could anticipate their turn at the trough.

3. A relentless, skillful and ultimately successful effort to win the nomination of what had become a nominating college of one person, Dr Azikiwe, in view of the unavailability of the three other potential Igbo grand patrons. His "package deal" was Azikiwe's support for his candidacy and his success in helping the Owelle get a presidential nomination. Nwobodo's operation of the patron-client relationship was direct, effective and largely devoid of subtlety.

4. The conducting of a campaign with Azikiwe in tow, characterized by frank appeals to pan-Igbo consciousness and interests. The sub-ethnic mobilization attempted, and then muted, by his strongest opponent in the election, C. C. Onoh, could be peremptorily dismissed: "as far as he [Nwobodo] was concerned, there was only one Anambra state."[30]

To conclude: the governor of Anambra State under the 1979 Constitution was to be the candidate who could win a popular mandate at the polls. However, as the perceptive journalist, Sam Ekpe, informed me even before any votes were cast, "the most decisive factor in the governorship races remains the power of attraction of Dr Nnamdi Azikiwe... All the people want to know is that Nwobodo is Zik's man and he'll get their vote... Nwobodo's greatest achievement is the securing of Zik's patronage."[31] Months of frenetic maneuvering and campaigning culminated in the uncomplicated linking of three factors into one absolute equation: the people, the wealth and skill of an ambitious politician, and the "blessing" of the Grand Patron.

THE NATIONAL ARENA AND THE IGBO VOTE

The fundamental thesis of this study has been that a pattern of political behavior has become established in Nigeria with a requisite set of norms and expectations about the probable actions of individuals and groups in the public domain. One clear indication of the centrality and continuity of such behavior and associated normative expectations has been the maneuvering that has taken place for control of the pivotal Igbo vote, whether we are speaking of pre-independence politics, that of the First Republic, or of the transitional years before the inauguration of the Second Republic. An awareness of this critical concern helps us understand the considerable efforts made by the NPN government of Shehu Shagari to forge a reconciliation with Odumegwu Ojukwu, the exiled leader of the Biafran secession, and to have him return to Nigeria in June 1982, followed by his declaration of support for the ruling party in January 1983. The NPN, in so doing, hoped it had at last obtained an Igbo Grand Patron who could challenge Azikiwe's monopoly of that crucial role.

The trading of a significant bloc of popular votes for strategic state offices is an equation which, for over three decades, has appealed with particular force to the Igbo political elite. The reasons for this phenomenon are several: the resource limitations of much of their home region; their emigration to form sizable communities throughout the Federation which then have a need for national representation; and a perception of being locked into a zero-sum struggle with the Yoruba for political and economic ascendancy. In this chapter I have directed attention to the behavior and strategies of key individuals who sought to win the support of the Igbo electorate and, as part of this process, to assist or prevent the return to open party politics of Dr Azikiwe. The tortuous avenues which the latter himself pursued before his final declaration for the NPP will not be traced here. The subsequent landslide nature of the party's performance in Imo and Anambra reflects the overriding importance of certain factors. By all accounts, the NPN was registering the most steady progress of the new parties in Anambra and, to a lesser extent, Imo State, before Azikiwe declared for the NPP in mid-November 1978. The NPN had won strong Igbo advocates, with national as well as local reputations. Prominent among these were Dr Nwafor Orizu, who served briefly as acting president after the first military coup of January 1966. Dr Orizu, backed by ranks of prominent Igbo individuals such as Jerome Udoji, Nwakamma Okoro, and J. O. J. Okezie, felt he had convinced Azikiwe of the wisdom of declaring for the NPN, and so at the launching of the Onitsha branch of the NPN, he proudly read a letter from the latter which he claimed demonstrated Azikiwe's support for the party.[32] Leading Igbo figures within the NPN were divided, however, between those like Dr Chuba Okadigbo, who sought to achieve the highest possible position within the party for Azikiwe, and others like C. C. Onoh, who had no personal commitment to Azikiwe and wished to see him given either a ceremonial position within the party or induced to remain on the political sidelines.

All attempts by the NPN to gain access to the sizable Igbo vote foundered, paradoxically, because of the party's confidence in its national strength. Individuals from the aristocratic northern leadership of the party who negotiated with Azikiwe, such as Shehu Shagari, Shettima Monguno and Umaru Dikko, were prepared to offer him any position in their party short of the presidential candidacy. The role of Grand Patron was offered to Azikiwe with the plan that all other senior statesmen in the party, such as Makaman Bida and Kashim Ibrahim, would be redesignated as Patrons to make clear Azikiwe's elevated status.[33]

The idea was floated for a while that Azikiwe would be the NPN presidential candidate but would only serve for two years before stepping down in favor of his vice-president from the North. Such an arrangement, however, held too many risks to be seriously pursued. The northern NPN leadership wanted to have Azikiwe on its side to complete the party's successful recruitment of leading Igbo politicians. However, this group believed that the presidency, even a temporary one, was too high a price to pay to achieve this goal.[34] Moreover, who could guarantee that Azikiwe would step down when the time arrived? The voices of those within the NPN such as Dr Ibrahim Tahir, who had done much to recruit Igbo adherents and now felt that Azikiwe should not be asked to stand aside or down for Shehu Shagari, could muster little support within the party. The failure to get Azikiwe on acceptable terms meant taking the risk of losing the Igbo vote. Such a dénouement was also equally unacceptable. Therefore, after Azikiwe declared for the NPP, talks were immediately arranged to see if an NPP-NPN alliance could be engendered. These probings were unsuccessful.[35] Immediately following the 1979 elections, however, they were resumed again, and concluded with an office-sharing arrangement in the federal cabinet.

CONCLUSION

This chapter, and the next two, take the reader into the more intimate dimensions of prebendal politics in Nigeria, into the relations among individuals, their attitudes, expectations and final political choices. What was striking to me was the close congruence between what the common Igbo people were discussing and the arguments they were using (as reported by my students during their field research and commentaries in the print media), and the premises on which Igbo politicians were devising their strategies as captured in personal interviews. It is for this reason that the general vote of this large community of people was essentially resolved as a result of the maneuvers which took place in a score of private homes. Yet, to settle for the judgment that what we have reported is merely a case of elite or class politics would be inadequate. The Igbo political elite, bolstered by the Igbo businessmen and women who were prepared to invest heavily in the 1978–9 campaigns and elections, found it necessary to devote a large part of their efforts to trying to discover Azikiwe's intentions, encouraging his affiliation to the party they personally favored, and, at the highest level, trying to forge a national strategy that Azikiwe himself would find irresistible.

"How can Dr Zik change the course of events for a large number of people?" Monyelu Ugolo asked. And he answered his question with the comment, "It shows [that the] Nigerian is still very deep in ethnic politics."[36] Elite and class action among the Igbo was constrained by an even stronger force: the capacity for collective action of their people. The fact that such a will could be summoned up among the Igbo, and that it could be reflected in an overwhelming vote for the fortunate party, meant that all political actors were caught between the tribune-in-reserve and the patient Igbo *demos*. Material considerations such as government appointments, public amenities and economic opportunities constituted a language shared by the aspirant political leadership and the popular masses. When Sam Mbakwe spoke of the need for the Igbo people to be allowed "to consummate the general amnesty," he was evoking a cry which Igbos of all socio-economic levels could reinforce with a common litany of events since the civil war: the twenty naira *ex gratia* payment ito Igbos after the war for their bank accounts, irrespective of size, which had been dissolved during the hostilities; the inability of Igbos to share equitably in the indigenization exercises in which vast holdings of company shares had been transferred to private Nigerian owners since 1972; the inadequate sums spent on rebuilding roads in Imo and Anambra compared with the vast sums spent elsewhere in the Federation; and the supposedly insufficient number of Igbos appointed to the Supreme Military Council, ambassadorial posts, the boards of parastatal companies, and so on.

If the consolidated ethnic politics which the NPP came to represent in Imo and Anambra was based on the "persuasive logic" that Igbos needed above all "to make up for lost time" and to have "a bulwark against oppression by rival groups," there were lurking dangers behind such a stratagem.[37] The first of these had to do with Azikiwe himself. Since he came to embody the political will of the Igbo people, it was important both that he make the right political choices and that he overcome any practical impediments to his full participation in the elections. The following statement, which seemed naive when first encountered, can now be fully appreciated: "What if Azikiwe is disqualified from the presidential race? How will the people select whom to vote for?"[38] The second danger was represented by the highly visible and continuous resort to monetary incentives at all levels of the party recruitment and then selection process. Few nominations for party positions or electoral office did not carry with them specific prior costs to both winners and losers. The commingling of mercenary exchanges with communal solidarity – a point I emphasized in

Chapter 5 – is a subtle yet significant dimension of these exercises. Consequently, individuals were often induced to issue warnings about the danger represented by this practice:

> The elite must discover for themselves which Nigerian groups are likely to agree to the permanent and equal sharing of power...
>
> Appointments as ambassadors, judges, ministers, board members are only of secondary importance, and relevant only in so far as the appointees protect these basic interests [stability, personal security, property]. The people cannot sacrifice their basic interests so that a handful can get political appointments or become wealthier.[39]

As we have seen in the case of Christian Onoh's redefining of the "language of relationships" within Anambra State, all elements of prebendal politics and ethno-clientelism are brought into play in such efforts. Just as, on the national level, Azikiwe was viewed as being certain to enter party politics if it became necessary to "stop Awolowo" (and the sectional group identified with the latter), so also Azikiwe's intervention can be seen as undermining Onoh's gambit at the sub-ethnic level. At each of these levels the operative factors were the forging of patron-client ties, the defining of the affective community, the fostering of a sense of group deprivation and the explicit promise by individuals both to serve as the personal embodiment of the community and to use political office to procure increased material benefits for their class allies and communal supporters. What Azikiwe, and his successful courtier and client, Jim Nwobodo, had to draw upon in their battles with Onoh, Ezenwa, *et al.*, was the logic that was most persuasive among the Igbo people in 1978–9 – namely, that the battle to bring sectional popular weight to bear on decisions at the federal level had to take priority over all other divisions, actual or potential, among them.

8

Ethnicity, faction and class in Western Nigeria

There is a relentless geographical logic to Nigerian politics that condemns the country to a triangular contest of North-versus-West-versus-East. All the pronouncements since the collapse of the First Republic in January 1966, including the division of the country into first twelve and then nineteen states, seemed so ephemeral as the nation entered the 1979 electoral competition with its three major parties being regarded as northern, western and eastern-led. Even more surprising, however, is the fact that one of these three geographical areas, the West, should be seen as the fulcrum on which is precariously balanced the fate of successive Nigerian polities.

Unlike all previous chapters in this book, this one and the three which follow have been written, from the outset, with the knowledge that the Second Republic has collapsed. Such a perspective will allow for special emphasis to be placed on observations which, in retrospect, clearly indicate the stress-points of Nigerian politics. For example, Chief A. M. A. Akinloye, the National Chairman of the NPN, and an individual who has figured in some of the most critical events of Nigerian politics since the early 1950s, gave the following response when asked in 1978 if Ibadan, the populous capital of Oyo State, was really "the center of politics in Nigeria": "That is a plain fact. During the civilian rule and even during the army regime, it has been the case. When there is peace in Ibadan, the country will sleep. But if there is trouble in Ibadan it has a way of spreading all over the country."[1] In this chapter I will therefore be examining the political struggles in an area generally regarded as the hub of the country's peace and stability. Even within this region the state of Oyo and its capital city, Ibadan, have earned reputations for being highly combustible.[2]

THE HISTORICAL BASIS OF YORUBA FACTIONAL POLITICS

The boundaries of what is regarded as Western Nigeria have shifted in recent decades with the excision of a Mid-Western Region (subsequently Bendel State) and as a consequence of the greater Yoruba presence in the federal capital of Lagos and in the border state with the "North," Kwara. In effect,

109

the West is defined ethnically, namely, where the Yoruba people predominate. Oyo, Ogun and Ondo fall unambiguously in this category. Lagos, which once seemed cosmopolitan in its composition and politics at the birth of the modern political era in the 1940s, is now essentially a Yoruba state embracing a federal capital city that is ethnically heterogenous. Finally, the struggle of the Action Group during the nationalist and post-colonial years to have much of what is today Kwara State excised from the Northern Region and attached to the West have since been achieved *de facto* as a consequence of the demographic strength of the slight Yoruba majority within its boundaries.

One has to be selective here since the politics of any one of these vibrant states would be worthy of a case-study in itself. My focus will be influenced by the pattern of struggle between the Unity Party of Nigeria, under the leadership of Chief Obafemi Awolowo, to establish political hegemony over this area, and the efforts of its opponents, notably the National Party of Nigeria, to deny the UPN and Awolowo a secure regional base. Professor Jacob Ajayi's oft-quoted remark that the colonial period will be seen in retrospect to have been little more than an episode in African history is especially pertinent here. It is impossible to study the lines of political division among the Yoruba from 1950 to 1983 without becoming increasingly conscious of the working out of the dynamics set in motion by the collapse of the Oyo Empire in approximately 1830. In the pattern of political alliances and conflicts that emerged in 1978–9, one can perceive many sequels to the nineteenth-century events of what are generally called the Yoruba civil wars: the Oyo-Ijebu confrontations in the Owu war of the 1820s; the rise to political prominence of Ibadan which began as a military encampment of elements of the decimated Oyo Empire; and the forced southward emigration of the Egba formerly subject to Oyo, to settle at Abeokuta and the resultant conflicts with their new neighbors such as the Egbado.

Increasing British intervention during the late nineteenth century – religious, consular, military – eventually brought peace to this area and arrested the large-scale movement of peoples. These experiences have left their mark in the patchwork of allegiances and oppositions among the dispersed ancestral groups and kingdoms of the Yoruba. The mutually intelligible language dialects of these peoples, their shared social customs and religious practices, and their relatively recent common name of "Yoruba," have not obliterated the collective memory of the historic lines of friendship and warfare. While keeping these still-relevant historical dynamics in mind, I shall show how politics in the predominantly Yoruba states reflects an interplay among the following factors, each of which, with careful attention, can be separated and analyzed even though it overlaps and interweaves with the others: (i) sub-ethnicity (or ancestral group identity); (ii) the persistence of what can be termed primary political factions, e.g., the NCNC and the Action Group; (iii) loyalty to or disaffection from Chief Obafemi Awolowo; and (iv) the deliberate resuscitation of the NNDP (Nigerian National Democratic Party) experience in 1963–5 as a legitimizing model for collaboration between

Yoruba politicians and northern leaders, reflecting a set of shared ideological positions.[3]

The universe that these factors represent among politically aware Yoruba of Western Nigeria is so widely known and acknowledged that there is considerable consistency between published reports in the mass media, academic treatises by student researchers, and the detailed and often candid interviews given to me by some of the principal political actors. Since the flow of information between leading political figures, subsets of active participants, and finally the general population through the mass media in English and the vernacular, is so thorough, political action in Western Nigeria can follow quickly on the heels of political expression. The pacification of much of Yorubaland by 1886, mainly through diplomatic efforts, followed six years later by the crucial military subjugation of the Ijebu, created the conditions for rapid economic and educational development in this region. What remained unresolved throughout the *Pax Britannica*, and after a quarter of a century of independent government, was the absence of a stable hegemony among the Yoruba dating back to the collapse of the Oyo Empire and the subsequent stalemating of a new political suzerainty centered on Ibadan. That the Yoruba continue to live through their history in the present is often culturally magnificent but also politically catastrophic.

PARTY POLITICS AND SUB-ETHNIC IDENTITIES

The favorable terrain for ethnic politics in Western Nigeria should be apparent from the brief survey above. Moreover, it is not surprising that what are inadequately termed "sub-ethnic identities" among the Yoruba inevitably re-emerge as the clearest lines of political affiliation and political competition.[4] After party politics was legalized in September 1978, Western Nigeria seemed to re-enact gradually its past conflicts and other occurrences. While Chief Awolowo and UPN militants often employed the metaphor of the new dawn that was coming, the light of political action and of public pronouncements often shone more sharply on past political formations and rivalries. As I have stressed repeatedly in this study, ethnicity is not a sufficient explanation of Nigerian political behavior. It is the most accessible yarn from which political cloth can be sewn. Moreover, fundamental to the ensuing discussion is the fact that ethnic threads can be combined with quite different ones, as will be seen when we consider the powerful appeals to class action in the populist program of the UPN.

"The Oyo people do not want Ijebus." The statement seemed mocking, half-serious. After all, an impressive gathering of political and legal talent in the country had been working for the past three years to devise the most appropriate constitutional provisions for the Second Nigerian Republic. Yet here was a Member of the Constituent Assembly, a legal practitioner and elected local government councillor, telling me that the newly formed Unity Party of Nigeria would fare badly in Ibadan because the Ibadan were an Oyo

111

people who (in some fundamental sense) "do not want Ijebus," the specific reference being to Obafemi Awolowo, an Ijebuman.[5] This language and all its historical referents – from the pre-colonial, nationalist and First Republic years – had to be quickly learned because it proved to be the language of political discourse, more or less explicit, of many major political actors in Western Nigeria during 1978–9.[6]

It is pertinent to compare the varying fortunes of sub-ethnic politics in the four "Yoruba" states in 1978–9. The break-up of the former Western Region has served to neutralize some of these conflicts and give new life, or potential salience, to others. Lagos State, which had been at the center of so many past conflicts – native Yoruba against Yoruba settlers, Lagos Island against the Mainland, supporters of one royal house of the Oba of Lagos against another, supporters of Lagos as a separate state against those favoring incorporation into the Western Region, etc. – was galvanized into giving overwhelming support to the UPN of Chief Awolowo and its gubernatorial candidate Lateef Jakande. The populist and pan-Yoruba politics of the UPN appeared to sweep underfoot the prior internecine and factional disputes of the 1923–65 period. Similarly, but in a less complex sociological terrain, the state of Ondo also fell resoundingly into the UPN camp. The fact that the septuagenarian gubernatorial candidate, Chief Michael A. Ajasin, belonged to a minor ethnic group in the state became a matter of less importance than the fact that he was the designated local leader of the UPN, a party which inherited the strong Action Group loyalties of the people of that state including the predominant Ekitis. Lagos, by evolution, and Ondo by persistence, demonstrate the continued process of pan-Yoruba consolidation launched by a group of intellectuals including the young lawyer, Obafemi Awolowo, in the Egbe Omo Oduduwa (sons of the legendary Oduduwa) in 1945.

Ogun and Oyo States were quite different political arenas with regard to sub-ethnic identities. With the sub-division of the western state in 1976, the spacial arrangement of intra-Yoruba competition was altered. In Ogun, where the two major sub-ethnic groups are the Ijebu and the Egba, the new state boundaries brought the elites of these groups into more direct confrontation and within a narrowed political arena. The NPN had great hopes of embarrassing Chief Awolowo in his home state as a result of the support it received, overt and covert, from several leading politicians, traditional rulers and businessmen, mainly Egba but including some Ijebu as well.[7] Awolowo treated such hopes with derision, and he seldom made remarks in his public statements that seemed deliberately intended to provoke ethnic or sub-ethnic identities.

The contest was never fully joined in Ogun. The NPN had put together an impressive line-up of "heavyweights" in the state: its gubernatorial candidate Chief Toye Coker, a lawyer and former Action Group Agent-General in London in the early 1960s, Chief M. K. Abiola, the affluent Head of ITT in Nigeria, and the highest traditional rulers, Oba Lipede, the Alake (Egba) and Oba Sikiru, the Awujale (Ijebu). The NPN hoped that its phalanx of prominent personalities would offset the towering presence of Awolowo. Here the parallel with Anambra State is apposite. A concerted attempt was made by the NPN to give new political force to the Egba/Ijebu ethnic division in the state's politics, paralleling the efforts being made in Anambra to politicize a Wawa identity to undercut Azikiwe's pan-Igboism. It was claimed that if Awolowo and the UPN gubernatorial candidate, Chief Bisi Onabanjo (both Ijebu), were elected, the location of the state capital – with all its attendant jobs, contracts and developmental impact – would be shifted from Abeokuta, that is, away from the Egba. Onabanjo responded to such a charge by contending that his government would enjoy no such powers since state capitals were written into the Schedules of the 1979 Constitution. Awolowo also seized on this charge to convey his own transcendence of such divisions by pointing out that his mother was from Egba-Ijeun: "I grew up as a child in Abeokuta, I schooled at Ibara, I taught in the same town, Abeokuta. Why should I then destroy a house that had already been built."[8]

The long list of political and business notables in the state who rallied to the NPN – Prince A. Adedoyin, Chief O. Awotesu, Chief Harold Sodipo, Alhaji Aileru, Chief Akin-Olugbade – contributed, paradoxically, to enhancing the UPN's appeal as the party of the popular masses, a point I shall explore later. The attempt to politicize sub-ethnic divisions can pay ample dividends in Nigeria; it can also fail ignominiously and be made to appear mean-hearted and self-serving. The attempt to galvanize the Egbas and Egbados of Abeokuta Province in Ogun against the Ijebus and (Ijebu-)Remos of the smaller Ijebu Province, was reflected in Toye Coker's choice of his running-mate from among the Egbados, Chief Y. A. B. Olatunji, Chairman of the Egbado South Local Government. The gambit did not work. Onabanjo was able to counter this strategy and bridge the Ijebu-Egba divide by appointing his running-mate, Chief S. Soluade, from among the Egba. Moreover, other prominent Egbas refused to substitute Egba solidarity for loyalty to Chief Awolowo and his new party, for example, Tunji Otegbeye, a socialist whose radical exploits belonged to the past, and Chief Soji Odunjo, who like Otegbeye had lost out in the contest for the gubernatorial nomination. When I put to Chief Awolowo the claim by the NPN national leadership that it was going to surprise him by its performance in his home-state, his response was one of wry amusement. In fact, he countered, the UPN was of a mind to let the NPN win at least a few seats in the state assembly so that the opposition would come from without rather than from within the UPN.[9] As it turned out, the UPN won all 36 of the state assembly seats in Ogun, Onabanjo garnered 94 per cent of the votes cast for governor, and Chief Awolowo won 91.38 per cent of the state's votes for President.[10]

In Oyo State, the terrain was more favorable than in Ogun for the restoration of ethnic battlements. One gubernatorial candidate, Areoye Oyebola, often graced many of his campaign speeches with a list of the areas in Oyo State which had formerly given strong communal support to the NCNC – Ibadan, Oyo, Oshogbo, Ilesha, Iseyin – in the hope that his party would compensate for its thin cadre of leaders by gaining legitimacy as the successor of the once locally powerful NCNC.[11] What Azikiwe was able to accomplish for the NPP in Anambra and Imo, however, could not be replicated in Oyo State. When Azikiwe finally made what was expected to be a triumphant appearance in Ibadan in February 1979, where the NCNC had been particularly strong, the sparse audience at the NPP rally signalled that time had diluted the personal appeal of Zik in Western Nigeria. In Ogun state, a clutch of well-known individuals had hoped to combine their personal prominence with aroused ethnic sentiments and the attraction of the NPN's national image to forge a strong state organization. Yet, they were stymied in 1979 by the fact that the Egba-Ijebu conflicts of the pre-colonial era never reached the same intensity in modern Nigeria. Both the Egba and Ijebu boasted numerous successful sons and daughters in the professions, in business and in the civil service.

In the broader arena of Yoruba politics, however, and particularly in Oyo State, anti-Ijebu feelings were more overt. The Ijebu were often accused of being economically aggressive, especially in the acquisition of land in Ibadan, of having – together with the Ekitis of what became Ondo State – monopolized civil service positions in the former Western state and, finally, of being the ethnic group to which Obafemi Awolowo belonged. It would be more agreeable to analyze Nigerian politics without having to refer to these perceptions and arguments, yet, as mentioned earlier, they constitute so much of the content of political discourse that it would be tantamount to distorting reality if such frameworks were overlooked or sanitized. Moreover, these twentieth-century schisms have deep historical roots, especially with regard to the Ijebu,, who had to be bypassed by the Oyo Empire in its involvement in the Atlantic slave trade, and who were involved against Oyo in one of the conflicts which immediately preceded the Empire's dissolution.

The NCNC, Nigeria's first nationist party, was able to win and retain the support of several Yoruba sub-groups which are peculiarly concentrated within the present state of Oyo. Following the break between Awolowo and his designated successor as Premier of the Western Region, S. L. Akintola, in 1962, a process was started in which intra-Yoruba conflicts of varying antiquity became commingled with party confrontations, class and ideological orientations, and then opposed strategies towards Northern hegemony in Nigerian national politics. The NPP's attempt to attract the former support bases of the NCNC in Oyo State failed, partly because of the intervening heritage of the NNDP and Akintola. The latter party, which emerged in 1963 after a complex series of developments, brought together former NCNC politicians, such as Richard Akinjide, and ex-Action Group members such as Chief A. M. A. Akinloye. The Akintola heritage combines opposition to the socialist leanings of Awolowo with a willingness to collaborate with the Northern political leadership. Much of northern Oyo, especially the extensive Oshun area around Akintola's hometown of Ogbomosho, became fertile terrain for the NPN which presented itself as the direct successor of the

NNDP. The battles between NNDP and Action Group supporters were the bitterest Nigeria had known during the First Republic. The NPN deliberately resurrected these ethnic and factional confrontations by such deeply symbolic acts as the placing of a wreath by Shehu Shagari on the tomb of Chief Akintola and his frequent praise of the latter as having been one of Nigeria's finest politicians.

In 1978, Chief Akinloye would make the following overt public appeals to these past confrontations which had won for the region the epithet of the "wild wild West": "we support a party which can deliver the goods and ... the ability of a person to hold an office. We should ask why Bola Ige has been imposed on Ibadan people. It's the same old A.G. policy and we won't go where we are not wanted."[12] Chief Akinloye's remarks are only slightly less blunt than the following by another Ibadan politician, Chief Lekan Salami: "remember that Chief Richard Akinjide is your own son, so you must all vote for him as governor of Oyo state."[13] The UPN had nominated Bola Ige, a lawyer from Ilesha and a well-known public figure in Nigeria, to be its gubernatorial candidate. Of the four UPN candidates for governor in the predominantly Yoruba states, Bola Ige was the only one who had secured the nomination by defeating the preferred candidate of Chief Awolowo, the Rev. Alayande of Ibadan. Moreover, despite Ige's reputation as a loyal and intellectually resourceful member of the Awolowo camp, his home town of Ilesha was one of the former strongholds of the NCNC. As we saw with regard to Ogun, but now even more strikingly in the once sharply divisive politics of Oyo State, the UPN was transcending communal divisions both at the level of its party leadership and in its areas of popular support.

The weak turn-out for Azikiwe's visit to Ibadan in early 1979, as mentioned above, indicated that one chapter of the city's politics had been closed. By contrast, the huge demonstration when Awolowo made his first campaign visit to the same city almost paralyzed certain quarters and demonstrated that a new era in Ibadan's politics had begun. The dominant political organization during the 1950s, the Mabolaje Grand Alliance, was a populist aggregation of residential, occupational, and protest organizations. Alhaji Adegoke Adelabu, the charismatic leader of the Mabolaje, had been one of Awolowo's most redoubtable political opponents. In 1978–9, however, the commanding role of the Mabolaje, like its former national affiliate, the NCNC, could not be revived in Western Nigeria. Several individuals claimed to speak for the Mabolaje, and they divided their support among four of the parties: the NPN, UPN, NPP and PRP. An important aspect of the nullification of the NPN's hopes for Ibadan was touched upon by Bola Ige when he contended that "someone like Adisa cannot be in the same party as Akinjide and Akinloye."[14] He was referring to Adeoye Adisa who had the most generally recognized claim to speak as Adelabu's successor and who eventually threw his support behind the NPP. The gist of Ige's remark also pertains generally to the inability of the NPN, throughout the West in 1978–9, to attract popular communal support to match its success in gathering under its banner leading

115

figures from the business and professional world and traditional rulers and former politicians.

Bola Ige's running-mate for Deputy Governor was Mr S. M. Afolabi of Oshun, which gave the UPN in Oyo state a political line-up composed of individuals from the strongholds of the parties which formerly opposed the Action Group. On another level, in spite of the sharp dismissal of the UPN as a party which sought to "enthrone the Ijebu." Awolowo successfully demonstrated his acquired position as a pan-Yoruba leader by the massive crowds which turned out for his political rallies throughout the state and in his commanding vote totals in the presidential election. Both the NPP and NPN were therefore unsuccessful in provoking sub-ethnic identities to undermine the UPN's drive to draw support – unevenly to be sure – from all areas of the state. The historic achievement of the UPN in 1978–9 was the blunting of its vulnerability to ethnic political strategies among the Yoruba, while simultaneously mobilizing support along class lines. It is a difficult strategy to implement because so much of Nigerian politics, and especially intra-Yoruba politics, rests on the capacity of an individual and his party "to deliver the goods," as I quoted from Akinloye.

The NPN, among the Yoruba as much as among the Igbo, had the personnel, the funds and the political machinery to continue to advance such claims. One of the structural weaknesses of the Second Republic during its brief life was that the 1979 elections in the two southern angles of the Nigerian triangle were decisive without being conclusive. The NPN in these areas would proceed to use the muscle of the national government to equalize gradually the contest between itself and the UPN in the West and the NPP in the East. To conclude this discussion: the UPN took 117 of the 126 seats in the Oyo State assembly, 84 per cent of the gubernatorial vote, and 86 per cent of the presidential vote. Indeed, of the 24 local government areas in Oyo State, the only one in which Shehu Shagari of the NPN won more votes than Awolowo was in the home town of the late Chief Akintola, Ogbomosho, where Shagari won 40,197 votes to Awolowo's 7,699. One of the closest margins was in Oyo itself, where Shagari's vote-total was approximately half Awolowo's. In Ibadan, however, Awolowo's nearly 200,000 votes to Shagari's 35,000 and Azikiwe's derisory 4,000 is suggestive of the shifts in the politics of that pivotal city discussed above.

THE CLASS APPEAL OF THE UNITY PARTY OF NIGERIA

It is unfortunate that, in order to stay close to the dynamics of Nigerian politics, it was necessary to discuss the attempts to politicize ethnic identities before exploring the factors of class, ideology and social policies. The two dimensions are not of equal force, especially over an extended period in Nigeria; the latter must constantly struggle to hold its own against the less demanding tactics of ethnic politics. When the Unity Party of Nigeria was formally launched in September 1978, it represented one of the most concerted

116

attempts to combine leadership, organizational cohesion, research and planning, and a progressive ideological commitment in post-colonial Africa. The fact that all of this effort ended in brutal street fighting in the Western states in the latter stages of the 1983 elections suggests the hard thinking that must be done in Nigeria to find ways of avoiding the decay, not just of the governmental system, but also of the political organizations that emerge to compete for the support of the electorate. More than those of any other party which obtained registration in Nigeria for the 1979 elections, the leading members of the UPN knew what they wished to achieve when they came to power (in the Federation) and how their electoral campaign should be conducted to prepare the electorate for this mission.

One has to distinguish the central thrust of the UPN, its defining dynamic, from the range of features it embraced which could also be found in the other parties. Depending on which prominent member of the UPN one consulted, a slightly different picture of the party emerged. According to Alhaji Lateef Jakande, the UPN included individuals committed to a range of different ideological positions, "from scientific socialists like [Dr Tunji] Otegbeye, to others who were less committed to scientific socialism, to people who were even rightists."[15] Yet the explicit commitment of the party was to the building of a socialist Nigeria although such a commitment was left ambiguous. Most of the party's campaign literature stressed the implementation of a series of populist welfare measures rather than the rapid socialization of the means of production. Intellectuals associated with Chief Awolowo could look back in 1978 to a decade of research, writing and theoretical planning that sought to give specific content to the Action Group's adoption of democratic socialism as its philosophy in 1962. It was therefore not merely political factionalism or sub-ethnic loyalties which explained why so many affluent and enthusiastically capitalist individuals in the Western states rallied to the emerging NPN rather than to the UPN.[16] While the UPN included in its ranks many affluent business people who contributed to its ample treasury, they either shared the welfarist spirit of Awolowo's "Committee of Friends" – the immediate forerunner of the UPN – or regarded such aspects of the party's work as mere politics, as the verbal trimmings needed to excite a mass electorate. The extreme left wing of the party, though graciously courted, enjoyed little real power. Their members served to give conceptual flavor to the party's programmatic statements. As for the extreme right of the party, it was largely symbolic of the inability of Awolowo to attract cadres of the quality and number that flocked to the party from its Western heartland. Typical of such recruits was the party's vice-presidential candidate in 1979, Philip Umeadi of Anambra State, whose mishmash of corporatist, if not fascist, ideas sat uneasily with the strong commitment to democratic socialism of the UPN "brain trust." The explanation of how the varying, and sometimes conflicting, strains in the UPN could be held together in one party organization must obviously be sought in the personality and politics of Obafemi Awolowo.

In 1979, the two individuals in the party hierarchy, apart from Awolowo himself, who spoke with the greatest authority regarding the UPN's ideological position were Ebenezer Babatope, the youthful Director of Organization, and Bola Ige, the party's gubernatorial candidate in Oyo State. Despite his superordinate position in the party, Chief Awolowo greatly relied on the input of close associates, such as Professor Sam Aluko, an economist at the University of Ife, in formulating the party's programs and actions. Some of the books which appear under his signature in fact incorporate the basic groundwork carried out by Ige, Aluko and other intellectuals. At the time that his new political organization was allowed to function openly and legally, the following approach and themes had been put into final shape: (i) the party would pursue socialism in Nigeria "but not in one fell swoop"; (ii) four "cardinal programs" would be put before the electorate in 1979 (Free Education at all levels, Free Medical Care for all, Integrated Rural Development, and Full Employment); (iii) one of these programs, namely free education, would be pre-eminent (reflecting a long-standing commitment of Awolowo) and treated as fundamentally necessary for the advancement towards full socialism.[17]

So the UPN was able to go to the Nigerian electorate with a program which ranged from the distant but vague goal of socialism, to four specified cardinal programs and, finally, to the major and immediate promise of free education at all levels. Free education was promised in a millenarian tone: it would become a reality on the very day that Obafemi Awolowo was inaugurated as the President of the Second Republic. What became increasingly apparent as the campaign unfolded in 1979, was that Awolowo's messianism on the subject of free education struck a vibrant response in Nigerians belonging to a range of social categories. Indeed, the "social meaning" of free education, especially in Western Nigeria, matched in significance the philosophical and quasi-religious commitment of Awolowo, throughout four decades of political life, to the freeing of his fellow citizens from the shackles of ignorance and illiteracy.

It seems implausible that the call for free education, and the associated promise of free textbooks, a secondary school within five kilometers of each Nigerian child, and the cancelling of educational loans, should have emerged as the overwhelming policy issues of the 1978–9 campaign and elections in Nigeria. In comparison with that in much of tropical Africa, education in Nigeria was highly developed, particularly in the Western states. Moreover, the federal military government had only recently implemented a universal primary education scheme (UPE) throughout the country. How do we then explain this apparently paradoxical development? The first reason, mentioned above, was Awolowo's almost messianic commitment to this issue and his ability, and that of his associates, to articulate it forcefully. The second was the historic achievement of Awolowo's Action Group government in introducing a free education scheme in the Western Region in 1955. Only personal commentaries can convey the degree of governmental legitimacy which Awolowo and the UPN could evoke with its call for free education at all levels.

Here is a summary from research notes made of the comments of a group of recent graduates of the University of Ibadan, recorded in the town of Oyo in October 1978, during the course of a lackluster NPN rally:

> They were strongly for the UPN, their enthusiasm seeming of recent birth. Great stress was placed on Awolowo's plans for education. Awolowo had promised to cancel student loans if elected – this carried great weight with them. They could remember the free textbooks used in schools still bearing the imprint of the Western Regional Government . . . Awo, they claimed, is identified with the real UPE, not the sad affair established under the Obasanjo regime . . . Oyo, they claimed, was backward because it was an old NNDP bastion: very poor roads, no industry, few schools. This situation was quite striking when compared with Ogun and Ondo states. In these areas there are many schools, a number of them built under Awolowo. In fact, they are often referred to as Awolowo schools.

This set of reactions to the UPN's call for free education was shared by at least two generations of educated people in Western Nigeria. The other Nigerian political parties, but especially the NPN, found it necessary to try and counter the attention that this issue was receiving on the campaign trail and in the media. Shehu Shagari took to referring to the products of UPE in the former Western Region as being semi-literates and "mere letter writers."[18] A more unfortunate counter-attack could hardly be imagined. Tens of thousands of Yoruba professionals – teachers, lawyers, doctors – who owed their educational training to policies of the Action Group government in the 1950s, felt directly insulted by such statements.[19]

The promise to institute free education and medical care enabled the UPN to formulate a class appeal which was more persuasive, more immediate, than the vaguer notion of creating a socialist Nigeria. The UPN had come into existence in September 1978 with its four cardinal programs, and an array of supporting documentation on how these would be implemented, that gave it a decisive advantage in appealing to the masses of voters in Western Nigeria. Lateef Jakande spoke of the burden which educational costs represented for the overwhelming majority of the Nigerian people and which the UPN now proposed to lift from their shoulders.[20] Bola Ige, to convey the impact of the UPN's proposals, contended that the people were now abusing the NPN leaders for opposing free education because "they want our children to be slaves of their children."[21] When Bola Ige and Richard Akinjide met in a televised debate during the campaign, Ige challenged Akinjide to translate into Yoruba the NPN's promise that, unlike the UPN program, it would provide "free and qualitative education." The UPN was able to attract a considerable amount of media attention, to stake out a policy that promised to combine fiscally resourceful government with social progress, and finally to arouse class sentiments which mitigated its assumed ethnic basis.

Wherever he travelled in the former Western Region, Awolowo was able to contrast the heavy burden of educational and medical costs, and the deteriorated state of roads and bridges, with memories of the achievements of the Action Group government two decades previously. The opportunistic politics of sub-ethnicity and faction could temporarily give way to one centered on a call for specific social welfare programs. Although the more complex programs of integrated rural development and full employment were seldom fully explained or debated during the campaign, they did give thematic coherence to the party's appeal to the rural and urban masses. During the oil-boom years of the 1970s, Nigeria's food and especially export agricultural economy had suffered greatly, and a ceiling had already been reached in the expanded employment opportunities for the swollen urban populations. What all commentators, including my students undertaking their research projects, emphasized, is that the UPN was receiving a positive response from the women of Western Nigeria, who shoulder the bulk of the responsibility for putting their children through school.[22] The UPN did not have to convince Western women of the importance of education: they had long demonstrated their priorities in the heroic sacrifices they made to educate their children. For what turned out to be too brief an episode, the politics of sub-ethnicity could be neutralized by the offer of direct budget relief for a whole class of people.

As I indicated in Chapter 5, political mobilization based on class, ideology and programs represents a virtual ideal model in the context of contemporary Nigeria. Had Western Nigeria been a nation unto itself, the achievements of the UPN's political campaign of 1978–9 – and the detailed planning that preceded it – could have established a new model of progressive party politics for tropical Africa. Those who opposed the UPN would have constituted a minority opposition without the power to impede the party leaders in their implementation of a program which had been diligently explained to the electorate. However, the Western states constitute only one fifth of the Nigerian Federation. And even though the same populist program of the UPN could be recognized as coherent and even praiseworthy by people in other areas of the country, other factors acted to prevent the party from obtaining anything but a derisory share of their electoral votes.

Clientelistic and ethnic politics presented impermeable barriers to the UPN's attempt to wean the masses of the people from their local "sons of the soil" outside the Western states. Moreover, the fact of the Federation acted to undercut the extraordinary electoral gains of the UPN in the West, especially in the light of the balanced strength of the opposing parties in this area during the previous civilian era. NPN politicians who were trounced by the UPN in their home states in the West lost, despite this defeat, not a jot of their political clout. A. M. A. Akinloye retained his commanding post of national Chairman of the NPN, and Richard Akinjide became the Federal Attorney General. Many others in the party hierarchy procured benefits, in political office and direct economic opportunities, as a result of their party's control of the national government and thus the national treasury. Also, the Akintola stratagem of 1963–5 returned in full force: an alliance with the nationally dominant party would be used to procure the means – economic and physical – to reverse the UPN's gains of 1979.

Another way in which the UPN's class gains were undercut by the very

120

structure of the Nigerian Federation concerns the UPN's goal of winning national power and thus being able to readjust the totality of government expenditure patterns to make possible the implementation of its social welfare and developmental programs. The failure to win federal power meant that the UPN did not have control of the financial resources needed to implement its far-reaching programs. Yet, having committed itself so messianically to this mission, it decided to proceed nonetheless with its program in the five Western states it controlled between 1979 and 1983, with largely negative consequences.

AWOLOWO AND HIS ASSOCIATES

I used the analogy in Chapter 7 of a card game in progress and of Nnamdi Azikiwe circling the players to decide whether he should join the game and on whose side. In the case of Awolowo, he represents the person who organizes the game and then invites others to join. Anyone is free to come and try his or her luck. No one is excluded on the basis of religion, ethnic identity, place of origin or prior political affiliation. Yet, the degree of "openness" of this process, however much it might have been proclaimed, was found unconvincing by many invitees. Some might come and stay for a few hands but then drift away accusing Awolowo of playing with a stacked deck. Others could never convince themselves that those who had spent years around the table would not have an unmatchable advantage over the newcomers. Even if the cards were fairly dealt, how could they ever be certain that the veterans would not use covert understandings, especially of the ways of the Master, to keep them off-balance and ineffective?

The efforts of Obafemi Awolowo in Nigerian politics over four decades is deserving of broader study and analysis. I cannot do better than a moderate injustice here in discussing his pivotal position in the struggle to succeed the military government in 1979. There were four major dimensions to the political movement which took the name of the Unity Party of Nigeria, three explicit and avowed, the fourth implicit and often disavowed. The first of these, as mentioned above, was the research and planning which went into full gear, according to Awolowo, as soon as he was convinced that Murtala Muhammed meant what he said in 1975 about returning the country to civilian rule.[23] Those individuals who regarded themselves as associates of Awolowo, as people loyal to his political leadership, set to work on a number of fronts – for example, in sponsoring the writing of research papers and in acting on directives of Awolowo in the local government elections of 1976 and in the subsequent election of delegates to the Constituent Assembly.

Within the Constituent Assembly in 1977–8, those delegates who belonged to "Awolowo's camp" functioned as one of the factions which divided their energies between attending to the Assembly's business and maneuvering to entice unaffiliated members into their pre-party organization. In short, a political machinery that was kept in reserve throughout the military era

121

rumbled into action. Its nerve centers were the personal residences of Awolowo, especially in Ikenne in Ogun State and Apapa in Lagos. The second dimension was the personal effort of Awolowo to reach out and recruit to his cause the individuals, especially from outside the Yoruba heartland, who were needed to give his party a broad national image. Letters were personally delivered to such individuals and then frequently followed up by personal visits from the Chief himself. The third dimension involved the meetings of what became known as the Committee of Friends.

There was, of course, a fourth yet unavowed dimension, namely ethnic consolidation among the Yoruba. This phenomenon for Awolowo and his closest associates was stimulated in subtle and often unarticulated ways. A contrast can be drawn with the Azikiwe operation here. After Dr Azikiwe declared for the NPP, even though numerous prominent Igbos, including some of his former associates, remained with the NPN, there was considerable uncertainty as to whether the "Zik mystique" would work as it did before 1966, especially bearing in mind Azikiwe's ambiguous role in the Biafran war. In the case of Awolowo, however, he was able to declare openly and frequently in his personal recruitment efforts of 1977–9 that he no longer wished to be regarded as "Leader of the Yorubas," a general title bestowed on him after his release from prison in 1967 and during his leadership of the Western delegation at the abortive constitutional talks that year. This fourth dimension of ethnic consolidation under the aegis of the UPN, which other commentators might be tempted to make primary, would be effectively secured via the pursuit of the other three: the political machinery of the "Awolowists," the personal diplomacy of Awolowo, and the general meetings of the Committee of Friends. The weapon of ethnic chauvinism was there to be unsheathed if the party needed it. Access to all the necessary instruments to make it a reality, including the class mobilization among the Yoruba masses discussed earlier, enabled the UPN leadership to take the high road of building a national organization, leaving it to its opponents to raise the issue of "Yoruba irredentism" in ways that suggested their own limited horizons.[24]

The party organization that Awolowo sought to construct was inherently contradictory in the context of Nigerian society, and this is why the party achieved an overwhelming success in its western redoubt and highly disappointing performances everywhere else except in the extreme north-eastern state of Gongola. The four point package that Awolowo put together could not be sold outside his home region. This point will be seen perhaps even more clearly in Chapter 9, when I discuss the successful national strategy of the NPN. The Committee of Friends was one of several pre-party recruitment organizations which flourished in Nigeria before the ban on political parties was lifted, some pertaining to a specific locality, others – like Waziri Ibrahim's National Unity Council and Club 19 – being more national in scope. The Committee of Friends, whose meetings often numbered over a hundred people, was open to all politically interested Nigerians. A comparative study of these groups, which set their own flexible agenda and rules, would show

how Nigerians pursued their political objectives in the shadows of a military government. On the basis of what is known to me, the successes and failures of Awolowo and his party loyalists in their recruitment efforts, either through Awolowo's own contacts or via the looser context of meetings of the Committee of Friends, were roughly balanced. Of crucial importance to the UPN's national aspirations was the failure, via these two avenues, to attract non-western politicians or intellectuals of recognized stature who also had access to independent bases of support.

The successes and failures of the UPN's recruitment efforts in 1978–9 are closely tied to the personal qualities, and deficiencies, of Awolowo as a political leader. On the one hand, he was able to evoke the intense loyalty of individuals and groups of people over decades. Thus Sunday Olawoyin, the UPN gubernatorial candidate in Kwara State in 1979, could unabashedly declare

> It was his sole aim and determination to work for any political party led by Chief Obafemi Awolowo ... I want to state very clearly and categorically that so far as Chief Obafemi Awolowo is alive and interested in political activities, I will not seek nor accept offer to contest election as President of Nigeria.[25]

Three of the four gubernatorial candidates in the predominantly Yoruba states in the 1979 elections had stood trial with Awolowo in 1963 for planning the violent overthrow of the government, two of them accompanying him to jail. Yet Awolowo could also reach out, in his words, "several times in 1977," to respected opponents, such as Adeniran Ogunsanya of Lagos State, whom he personally invited to attend the Committee of Friends.[26] It was no secret that Chief Ogunsanya, who had held numerous local, state and federal positions since his early affiliation to the NCNC in the 1940s, greatly desired to be Governor of Lagos State. Awolowo's explanation of his disagreement with Ogunsanya also applied to other unsuccessful recruitment efforts: "the governor for Lagos had not been nominated ... if he [Ogunsanya] expected us to prepare an office for him, our attitude is not to allow that kind of thing."[27] Awolowo and his top associates could righteously reject politicians such as Ogunsanya who appeared selfishly interested in running for a particular office rather than in joining a party which saw itself as a progressive movement. Yet how fair a chance would Ogunsanya have had to obtain the nomination to contest for the Lagos governorship against Lateef Jakande, the eventual UPN candidate, and an acknowledged strong-arm man of Awolowo for decades?

Awolowo's most bitter critics, such as Akinloye, were thus able to appear reasonable when they complained about his methods:

> He more or less formed his own party and put himself as the leader. There happens to be some who resent anybody lording it over them. Maybe if he had called people together and said "let's talk", things might have been different.[28]

Of course, things are not likely to have been different between Awolowo and Akinloye because of their deep political disagreements dating from the early 1960s. Femi Okunnu of Lagos, a former federal commissioner under Gowon

123

and, like Akinloye, a doubtful contestant for political office in 1979 because of past financial probes, had the following comment to make: "If Awolowo had been genuinely interested in reconciliation, I would have followed him. What keeps Awo from breaking out and drawing others under his banner is the circle of friends he has around him, Jakande and others."[29]

It is not possible to separate cogent critiques of Awolowo's Committee of Friends from self-serving statements based on aspirations for political office and past factional battles. Within the Committee of Friends, those invited could perceive a tighter "circle of friends," and nothing was done to alleviate that suspicion. According to Ogunsanya, he had earlier advised Awolowo to make his party as broadly based as possible "by bringing to his fold members of former political parties opposed to his former party."[30] Awolowo would not, perhaps could not, leave behind the traits of a factional political fighter surrounded by devoted lieutenants, in order to become in fact, rather than in aspiration, a unifying national leader. In his strengths therefore were also to be found his limitations. Yet, as was mentioned above, these complaints had little effect on the UPN's appeal among the Yoruba population. Outside the West, they were fatal to the party's hopes. Here is the personal commentary of Shettima Ali Monguno of Borno State in the north-east, a leading figure in both the former NPC and in the NPN:

> Like many of my northern colleagues, I was invited by Awolowo to come and talk with him. He indicated that he wanted to be President and that he had already even formed a group for this purpose. I told him that was premature. If he had wanted to form a party he should have waited until the ban was lifted. He had written me a letter that he wanted to see me but I didn't like the idea of one person setting himself up like that, and expecting the others to fight for the other jobs.[31]

Awolowo was later to comment that the rebuffs he received from all the prominent Northerners he tried to attract suggested that they were under oath to the late Sardauna or Balewa not to join forces with him. More trenchantly, he interpreted this rejection in personal terms which also bore communal implications: "all those I thought were qualified from the North ... though it was an affront to offer to them the post of a Vice-President. They all thought it was their birthright to be Number One and so they spurned my offer."[32] His keen efforts to recruit respected Igbos, especially the former Premier of the Eastern Region, Dr Michael Okpara, then still in exile in London, met with similar results.

One can repeat this observation for other areas of the country. The UPN found itself settling for unimpressive Northerners and Easterners, such as the national vice-chairman from Sokoto State, Alhaji Ali Nakura, and the vice-presidential candidate, Philip Umeadi.[33] Such individuals were representative of the generally weak cadres of the party in many areas outside the West.[34] In the absence of the intra-regional conflicts of the 1950s and 1960s which had brought under the Action Group's umbrella minority populations seeking political support outside their region, the strengths of Awolowo and the UPN

124

appeared in 1978–9 to be more of a threat than a haven to these same peoples and to the politicians who acted as their *interlocuteurs*. Awolowo even prided himself on the politicians he had chased away who had come in search of guaranteed offices for themselves. This denial of one of the precepts of prebendal politics left a clear path open to the NPN. The Unity Party of Nigeria was therefore caught midway between the clientelistic politics of the past, which it claimed to have abandoned, and elements of a more national, ideological and class-oriented system which it hoped to help bring into existence. Both the party's loyal supporters and its critics could strongly substantiate their opposing claims regarding its virtues and vices, a fact which mirrored the sharp contradictions in the party's composition and posture.

NIGERIAN GENERAL ELECTIONS, 1979

Table 1 *Senate Election*

State	GNPP	UPN	NPN	PRP	NPP
Anambra	12,832	10,932	210,101	19,574	699,157
Bauchi	188,819	28,959	323,392	127,279	39,868
Bendel	38,332	316,511	250,194	2,055	60,639
Benue	46,452	14,769	332,967	—	75,523
Borno	278,352	22,145	184,633	31,508	—
Cross River	161,353	77,479	310,071	—	68,203
Gongola	223,121	124,707	203,226	30,708	17,830
Imo	101,184	7,553	145,507	8,609	750,518
Kaduna	233,824	85,094	410,888	278,305	61,807
Kano	35,430	13,831	233,985	683,367	—
Kwara	32,383	126,065	54,282	328	1,020
Lagos	14,480	428,573	35,730	2,556	52,738
Niger	71,498	13,860	175,597	8,139	207
Ogun	1,018	230,411	31,963	—	119
Ondo	4,905	501,522	49,612	—	6,417
Oyo	9,472	758,696	200,372	2,497	4,397
Plateau	41,287	20,024	154,792	19,017	220,278
Rivers	46,985	20,106	153,454	30	86,138
Sokoto	305,292	34,145	571,562	38,305	—
Seats won out of 95	8	28	36	7	16
Per cent	8.4	29.5	37.9	7.3	16.9

Table 2 *House of Representatives*

State	Number of seats	GNPP	UPN	NPN	PRP	NPP
Anambra	29	—	—	3	—	26
Bauchi	20	1	—	18	—	1
Bendel	20	—	12	6	—	2
Benue	19	—	—	18	—	1
Borno	24	22	—	2	—	—
Cross River	28	4	2	22	—	—
Gongola	21	8	7	5	—	1
Imo	30	—	—	2	—	28
Kaduna	33	1	1	19	10	2
Kano	46	—	—	7	39	—
Kwara	14	1	5	8	—	—
Lagos	12	—	12	—	—	—
Niger	10	—	—	10	—	—
Ogun	12	—	12	—	—	—
Ondo	22	—	22	—	—	—
Oyo	42	—	38	4	—	—
Plateau	16	—	—	3	—	13
Rivers	14	—	—	10	—	4
Sokoto	37	6	—	31	—	—
Total	449	43	111	168	49	78
Per cent	100	9.6	24.7	37.4	10.9	17.4

Table 3 *State Assembly*

State	Number of seats	GNPP	UPN	NPN	PRP	NPP
Anambra	87	1	—	13	—	73
Bauchi	60	9	—	45	2	4
Bendel	60	—	34	22	—	4
Benue	57	6	—	48	—	3
Borno	72	59	—	11	2	—
Cross River	84	16	7	58	—	3
Gongola	63	25	18	15	1	4
Imo	90	2	—	9	—	79
Kaduna	99	10	3	64	16	6
Kano	138	3	1	11	123	—
Kwara	42	2	15	25	—	—
Lagos	36	—	36	—	—	—
Niger	30	2	—	28	—	—
Ogun	36	—	36	—	—	—
Ondo	66	—	65	1	—	—
Oyo	126	—	117	9	—	—
Plateau	48	3	—	10	—	35
Rivers	42	—	1	26	—	15
Sokoto	111	19	—	92	—	—
Total	1,347	157	333	487	144	226
Per cent	100	11.7	24.7	36.1	10.7	16.8

Table 4 *State Governors*

State	Party	Governor
Anambra	NPP	Mr Jim Nwobodo
Bauchi	NPN	Alhaji Tatari Ali
Bendel	UPN	Prof. Ambrose Alli
Benue	NPN	Mr Aper Aku
Borno	GNPP	Alhaji Mohammed Goni
Cross River	NPN	Dr Clement Isong
Gongola	GNPP	Alhaji A. Barde
Imo	NPP	Mr Samuel Mbakwe
Kaduna	PRP	Alhaji Balarabe Musa
Kano	PRP	Alhaji Abubakar Rimi
Kwara	NPN	Alhaji Adamu Atta
Lagos	UPN	Alhaji Lateef Jakande
Niger	NPN	Alhaji Awwal Ibrahim
Ogun	UPN	Chief Bisi Onabanjo
Ondo	UPN	Mr Michael Ajasin
Oyo	UPN	Mr Bola Ige
Plateau	NPP	Mr Solomon Lar
Rivers	NPN	Chief Melford Okilo
Sokoto	NPN	Alhaji Muhammadu Kanjiwa

Table 5 *Presidential election*

State	Total Votes Cast	Waziri Ibrahim (GNPP) % Votes Rec'd	Obafemi Awolowo (UPN) % Votes Rec'd	Shehu Shagari (NPN) % Votes Rec'd	Aminu Kano (PRP) % Votes Rec'd	Nnamdi Azikiwe (NPP) % Votes Rec'd
Anambra	1,209,038	1.67	0.75	13.50	1.20	82.58
Bauchi	998,683	15.44	3.00	62.48	14.34	4.72
Bendel	669,511	1.23	53.23	36.19	0.73	8.60
Benue	538,879	7.89	2.57	76.39	1.35	11.71
Borno	710,968	54.04	3.35	34.71	6.52	1.35
Cross River	661,103	15.14	11.76	64.40	1.01	7.66
Gongola	639,138	34.09	21.67	35.52	4.34	4.35
Imo	1,153,355	3.00	0.64	8.80	0.89	86.67
Kaduna	1,382,712	13.80	6.68	43.12	31.66	4.72
Kano	1,220,763	1.54	1.23	19.94	76.41	0.91
Kwara	354,605	5.71	39.48	53.62	0.67	0.52
Lagos	828,414	0.48	82.30	7.18	0.47	9.57
Niger	383,347	16.50	3.69	74.88	3.99	1.11
Ogun	744,668	0.53	92.11	6.23	0.31	0.32
Ondo	1,369,849	0.26	94.51	4.19	0.18	0.86
Oyo	1,396,547	0.57	85.78	12.75	0.32	0.55
Plateau	548,405	6.82	5.29	34.73	3.98	49.17
Rivers	687,951	2.18	10.33	72.65	0.46	14.35
Sokoto	1,348,697	26.61	2.52	66.58	3.33	0.92
Per cent		10.0	29.2	33.8	10.3	16.7

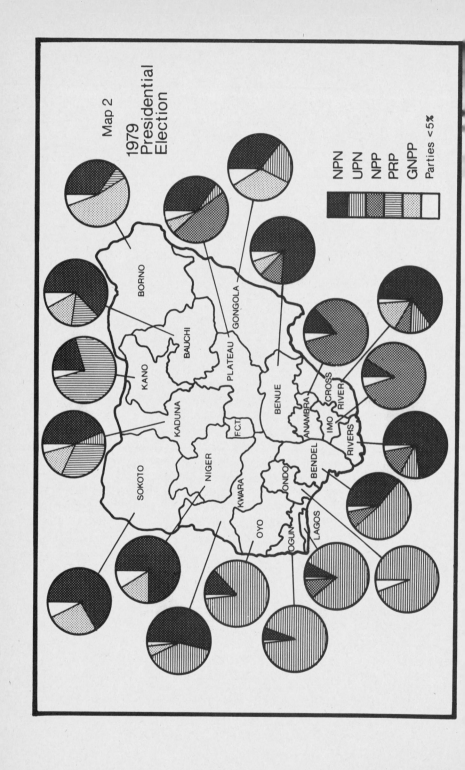

Map 2
1979
Presidential
Election

NPN
UPN
NPP
PRP
GNPP
Parties <5%

9

Northern primacy and prebendal politics: the making of the NPN

The emergence of the National Party of Nigeria (NPN) shortly after the lifting of the ban on politics in September 1978, and its triumph in all five elections a year later, represent an impressive demonstration of the range of strategies available to Nigerian political actors. Yet it was a success which incorporated the seeds of its own undoing. A castle built of cards is impressive as long as we do not plan to do anything but admire it. The success of the NPN was of such a nature. Its rationale was pre-eminently that of prebendal politics in all the dimensions I have discussed earlier. Its demise was foreshadowed by the ultimately destructive logic of this very set of practices.

When power was handed over on 1 October 1979, the victorious parties stepped into the vacated offices of the state or the new ones mandated by the new constitution. Nigeria needed a few cycles of civilian government in the Second Republic to overcome the immediate consequence of the accession of the NPN, and the other parties, to political power. Those who emerged triumphant in the internal struggles for position within the party, in manipulating ethno-clientelistic ties and identities, subsequently took the same attitudes, objectives and tactics into the operation of the offices of the state itself. Nigeria lacked the resources – material and constitutional – to survive the crisis of the institutions of the Second Republic that was forewritten in the very nature of the maneuvers that rendered the NPN such a formidable force in the 1979 elections.

This review of the key features in the making of the NPN is therefore the story of an offspring which is ushered into life but with fatal weaknesses. From this perspective, the demise of the Second Republic can be explained not so much on the basis of imperfections in its written constitution or institutional structure but rather on its inability to survive the machinations of those empowered by elections to act and speak in its name. By exploring the socio-political practices of Nigerians, the nature of their economic activities and institutions, and now the essentials of party formation in 1978–9, I shall have covered much of the road in explaining why the cycle from political renewal to political decay was so quickly traversed.

THE PRINCIPLE OF NORTHERN PRIMACY

There are many layers to the significant phenomenon in Nigerian politics of what can be called "northern primacy." Much of the dynamics of national political alignment and opposition can be traced to a willingness to acquiesce to, or reject, the contention that the political elites of the former Northern Region should hold a position of primacy in any national government. The roots of this sentiment cannot be fully explored here, but they include the early nineteenth-century Islamic revolution and the establishment of Fulani hegemony over a vast area under the Sokoto Caliphate. They include the close collaboration which evolved in the twentieth century between British colonial administrations and the ruling Hausa-Fulani aristocracies. They include the extensive size of the Northern Region, which was kept intact well into the independence era, the advantage of having the Hausa language as a lingua franca, and the related cultural and religious bonds created by the spread of Islam. Lastly, they include the practical instruments of incorporation and repression developed to a fine art under the rule of Alhaji Sir Ahmadu Bello, the Sardauna of Sokoto and Premier of the Northern Region, until his death in the first military coup of January 1966.

Northern primacy has not been dislodged, merely rendered more complicated, during the quarter-century of political independence. The "North" was broken into seven states by the Gowon regime on the eve of the civil war in 1967, but it was a northerner (Gowon) who was able to declare such a change and the count still remained in the North's favor with seven states to five.[1] When more states were created in 1976, the margin of numerical advantage was reduced to ten states to nine. Significantly, it was Murtala Muhammed, a scion of the traditional establishment of Kano, who was able to replace Gowon, and the actual coup against him was engineered by northern officers such as Joseph Garba and Shehu Yar'Adua. After Muhammed's death in the attempted coup of February 1976, his succession by the reluctant Olusegun Obasanjo never disrupted this principle of northern primacy because of the strategic positions given to northern officers within the regime and, in particular, the appointment of Yar'Adua to be second-in-command as Chief of Staff, Supreme Headquarters. Yar'Adua, like Muhammed, was a member of the northern Fulani establishment, in his case of Katsina in northern Kaduna. More generally, General Obasanjo, the second non-northern leader of Nigeria since the brief rule of General Ironsi in 1966, knew that the stability of his regime depended on his retention of support from the traditional and modern elites of the North and he was assiduous in ensuring that this support never wavered.

As Nigeria entered the final two years of the transition to civilian rule, the process of ensuring northern primacy in the successor government was a tortuous one. Yet, so strong is this phenomenon, being a virtual axiom of the country's political life, that it was little weakened by the many changes which had occurred since the civil war, even in the far-flung societies of what constituted the former Northern Region. In the various states of this region there emerged, as elsewhere in Nigeria, *ad hoc* groupings of old and new political actors bearing such names as "Improvement" or "Unity" or "Solidarity" Associations. In the case of Borno State, to take one example, such an association was able to function in a relatively coherent manner, putting forward a list of preferred delegates for the Constituent Assembly, and successfully arranging their election by the various local government councils which served as electoral colleges.[2] There was never a question that at least one of the parties competing for national power in 1979 should represent the political establishment of the North. Therefore, both within the Constituent Assembly in 1977–8 and in meetings usually held in Kaduna and Kano, self-designated leaders and the more authoritatively designated MCAs (Members of the Constituent Assembly), assembled to establish the structures, ideas, policies and personnel of what would become *the* party that would be the new vehicle of northern primacy.

SECTIONALISM AND THE NPN

In less than a year, the transition of the former Northern People's Congress into the Nigerian National Alliance (NNA) in 1964 was recapitulated, and then carried forward, in the creation of the NPN.[3] By May 1978, numerous encounters among Nigerian politicians from the former Northern Region had condensed into the creation of a Northern Movement which embraced an impressive array of individuals from all the former political groupings in the region. Politicians who represented the surviving leadership of the NPN such as Inua Wada, Sule Gaya, Shehu Shagari, Nuhu Bamalli, Aliyu Makaman Bida and Shettima Ali Monguno, were brought together in a loose political framework which also included former staunch opponents of the NPC such as Aminu Kano and Joseph Tarka.

Many of these individuals had continued to enjoy some political power during the thirteen years of military rule. However, a new group of northerners who had not figured in any of the political groupings of the First Republic were also regular participants in the evolving Northern Movement. Individuals such as Umaru Dikko, Ibrahim Tahir, Iya Abubakar and Adamu Ciroma, whose achievements were within institutions of the public sector – universities, ministerial posts at the state level, and regulatory agencies – acquired new prominence through their selection as delegates to the Constituent Assembly on the strength of their educational credentials. I shall explore later how the hopes of this younger group of assuming leadership positions in the emerging national party were partially frustrated by the older politicians.

There was no single blueprint followed in the creation of this political organization. Rather, there were constant adjustments made in response to external events as well as to the shifting pattern of internal alliances and oppositions. If the most important reference point of this movement was the NPC-NNA experience of 1964, its most apparent weakness in comparison

131

with its predecessor was its lack of a recognized leader. No one had emerged since the Sardauna's demise to assume the position of Leader of the North. Strangely enough, the individual who was most widely recognized as having such a claim was Malam Aminu Kano, the populist opponent of the NPC throughout the late colonial and independence period. In the uncertain years 1966–7, before the outbreak of the civil war, Aminu Kano had won recognition as a spokesperson for northern interests. His subsequent appointment to Gowon's cabinet, and his responsibility for overseeing arms procurement during the civil war, gave him as much entitlement as his counterpart, Awolowo, in the West, to seek the leadership of first his region and then the country in any post-military government.

The decade and a half during which Aminu Kano had opposed the oppressive features of emirate rule in northern Nigeria could not, however, be so easily disregarded by former NPC stalwarts. A decision was made around May 1978 to postpone the issue of leadership within what was then called the National Movement. Joseph Tarka, another redoubtable NPC-opponent, was chosen as Chairman of its Steering Committee, a gesture aimed at neutralizing fears about Hausa-Fulani hegemonic aspirations. An important practice introduced by this grouping, and which was to become an institutionalized feature of its successor, the NPN, was the use of formal representation by state delegations. Each of the ten states of the former Northern Region were authorized to send five representatives to meetings of the "Movement." This practice of promoting formal equality among the geographical components of the Federation gave the emerging party the appearance of seeking full compliance with the provisions concerning the leadership of parties in the draft constitution of 1976.

The process of party formation before the lifting of the ban on politics in September 1979 took place principally within two arenas: the halls and meeting rooms of the Constituent Assembly and the private dwellings of former and aspirant politicians. Alhaji Shettima Ali Monguno, an MCA and leading figure in both the NPC and NPN, attests that a group of delegates, two per state, started meeting shortly after the Constituent Assembly began its deliberations.[4] Its efforts were soon disrupted, however, by a series of events which brought the work of the Constituent Assembly to a halt and also generated a wave of anxiety throughout the country over the possibility of renewed sectional conflict. The idea of the "North" involves a reality as well as a myth. These two features are reflected in the slogan of the former NPC, "One North, One People." For many individuals, especially those who were Christians and resided in the lower or non-Emirate North, northern unity was an ideology which masked, and provided legitimacy for, their domination by members of a quasi-feudal aristocracy. Before the Constituent Assembly convened in October 1977, aspirant politicians from the lower North had already come together to form a Council for Understanding and Solidarity (CUS). They saw their mission as that of opposing any attempt to reimpose "Hausa-Fulani domination" and, in particular, to roll back the concessions that had been included in the draft constitution for the upgrading of Shari'a or Islamic law in Nigeria through the creation of a Federal Shari'a Court of Appeal.

One other issue should be mentioned here. After much debate in Nigeria over the reasons for the collapse of the parliamentary governments of the First Republic, a consensus had emerged that the country needed to adopt the basic features of the system of government of the United States, including the office of an "Executive President." In the interim period between the incorporation of such a proposal in the draft constitution and the convening of the Constituent Assembly, the tide of opinion concerning this latter proposal had shifted significantly among the leading members of the Northern Movement. Ibrahim Tahir, a sociologist from Ahmadu Bello University in Kaduna State and a forceful and articulate speaker, had provided an academic rationale for opposing such a post, behind which lay, quite frankly, the anxieties of northerners about such a powerful post being won by a southerner. When the proposal for the Executive Presidency came before the Constituent Assembly, therefore, sectional divisions were apparent in the general weight of opinion for and against the proposal and, moreover, many MCAs from the emirate North found themselves placed in the numerical minority. The Shari'a issue only served to deepen this incipient division, to such an extent that 93 MCAs staged a boycott of the Assembly when they were later confronted by certain defeat on the issue of the Court of Appeal.

The pursuit of northern interests, and the insistence on northern primacy in the new political order, therefore, seemed stymied just a year before the elections were to be held to form the first post-military federal and state governments. That a complete rebound would occur from such initial setbacks, and that northerners would achieve a commanding position within the dominant party and in the Federation, reflects, in its plainest form, the mechanisms of national political control in Nigeria. The creation of the NPN, and its capacity to serve as the vehicle for northern primacy, required a shift from the rigidities of the early battles in the Constituent Assembly. The need to reassert the NPC heritage, as well as to introduce a new spirit of accommodation that would facilitate the widest possible national recruitment, eventually favored the "old guard" of the northern leadership over their more "aggressively northern" colleagues among the younger generation.

THE "KADUNA MAFIA" AND THE "OLD BRIGADE"

One of the key terms in the contemporary Nigerian lexicon is the "Kaduna Mafia." It is, curiously, a term of abuse, yet one which is not rejected by those to whom it is alleged to apply.[5] It regularly occurs in the opinion columns of Nigerian newspapers, and its popularity has perhaps pre-empted more careful categorization by social scientists. Who or what is the "Kaduna Mafia"? In a general sense, it refers to members of the northern intelligentsia who assumed positions of political and social influence during the decade of military rule after the civil war. These individuals are, on the whole, better educated than their predecessors in the emirate North who held similar positions in the first decade after independence. They can also be distinguished from the latter by the fact that they were less dependent on the patronage of the traditional rulers to advance in their careers. A more appropriate, but less colorful, term for this group would be an "embryonic state class," to emphasize the political base of its members within the expanding institutions of the Nigerian state.

Kaduna was the capital of the former Northern Region, and it has remained the *de facto* administrative center of the North because of the concentration of parastatal organizations in that city, which serve a wide area now subdivided into several states. It became apparent that a group of "young Turks" had emerged to exercise considerable influence by the mid-1970s in the affairs of the northern states, and that they were linked by ties of educational background, social outlook and the practice of providing mutual assistance to one another as they advanced in their bureaucratic careers. The career paths of individuals such as Adamu Ciroma, Mahmud Tukrur, Mamman Daura, Suleiman Kumo, and Turi Muhammadu seem to include several common elements or features: appointment to executive positions in the universities, to the management of the *New Nigerian* newspaper, to supervisory posts in development corporations, as well as to the governing boards of publicly owned businesses or utilities. These offices, which usually carried a significant array of material perquisite and flexible budgets, seemed to circulate among an increasingly familiar set of names. Since this group never took on a formal organizational character, there will never be an agreed list of those who belonged to it. Moreover, there are differences of outlook among people who will be designated as belonging to the Kaduna Mafia. For example, Adamu Ciroma, a former Managing Director of the *New Nigerian* and Head of the Nigerian Central Bank, is a much more national-minded individual than Suleiman Kumo, the former Head of the Institute of Public Administration in Zaria.[6] And Ibrahim Tahir, former Head of the Sociology Department at Ahmadu Bello University and Chairman of the Board of Nigerian Railways, is a much warmer and more broadminded political broker than is the curt and haughty Umaru Dikko, a former appointed Commissioner in the North Central State during the Gowon period, who remained on the fringes of this group.

Two final points about the "Kaduna Mafia" worth noting before I discuss their political involvement in 1978–9: first, they can be clearly distinguished from a radical intelligentsia which emerged simultaneously in the far northern states and included such academics as Ali Yahaya and Bala Usman and academic-cum-journalists like Haroun Adamu. Secondly, what also characterized members of this political and social clique is an accommodating attitude towards the ruling structure in the North, and the sense of having become the main defenders and advocates of northern interests. They are often very outspoken on such issues as the allocation of federal resources to the northern states, the degree of recognition accorded to the credentials

134

conferred by northern schools, and the level of respect that should be paid to far northern (i.e., Islamic/Hausa-Fulani) culture in various dimensions of Nigerian life.

The "Old Brigade" is one of the many terms often used in Nigeria to designate the politicians who held prominent party and government positions in the terminal colonial period and in the First Republic. As important as were some of the divisions between major politicians in the emirate North, they can be said to have benefited, as a group, from the dividing of sets of politicians along generational lines within the emerging national party. Before explaining the triumph of the "seasoned" veterans over the relative newcomers, I should indicate some of the enduring lines of division which the former had to transcend or neutralize. The death of the Sardauna, and the failure of any of his former lieutenants to assume his mantle, had left the Northern Region with an unresolved balance between strong centrifugal and centripetal tendencies. Thus, historical rivalries between emirates, such as Sokoto and Kano, or between conquered and dominant groups, such as the Zamfara and Fulani in Sokoto, underlay the tendency of certain leading figures from the NPC – such as Inua Wada of Kano and Yaya Gusau – to drop away from the emerging party in 1978–9. And the independent spirit of some of these emirates, such as Katsina in northern Kaduna State, provided a tacit sanction for the efforts of "opposition" parties in the North, such as the GNPP and the PRP.

Yet despite the many lines of potential and actual division among the ruling strata of the emirate North, the forces making for cohesion – or at least inducing quiescence among disaffected individuals and ruling houses – were so great that once a group of former NPC politicians began acting in collaboration within the councils of the emerging party, they quickly emerged as the core of the party leadership. And here we must return to an interesting paradox about the divisions between the older and younger political cadres in the emirate North. The defeat of the northern MCAs on the issue of the Executive Presidency and, even more crushing, their defeat on the Shari'a provision, helped swing the advantage away from the "Kaduna Mafia" and towards the "Old Brigade" within the national party. The younger political actors found themselves being treated as political novices who had mishandled these efforts. They were dismissed as demonstrating "a very limited perspective on politics." "The reason we sent them to the Constituent Assembly," it was asserted, "was because of their education. Making the Constitution was paperwork, bookwork for which they had been trained. But politics calls for more than that."[7]

It took a while before I was able to transcend the obvious expectation that the younger and better educated northern politicians would tend to be more national and broad-minded in their attitudes than their predecessors. Although no simple dichotomy can be advanced here, a wide range of knowledgeable commentators independently cited the deficiencies of the younger generation when it came to functioning within the re-emerging national political arena in Nigeria. Here is the fullest account, drawn from an interview with Alhaji Nuhu Bamalli, a key actor in the shaping of the NPN and a member of the northern aristocracy, with wide political and administrative experience:

> The Kaduna Mafia is essentially "inward-looking." It is this which caused us so many problems in Lagos over Shari's. They are unable to accommodate other views. In order for Nigeria to work as a nation, it is necessary that all share proportionately. All sections and areas must be included and their views and feelings harmonized. It was therefore a good decision on our part to keep them out of the top positions in the party otherwise they would have made a mess of things just as they did over Shari'a.[8]

Other interviews, for example with Chief Simeon Adebo, who chaired a committee appointed to try and resolve the Shari'a deadlock, as well as with Alhaji Sule Gaya, an ex-NPC leader, also reinforced this critique of the younger northerners as sharing much of the responsibility for the crushing defeat of the Shari'a proposal.[9]

So, in the transition from military to civilian rule in Nigeria, the veteran politicians within the northern establishment were able to use the crisis within the Constituent Assembly as proof of the inexperience, and inappropriate tactics, of their younger colleagues. While the latter would speak of their competence and ability in managing "the institutions of the modern state," the former would dismiss such claims as the "arrogance of youth and education." It was a disagreement over tactics and attitudes in pursuit of a shared commitment to northern primacy and the promotion of northern interests within the Nigerian federation. The most sectionalist and uncompromising members of the younger group, such as Suleiman Kumo, fell away from the emerging party leadership. Those who remained, like Adamu Ciroma and Iya Abubakar, found themselves being out-maneuvered when the process of party formation shifted from the creation of a Northern Front to the fashioning of a national party. One younger political operative, Umaru Dikko, who had developed his skills in ministerial appointments at the state level rather than in the more bureaucratic parastatal agencies as did most of his peers, became a key ally of the team of older politicians who eventually seized control of the national party. This team consisted principally of Makaman Bida of Niger State, a septuagenarian and former northern regional minister who became the pro-tem Chairman of the NPN, Nuhu Bamalli, who served on various steering and selection committees of the party, and Shehu Shagari, their presidential candidate, who adopted the guise of not wanting to be president while assiduously working towards this goal.

SHEHU SHAGARI, "ZONING" AND THE "MIXED BAG" PARTY

It took a direct threat by the Federal Military Government to compel the Northern MCAs to end their boycott and return to complete the work of the Constituent Assembly in 1978. This action not only favored a more pragmatic and less sectionalist line of political mobilization, but also brought to an abrupt conclusion a religious conflict that could have imperilled the final stages of the transition to civilian rule. I shall take up later the more organizational details of the creation of the NPN. At this point, three specific elements must be explored: the gradual emergence of Alhaji Shehu Shagari as the presidential candidate of this party; the notion of "zoning" for the top party positions; and the gradual erosion of any ideological or programmatic content to the party (appropriately reflected in its categorization by Shehu Shagari and Joseph Tarka as a "mixed-bag party").[10]

Shehu Shagari is an individual who has had one of the broadest ministerial careers at the federal and state levels in Nigeria, yet he is a politician who has never had a wide popular following even in his home state of Sokoto. In any gathering of public figures, Shagari would speak seldom, and then in a soft voice. Nevertheless, although he had little of the charismatic presence of Awolowo and Azikiwe, and could not generate the fervor they did among both supporters and enemies, he was still regarded as one of the few northerners with a strong claim to national leadership. Yet, Shagari had to earn the position of northern "flagbearer" in 1978–9. He was felt, by virtually the entire contingent of younger politicians, to be intellectually weak. For Dr Suleiman Kumo, Shagari was the epitome of the "old guard politician," a person whose full-time job was that of being a politician, and who was often vacillating and indecisive.[11] For the radical intellectual, Haroun Adamu, Shagari's intellectual weakness showed up in the vacuity of his campaign speeches.[12]

One of the sharpest critiques made of Shagari was by Dr Datti Ahmad, a Kano physician who typifies the technocratic northerner who would not kowtow to the cabal of old politicians that was winning control of the national party. For him, the basic weakness of Shagari was that he would not be able to work with men more capable than himself. As a consequence, he contended, "Shagari will only share out the jobs among the rogues."[13] How can such an issue, about which there are such strong subjective attitudes, be tackled in a reasonably objective way? Perhaps it cannot. At a time when it became apparent that the "old guard" had the upper hand in party affairs, Dr Ibrahim Tahir would frequently exclaim: "I have no chance of leading the party. I have never been probed!"[14] The shift to a more pragmatic national approach meant that the old guard in the North could join hands with established politicians elsewhere in Nigeria. These were the individuals with whom they had had the greatest personal contact, outside their own region, during the late colonial period and early years of independence. They were also the politicians with whom they shared the most uncomplicated approach to the political tasks of forging alliances, raising funds, and linking support networks. Moreover, their discussions were facilitated by the existence of a common vocabulary: the promise of jobs, public amenities and the even distribution of the state's monetary resources after the elections. From the time the Northern Movement evolved into a National Movement around July

1978, respectable political figures like Nuhu Bamalli and Shettima Ali Monguno had entered into close collaboration with men of questionable probity such as A. M. A. Akinloye of Oyo State in the West, Anthony Enahoro of Bendel State in the former Mid-West, and K. O. Mbadiwe of Imo in the East.

Expediency, and a willingness to co-operate in building a party with the maximum national appeal, became the guiding considerations in the formation of the party. "Combining the combinables," to use just one of the colorful expressions of Mbadiwe, became the prevailing rule. To its credit, the directing northern core of Shagari, Aliya Makaman Bida, Nuhu Bamalli, Sule Katagum and Umaru Dikko, arrived at the intriguing notion of "zoning" to legitimize a practice that would facilitate northern primacy as well as make possible the creation of the NPN as a confederal party with each of its major sectional components having a specific allocation of one of the top party offices. When the idea of "zoning" was first announced in November 1978, it was promptly rejected by some party activists in the West and East: "The party is not a zonal party but a national party" (Sola Saraki); "Presidentialism is not regionalism and zonalism is a manifestation of regionalism" (Chuba Okadigbo).[15] Yet, as Richard Akinjide was able to counter, the practice of zoning the party's leading positions was a case merely of "obeying the provisions of the Constitution."[16] Contrary to Akinjide's contention, what the Constitution had called for in this regard was something much looser than the purely political stratagem of zoning:

> the members of the executive committee or other governing body of the political party shall be deemed to reflect the federal character of Nigeria only if the members thereof belong to different States not being less in number than two-thirds of all the States comprising the Federation.[17]

There were several versions of what zoning was supposed to imply but basically it was that the top positions of the party would be allocated to four "zones" of the country: North, West, East and the "minorities." The "minorities" did not really constitute a zone and, in practice, they became subsumed with the "East" and thus the designation applied mainly to the eastern or non-Igbo minority groups. Also, one aspect of the zoning package was the provision that in 1979 the northern zone would choose the party's presidential candidate, the West the party Chairman and the East the vice-presidential candidate. Clearly, the principle of zoning was a way of rationalizing the dynamics of the struggle for control within the national party. All the nominees short-listed for the presidential nomination came from the northern zone: Shehu Shagari, Adamu Ciroma, Olusola Saraki, Maitama Sule, Iya Abubakar, Ibrahim Tahir, and Joseph Tarka. The fact that the northern caucus of the party could not put forward a single nominee for the Presidency is indicative of the strength of the competing factions within the North. Still, it was an unequal contest which greatly favored Shagari.

Most of Shagari's opponents would be given the designation of "favorite sons" in a United States presidential convention. Their candidacy allowed delegates from various sections of the North to feel that they counted at the highest level of the party: Maitama Sule (Kano), Sola Saraki (Kwara), Iya Abubakar (Gongola), Adamu Ciroma (Borno) and Joseph Tarka (Benue/Plateau). A more challenging race would have ensued if two of the three candidates who represented the younger generation – Abubakar, Ciroma and Tahir – had stood down for the strongest among them, namely Ciroma, or had thrown their combined weight behind a viable alternative to Shagari from the older generation, such as the gifted Maitama Sule. When Shagari failed to achieve the 50 per cent of the votes required for nomination on the first ballot at the party convention, the second and third placed candidates, Sule and Ciroma, quickly conceded to him and thus positioned themselves for prominent positions within the party and government.[18]

Since Shagari lacked the broad base of popular support enjoyed by an Azikiwe or Awolowo – which might have enabled him to discourage challenges for the top position within his party – he had to strengthen his position through alliances with political brokers from other regions of the country. It was with considerable bitterness that Shagari's younger opponents for the presidential nomination regarded his ability and willingness to collaborate with southern politicians of doubtful probity, such as A. Akinloye, R. Akinjide, A. Enahoro, and K. Mbadiwe. The first three of these men virtually ran the final session of the NPN convention on 9 December 1978, and played a critical role in helping Shagari obtain the presidential nomination. In exchange, Akinloye was assisted in trouncing his four opponents for the Chairmanship from the West, by the large blocs of northern votes that were cast in his favor by state delegations acting on instructions from their leaders.

The NPN therefore began the electoral year 1979 as a party which was most impressive on paper, with a large number of "heavyweights" gracing its National Executive Committee and state committees, and with prominent figures declaring their affiliation in all nineteen states of the Federation. However, it was a success that had serious implications for the future of the Federation; and it is a credit to the Military Government that it held firm to its promise to hand over power by 1 October of that year, despite its knowledge of the character of many of the individuals who had maneuvered themselves into strategic positions within the leadership of the party with the strongest electoral prospects. The party with the greatest chance of winning power in the 1979 elections, in view of the ethno-clientelistic pattern of affiliations in Nigeria, was the one able to assemble the largest contingent of influential political brokers. Not only did the NPN's success in this regard mean the return to center-stage of "discredited" politicians of the previous era, it also made possible a pivotal role for those younger politicians who were prepared to play the "old game" without qualms, men like Chuba Okadigbo of Anambra, Joseph Wayas of Cross River, Mvendaga Jibo of Benue and Umaru Dikko of Kaduna.

The choice of Shehu Shagari as the presidential candidate must be interpreted as part of this wider process of political recruitment which

139

rendered the designated "leader" of the party so incapable of controlling the subsequent abuse of governmental power. Northern primacy, Shagari's presidency, and the NPN as a "mixed-bag party" in its personnel and policies, were linked features of the package which was put together in the course of intricate bargaining arrangements summarized above. The overriding principle that kept the participants at the table was the prime goal of winning the 1979 elections and therefore constructing the party that would be virtually unbeatable in the context of Nigerian social dynamics. Any questionable compromises made along the way could be dealt with after this goal was achieved. Less venal individuals within the NPN leadership at the federal and state levels, who had also helped create this political instrument, probably felt they could subsequently refine upon and improve it. However, at a time in which Nigeria so greatly needed a definite sense of direction in order to entrench civilian rule, and formulate new socio-economic policies for the post oil-boom era, the most national party in the country had chosen as its flag-bearer an individual whose public pronouncements seldom exceeded the following banalities:

> As a matter of principle, we are opposed to dogma. As such, the ideological and philosophical position of the NPN shall evolve shortly. Fundamentally, we stand for nationalism and patriotism ... We are a mixed-breed party of young and old, men and women, rich and poor. We are a party of the people, a party of the masses. Therefore, our national philosophy is populist-oriented.[19]

It was not necessary to subscribe to any ideological or policy position in order to be a member, or even acknowledged leader, of the NPN. As long as an individual was willing to echo the need for national unity, vigorously criticize the sectional roots of the other parties, and not be unduly concerned about the probity of many of the leading party figures, then the NPN appeared to be the party with the widest embrace and, moreover, to have the greatest chance of capturing the golden fleece in the 1979 elections.

ALTERNATIVE NORTHERN LEADERSHIP: CUS, PRP, GNPP

The Northern Region was the cradle of four of the five parties which competed for power in 1979. The determining force of Nigeria's political geography could be seen once again in the emergence of the NPN as the dominant party in the North and throughout the country, despite the strong challenges it faced within its core area. My account of these alternatives will begin with the Council for Understanding and Solidarity (CUS), formed in 1977 to act as a caucus within the Constituent Assembly as well as in the pre-party formations which were emerging in the major regional capitals. It was the CUS which provided the initial impetus and set of ideas which led to the formation of Club 19 and then the NPP, as discussed in Chapter 7.

CUS had a well-defined geographical and political identity. Its members included individuals such as Paul Unongo, Solomon Lar, Paul Belabo, Ayuba Kadzai and Ambrose Gapsuk, who came from the Middle-Belt or southern, predominantly Christian, fringes of the former Northern Region: Benue, Plateau, Gongola, southern Kaduna and southern Bauchi states. They were the younger, relatively well-educated, generation who, with a few exceptions (such as Lar), had played little part in First Republic politics. They were most clearly identified by what they opposed – the continued domination of their sub-region by the Hausa-Fulani establishment. Finally, they had little reason to make common cause with the "Kaduna Mafia," whom they regarded as just a younger, and modernized, off-shoot of that same establishment.

A determination to defeat the Shari'a proposal in the draft constitution provided this group with its immediate objective. They presented themselves as the people who knew first-hand how religious institutions had been used as agencies of social oppression in the North, and as having a duty to share such an awareness with the southern Christian delegates in the Constituent Assembly. More generally, they believed that the Middle-Belt could play a strategic, even leading, role in the new political system. Since it was this region which had supplied the country with leading members of the military governments of the past decade, such as Yakubu Gowon, Theophilius Danjuma and Joseph Garba, it was reasonable to suppose that there could be a civilian equivalent of this military elite. Finally, the members of the CUS were motivated by the idea that they could provide the impetus for a realignment of political forces in Nigeria in which the ethnic and linguistic minorities would come together to create a "majority of minorities," thereby bringing an end to Nigeria's tripartite division of power.

The CUS, which lost its separate identity early in 1978, achieved only a part of its assigned mission. It spearheaded the early confrontation with the far northern delegates in the Constituent Assembly and contributed to their defeat on the issues of the Executive Presidency and the Shari'a Court of Appeal. It also served as the catalyst of a political grouping first called "Club 14" (to emphasize its opposition to the far northern states) that was meant to evolve into the new and dominant party of Nigeria. Yet, the idea of creating an entirely new political movement to challenge the three regional centers in Nigeria, crumbled in the face of the revival of regionalist strategies which I have already discussed. Younger politicians from the Middle-Belt often found they could not carry along their local supporters who had championed their election to the Constituent Assembly from local government councils. Some of these politicians – for example, Paul Unongo and Ayuba Kadzai – were accused of being as venal and manipulative as the older politicians they assailed. Finally, the political operators from the far northern group succeeded in nurturing a set of political brokers from the Middle-Belt who argued convincingly to their people that there was no point in their being "in opposition" once again, since they now had their own states and therefore could participate fully in what was destined to become the national party. Where the Middle-Belters were able to maintain drawing power independent of the northern establishment, namely in Plateau State with its sharp resentment of Hausa-Fulani hegemony, they ultimately had to bolster this

141

independence by entering into a tactical alliance via the NPP with the eastern Igbo angle of the Nigerian triangle.

The second political alternative within the northern states had a pedigree as old as the former ruling NPC itself, namely the People's Redemption Party (PRP) led by Aminu Kano. This party could be said to have resumed in 1978–9 the ardent struggles of the former populist opposition party of the North, the Nigerian Elements Progressive Union (NEPU). The connections between the political support won by the PRP in the 1979 elections – enabling it to control the largest northern state, Kano, and to seize the governorship and two of the five senatorial positions in Kaduna – and the complex layers of socio-economic change in the "traditional polity" of northern Nigeria, are so intricate, and are of such broad historical significance, that even an entire chapter would not suffice to cover them satisfactorily here. We must settle then for an overview of these processes in which I shall confine myself to pointing out the roots and breadth of the political challenges to the NPN within its very heartland.

Aminu Kano points out that "he could have been the second-in-command to the Sardauna if he had been prepared to compromise with the NPC."[20] Instead, his party (NEPU) entered into alliances with southern parties, especially the NCNC, to wage a relentless struggle against the oppressive features of the northern emirate system. As mentioned earlier, during the Gowon era Aminu Kano had reasons to assume that he would be recognized as the new "leader of the North" in any new round of civilian politics. An important signal of this possibility was a highly publicized meeting between the former NPC federal Minister, Inua Wada of Kano, and Aminu Kano in 1977, ostensibly to mark a historic reconciliation between the two major northern political families. When the Northern Movement evolved into a National Movement in mid-1978, Aminu Kano surfaced as an active participant in its deliberations. However, in September 1978, as the NPN entered the final stage of selecting its pro-tem officers to serve until the first party convention in December, the announcement was made that Aminu Kano had been offered the position of Publicity Secretary. This was seen as a humiliating gesture towards a man who was one of the country's most important political leaders since 1950. Yet this slight was not an oversight or inadvertent error: it reflected the fact that the radical populism to which Aminu Kano subscribed was still unacceptable to the core of northerners holding sway in the NPN.

Aminu Kano thereupon left the party and returned to what was now a second-best option for him; namely, rebuilding a party which adhered to his ideas and accepted his leadership. From the NPN, he took with him the easterner, S. G. Ikoku, who had also been prepared to tone down his socialist convictions in exchange for the opportunity to participate in the emerging national party. The young radical intellectuals who had been hoping to have Aminu Kano lend them the vote-pulling power they lacked – men like

142

Abubakar Rimi, A. D. Yahaya, Balarabe Musa, and M. T. Liman – were the real creators of the PRP.[21] As Aminu Kano pulled out of the national party, most of his loyal supporters from the NEPU days moved with him. Shorn of his NPN ties, Aminu Kano was able to articulate his profound insights into the ways in which the many judicial, police, administrative and economic reforms in the North during the military era had created the *possibility* but not the reality of true liberalization.[22]

Of all prominent politicians in Nigeria in 1978–9, Aminu Kano was the one who most directly and convincingly argued the case for the freedom and equality of women. Despite its lack of funds and other material necessities, the PRP under Aminu Kano's leadership quickly mobilized the kind of enthusiastic popular following in the north that could not be matched by Shehu Shagari and the NPN. Yet it never became a fully national party. It won the adherence of enough party splinters in the West and East to enable it to win registration according to the requirements of the Electoral Decree. However, its voting strength tended to be concentrated in the two key states of the North, Kano and Kaduna. Its material limitations and the effective competition it faced from the GNPP and, to a lesser extent, the UPN, prevented it from regaining the breadth of implantation of the former NEPU. Apart from the progressive measures it could push through in the one state government entirely under its control, Kano, one consequence of the PRP's efforts was the highlighting of the shortcomings of the NPN as the probable successor of the military government. The PRP–NPN divide closely mirrored the sharp class division in the emirate North. Here, status, privilege and wealth were arrayed against subordination, poverty and powerlessness to a much greater extent than elsewhere in Nigeria. By drawing from the emerging national party those intellectuals and other political activists who were committed to the rapid democratization of wealth and power in the North, Aminu Kano and the PRP acted to sharpen the NPN's appearance as the party of the ruling establishment.

Aminu Kano's initial attempt to bring about a "historic compromise" between these two major political families in the North could have given the national party a quite different orientation had it succeeded. Of course, I am arguing against the facts here: Aminu's gambit failed because those in control of the national party preferred to risk losing Kano State (a sharing of power in Kaduna was not anticipated) rather than give legitimacy to the demands for direct radical social reforms which Aminu Kano and his old and younger confederates represented. The tension Aminu Kano personally experienced between his wish to co-operate with the likely governing party, after decades of opposition politics, and his advocacy of radical social progress, was carried over into the Second Republic. While his younger associates insisted on following through with the logic of their party's reformist program and popular bases, Aminu Kano had no wish to co-operate with other parties in a campaign of organized opposition to the NPN government. These tensions eventually provoked a break within the PRP during the Shagari Administration between an Aminu Kano faction and a radical one led by the PRP governors.

The fourth political formation to emerge from the former North was the Great Nigerian People's Party (GNPP). It was created following the failure to bring about a merger between the pre-party formation led by Alhaji Waziri Ibrahim, the National Union Council, and some of the members of Club 19. The latter, together with the Igbo contingent grouped around the presidential candidacy of Nnamdi Azikiwe, retained the name of the Nigerian People's Party after the merger floundered, while the Waziri group was obliged to abandon its use of it. For a brief period in late 1978, it seemed as if the established pattern of Nigerian party politics was about to undergo a profound change. Young political aspirants from the minorities of the Mid-West, Middle-Belt and East, who had forged a working alliance with former NCNC politicians from Igbo and Yoruba states within Club 19, were moving to join forces with a liberal northerner, with a strong NPC background, and his personalist following.

As I discussed in Chapter 7, the presidential aspirations of Dr Azikiwe, based on the push for an identifiable Igbo presence in one of the competing parties in the 1979 transition, significantly altered the "Club 19" spirit of the NPP and, moreover, undermined the emerging pact with Waziri Ibrahim. The political efforts of Waziri Ibrahim can be contrasted with those of Chief Awolowo and the UPN. Waziri, like Awolowo, greatly desired to be Nigeria's President, and his party was in large part the instrument fashioned to achieve this end. Unlike Awolowo, however, Waziri had the appearance of a "maverick" on the Nigerian political scene, yet one whose party could pull together heterogenous strands of political support to win approximately 10 per cent of the national vote in the 1979 elections, two of the 19 governorships and eight of the 95 senatorial seats. The GNPP's performance almost matched that of the PRP, even though it was the party which suffered most from the electoral fraud conducted by agents and supporters of the parties in command of specific regions, especially the NPN, UPN and NPP.[23]

Waziri Ibrahim and the GNPP presented a diffuse challenge to the NPN in the northern states and one which could have achieved greater precision if the framework for party politics had not decayed so rapidly after 1979. Waziri had been a Minister in the NPC government in the 1960s, first Minister of Health and then of Economic Development. Before entering politics he had risen rapidly within the large colonial firm, the United Africa Company, and, following the collapse of civilian rule, had turned his energies to building an extensive financial organization within the country. Waziri is a complex, somewhat eccentric individual, whose diverse talents and personal attributes enabled him to attract a variegated set of political associates.

He was a man of great wealth yet one who castigated the NPN for being "a party whose composition was exclusively made up of powerful rich men and highly placed officials."[24] He was usually described by others as being "of the pure leadership group in the north," married to the daughter of Sir Kashim Ibrahim, the former Governor of Northern Nigeria.[25] This latter perception did not prevent Waziri from putting himself forward as a humble and simple man with little concern for the trappings and privileges of the class to which he belonged. In 1978–9, Waziri drew on these seemingly contradictory traits to create a party which lacked any specific roots in the politics of the pre-1966 era. Even before the final stage of party formation, he used his right of access to woo the support of numerous chiefs and emirs in the North. He was, after all, as much a legitimate claimant to their support as was Shehu Shagari and other former ex-NPC Federal Ministers. Moreover, he and his lieutenants were able to use their knowledge of the historical conflicts among emirates, or between competing families within particular emirates, to line up support, often covert, for their party.[26]

As a result of his travels throughout Nigeria in pursuit of his business interests, Waziri was able to attract associates from virtually every part of the country. Indeed, the GNPP was the party with the second-best spread of electoral support in the 1979 elections after the NPN. And this national appeal, thin though it might have been in places, can be attributed to the relentless travels of this determined individual, as well as his ability to convince Nigerians of all religions, ethnic groups and regions that he identified with them and shared little of northern aristocratic chauvinism. In his business activities, Waziri Ibrahim earned a considerable fortune and he also earned the reputation of being a vigorous spender of his income. He contributed readily to charitable projects all over the country, and especially to the building of mosques and churches. It is, therefore, difficult to assess how much it was his seemingly limitless bankroll, rather than the ideas and proposals he advanced, which contributed to his far-flung political network.

Two important ways in which Waziri and the GNPP differed from Awolowo and the UPN are in the absence among the former of a definite program or core of ideas for the first civilian administration and the absence of a cadre of long-standing party leaders who could counterbalance the "one-man" appearance of Waziri's party. All of his associates appeared in the role of subordinates: Waziri seemed to run his party as autocratically as he did his businesses. The various ideas he and his party put forward during the campaign can be grouped under the loose rubric of "better government": improved amenities, better use of available resources, and greater accountability of public officials. Indeed, his party became most associated with Waziri's slogan, "politics without bitterness." If Nigerian politicians could be less bitter in the way they conducted their disagreements and conflicts, the Nigerian people would be better served. It was a true statement, but hardly a politically stimulating one. When we rule out the financial opportunism his wealth encouraged, the appeal of Waziri was largely that of providing an alternative umbrella for individuals who were dissatisfied with the available party options in their areas.

As open party politics returned to the northern states in 1978–9, the GNPP

145

represented a haven for political aspirants who, for reasons of family ties or pre-existing political divisions, did not wish to associate with the individuals who had won control of local NPN organizations. Buttressing this factional pattern of alliances, however, were the substantial socio-economic changes that had occurred in the North since the mid-1960s. Younger professionals, business people and government officials found the GNPP to be an appropriate vehicle which enabled them to avoid allying themselves either with the people of privilege and power who were grabbing control of the NPN, or with the popular masses whom the PRP actively championed. The GNPP could therefore be regarded from their standpoint as a potential liberal party of Nigeria, which was ideologically intermediate between the conservative NPN and the radical PRP.

The more distinctly class-based pattern of party affiliation in the emirate North overlapped with the region's ethnic and linguistic divisions. The NPC notion of "One North, One People" embodied, as I have discussed, a definite reality in the tradition of elite recruitment throughout this vast area, whose roots can be traced back a century and a half. The slogan, however, also covered up a significant contradiction. This contradiction existed between the ethos of equal access to modern elite positions and the important differences in status attached to an individual's home area within this region. Partly for this reason, Waziri Ibrahim, from Borno State, deliberately bypassed the political caucusing discussed earlier, whether of the Borno State Advisory Committee which co-ordinated the choice of MCAs, the efforts of such strong figures within the emerging NPN from Borno State as Shettima Ali Monguno, Adamu Ciroma and Kam Salem, or the battles in which the Northern Movement became embroiled in the Constituent Assembly over the Executive Presidency and Shari'a. As a consequence, Waziri drew the ire of other establishment northern politicians of both old and new generations for his insistence on "going it alone," and for his unwillingness to compete for positions, including the presidency, within the broader framework in which they had agreed to work. Yet Waziri's gambit had its own logic within the North: he was able to make a strong appeal to the submerged antagonisms within the ten northern states on the basis of a combined class and sectional appeal directed at the subordinate peoples and peripheral areas within the "traditional northern polity."[27]

In the southern states, Waziri and the GNPP had their strongest implantation among the eastern minorities of Cross River and Rivers States. Among the Yoruba and Igbo, the GNPP remained a weak option for those political aspirants who had lost out in the nomination battles in the UPN, NPP and NPN. Yet, before the split occurred in the NPP, as I have pointed out, there was a recognition that Waziri's NUC and Club 19 were mirror images: the southern weakness of the former was counterbalanced by the southern strength of the latter, and vice versa. The subsequent failure to hold this burgeoning alliance together, therefore, deprived Nigeria of its only potential new party formation in 1979. After their attempt at unification failed, Waziri Ibrahim and the GNPP were able to pose a stout challenge to the NPN in many areas of the North. To keep the GNPP from getting the significant share of the electoral votes to which it was entitled in 1979, including in the home state of the NPN presidential candidate, Shehu Shagari, NPN agents falsified the vote to such an extent that Waziri Ibrahim was driven to become the most relentless challenger of the election results.[28] In 1983, the elections were even more disfigured by electoral malpractices, which provoked Waziri to take his case, unsuccessfully, to the Nigerian Supreme Court. Northern primacy had by then become national primacy: the North as a bastion of the ruling NPN had to be maintained at all costs and by all means.

CONCLUSION: THE NPN AND PREBENDAL POLITICS

The specific outcome of the events and activities I have described is that the party which gave itself the name of the National Party of Nigeria took the most direct route to make this name a reality. Its victory in the 1979 elections meant that it would not only determine the policies and programs of the nation for the next four years, but also that it would set the standard for achieving electoral success in Nigerian party politics. The surest basis of such success is the implementation of what I have characterized as prebendal politics. As I explained earlier in this study, the behavior of Nigerian political actors, who achieve for themselves the recognition of being "heavyweights," is sustained, not simply by their own ambition and cupidity, but also by the ways in which their self-interest coincides with the normative framework and material concerns of subordinate political brokers. Moreover, as part of this general process, political aspirants who lack popular support can still win grudging acceptance of their role as political brokers if they can insinuate themselves into the party hierarchy at the federal, regional or state levels. Such an option places a premium on manipulative skills, usually at the expense of probity.

Let me illustrate this universe of thought and action as it was reflected in several dimensions of NPN politics. We can begin with the response of Shehu Shagari when asked during his campaign, "How fair would the NPN be in the sharing of the national cake – whatever remains of it – to all Nigerians, including those who oppose your party?"

> SHAGARI: I don't like the description of national cake. Nigeria's wealth isn't something that is there to go and share out... I want to forget this expression because it gives the impression of a booty. The task of a government is not sharing booty but to share in developing a national wealth. The distribution of amenities is not national cake. We shall give every community and every Nigerian the opportunities to have all the amenities that all the others have. There will be even distribution of positions in government as has been provided [for] in the constitution.[29]

The obvious contradiction between the first section and the last lines of Shagari's response mirrors the fact that, beneath the high-flown rhetoric, the operating basis of the NPN was the even sharing of amenities and government positions among sectional groups via their recognized *interlocuteurs*. This orientation rendered the party, and later the state, highly vulnerable to the depredations of venal politicians. The pronouncements meant for public consumption could hardly disguise the crude bartering that often took place within the NPN's councils. One can consider, for example, the selection of Shagari's running-mate for the position of Vice-President of the Federation. According to the zoning formula, it had been agreed that an easterner would have this position. For several weeks after his nomination in December 1978, Shehu Shagari was trailed by three ardent candidates, K. O. Mbadiwe and J. O. J. Okezie of Imo State and Joseph Wayas of Cross River State. Mbadiwe had earlier offered the party the use of one of his buildings in Lagos, which enabled it to move from its initial headquarters in a suite of offices owned by Joesph Wayas. (A more appropriate metaphor for the exchanging of property rights in real estate for property rights in party positions could hardly be imagined!) All these men, however, lost out to a virtually unknown candidate, Alex Ekueme, a wealthy architect from Anambra State, who had earlier been defeated in the contest for his state's gubernatorial nomination. The only question that the choice of Ekueme raised in public commentaries was whether his promised contribution to the party's treasury was one or two million naira.

The NPN, even before it came to power, found itself mortgaged to the avarice of such individuals. Mbadiwe's reputation for corruption was so great among his own people in Imo State that he was constantly shunted aside in 1978 as he sought to maneuver himself into a leading position in the state branch of the party. Nevertheless, he was eventually able to procure for himself a position as political adviser to President Shagari, with all that such a position implies in a prebendalized state. Joseph Wayas, whose pursuit of a senior position within the NPN government was relentless, was compensated for being passed over for the Vice-Presidency by being awarded the Presidency of the Nigerian Senate. As a representative of the "minorities," he could lay claim to what in effect was a fourth "zonal" office. It also meant, however, that politicians such as Wayas, who acquired such positions on the basis of their personal tenacity and capital investment, were now in a position to impose themselves as the patrons of their state or ethnic communities and to act as conduits for their people's share of national expenditures.

What gave special legitimacy to such a pattern of political behavior within the NPN is the fact that it was sustained by a parallel set of attitudes and choices within lower levels of interaction between party, state and community "representatives." Any region or set of states in Nigeria can be used to illustrate this phenomenon. Let us consider Benue State in the Middle-Belt. The three main ethnic groups, in descending order of size of population, are the Tiv, Igala and Idoma. During the former civilian era, the Igala and Idoma gave their support mainly to the NPC, usually through the intermediary of their local "ethnic unions," while the Tiv became one of the strongholds of the opposition party, the UMBC, allied with Awolowo's Action Group. In 1978–9, the Tiv were brought over to the NPN by Joseph Tarka, despite the active involvement of several younger Tiv intellectuals, such as Paul Unongo, in the CUS movement discussed above. The message delivered by Tarka to his people, and repeated at every turn by Tiv interviewed by me, was that his people had suffered greatly from being in opposition during the First Republic and he did not want them to suffer again. By suffer, he meant physical suffering as well as being deprived of a fair share of public amenities and other social goods.[30]

The widespread expectation that Joseph Tarka had lost his influence with the Tiv people as a result of his resignation from a ministerial appointment in the Gowon government on charges of corruption, was not borne out. During 1978–9, Tarka was accorded positions of high respect during the formation of the NPN and was included on the short-list of candidates for the presidential nomination. He was subsequently elected an NPN senator from Benue State. The Tiv, therefore, followed Tarka's lead and changed their alignment within Nigerian politics *en bloc*. Tarka's impact among the Tiv therefore matched that of Azikiwe among the Igbo. Most aspirant Tiv politicians, such as the young journalist, Mvendaga Jibo, felt obliged to fall into line, even if they were formerly highly critical of the Hausa-Fulani now at the helm of the emerging party. Even more ironically, Aper Aku, the NPN candidate for governor in Benue State, who had been imprisoned under a detention order by General Gowon after he had filed affidavits detailing the corruption within Gowon's regime, was now to be found in the same party as his fellow Tivman, Joseph Tarka, who had relinquished his government position after his corrupt activities had been exposed.

The leading political figures from the Igala continued unchanged from the First Republic their affiliation with the emirate North through the NPC. The Idomas, however, were pulled in two directions. There were invariably two opposing arguments about which way the votes of the Idomas should be cast: the first concerned the importance of the religious issue (i.e., Shari'a), and was indicative of renewed Hausa-Fulani hegemony, and therefore the NPN (as formerly the NPC) would not give their non-Islamic northern affiliates a fair share of government patronage; the second ran, "our young intellectuals are obsessed by Shari'a which is of little importance to the people who sent them to the Constituent Assembly, and the only way for the Idomas to advance is by rallying behind the strongest party."[31] There was clearly a well-spring of support waiting to be tapped by northern leaders once they put aside the divisive issue of the Shari'a Court of Appeal. What I learned in extensive travels and interviews across Nigeria in 1978–9, was that the promise of the NPN to be the party which would be most capable and willing to give "every community and every Nigerian the opportunities to have all the amenities that all the others have" was the one which had the greatest resonance and the widest appeal.

There was a remarkable concreteness to the claims of NPN supporters as to

149

why an ethnic group like the Idoma should support their party. The provision of electricity and water supplies, of tarred roads and a hospital, of the appointment of Idomas like Dr Edwin Ogbu and Mr J. C. Obande to high office – these were the alleged benefits of former NPC rule which were contrasted with the limited gains, and even setbacks which included the retirement of prominent Idomas such as Colonel Ochefu and Commissioner of Finance Vincent Okwu during the most recent military government.[32] Those who opposed the NPN used virtually this same set of contentions to argue the opposite case: the Idomas were only being regarded as a retriever by the NPN hunter: "the dog would get those prey [i.e., votes] the hunter misses, but the dog has to turn it over to the hunter and wait for scraps the hunter doesn't want."[33] Yet the Nigerian state was so demonstrably the prime source of whatever largesse, or access to commercial circuits, existed, that the argument that particular groups were certain to use their strategic positions to obtain a disproportionate share of these goods and opportunities had less force than the fear of being left out of the sharing altogether by having backed the wrong party.

There was considerable congruence, therefore, between the assembling of a party which could bring under a single umbrella the widest array of representatives and the desire of Nigerians of all socio-economic strata for access to the means of improving the material endowments of their families and communities. "I Chop, You Chop" (meaning "I eat, you eat") was the name proposed for a party in 1978 which aroused the ire of the Obasanjo Government. This pre-party group provided a moment of comic relief for Nigerians; yet the laughter it provoked – like the political cartoons which flourished in the newspapers during this period – reflected an awareness of the mundane reality beneath the rhetoric of party formation. The most successful party in 1979 would not be the one with the most perceptive leaders, or the most innovative proposals for Nigeria, but rather the one most likely to institute an "I eat, you eat" policy between the ethno-linguistic, regional and religious communities, as well as between individuals who managed to push their way to the top rungs of the party's hierarchy. The promise of Shehu Shagari and the NPN, echoing provisions of the 1979 Constitution, to undertake an even distribution of amenities and positions in the government, was a fair-minded statement with devastating implications. To implement it, aspirant politicians had first to get their share of party and government jobs, that their people would subsequently obtain "the opportunities to have all the amenities that all the others have." It is a principle I have called "prebendal politics," and which knits together the main features of Nigeria's contemporary socio-political system. It is also a principle whose logic eventually undermines the competence and legitimacy of state institutions, and finally saps the authority of those who have successfully appropriated its strategic offices.

Part IV

The crisis of Nigerian democracy

10

The challenge of the 1983 elections: a republic in peril

There are many dimensions of the brief life of the Second Republic that one can examine to demonstrate that the new system never became entrenched, never achieved stability nor even a reasonable degree of legitimacy. Several works have already been published which adequately document these failings, and many others will surely be added to the list before long.[1] Since I must select some dimension of the system's decay on which to focus my attention, the most critical and revealing appears to be the conduct of the 1983 elections to establish, and then renew, the federal and state governments of the Second Republic. In 1981, at the midway point in the first Shagari administration, I wrote:

> Two years from now, in 1983, an even more difficult challenge than the initial transfer of power will be the task of administering general elections under civilian – and hence partisan – auspices. Very few countries in Africa have conducted such a set of elections in accordance with the provisions laid down at the time of the hand-over of power from colonial or military government... The many incidents of fraud and intimidation which accompanied federal and regional elections in Nigeria during the 1960s eventually led to the collapse of the post-independence government in January 1966 with the seizure of power by the armed forces... If the 1983 elections are not to take place in an atmosphere of uncertainty and even disorder, of oppression of opponents and, conversely, of attempts to undermine governmental authority, of widescale rejection of election results for reasons of fraud and misconduct, then the right pathway among the many now available must be taken.[2]

A pertinent conclusion, drawing on concerns similar to the above, was reached by Alhaji Ahmadu Kurfi, Executive Secretary of the Federal Election Commission (FEDECO) for the 1979 general elections: "A truly representative system of government absolutely depends upon the integrity of elections."[3] The minimum requirement of a functioning constitutional democracy is that there be rules of right behavior which are honored much more in the observance than in the breach. In Nigeria, however, party politics as a relentless struggle to procure individual and group benefits via the temporary appropriation of public offices eventually reduces the electoral process to a Hobbesian state-of-war. In 1979, this process retained some semblance of

153

being an event of civil society. During the 1983 election, however, a situation of near chaos developed as the party campaigns and subsequent elections became marked by acts of increasing violence and lawlessness.

At the handing-over of power on 1 October 1979, the question still to be answered was whether the moments of crisis during the previous two years of the transition from military to civilian rule would increase in frequency, or whether those of consensus (such as the broad-base support won by the NPN) would come to characterize the new system.[4] Other indications of a "systemic" consensus in 1979 included the salutary spread of votes won by the other four parties, and the legislative and elected positions these yielded, giving all the parties a stake in the new Republic. There was a striking consistency throughout the five elections, with the parties achieving both votes and elected positions within the following percentage bands: NPN 34–37%; UPN 25–30%; NPP 16–17%; GNPP 8–12%; PRP 7–11%.[5] Moreover, the leading party was able to win an impressive spread of votes and positions throughout the country, which rendered it either the dominant party, or the second best, in all 19 states of the Federation.

The moments of crisis during the 1978–9 electoral period were equally significant. What kept them in check was undeniably the fact of military rule. The Federal Electoral Commission (FEDECO) was meant to be an independent agency and, in keeping with an unavoidable feature of governmental affairs in Nigeria, it was entrusted with implementing the numerous regulations devised to prevent every imaginable form of electoral misconduct. Invariably, many of the important decisions of FEDECO reflected a subjective element subsequently open to challenge by those adversely affected by them. For example, of the more than forty associations which sought registration as political parties in 1978, only five were approved by FEDECO. Then, hundreds of individuals who had hoped to contest the 1979 elections found themselves barred because of prior convictions for abuse of office, or for not satisfying such technical requirements as providing proof of income tax payments. The actual date on which the elections were to be held was not announced promptly, and then the timing seemed inappropriate in the light of the country's climate. Finally, when it seemed that Shehu Shagari had failed to win the presidency on the first ballot, and thus an electoral college would be convened to choose from among the leading contestants, an interpretation was announced which in effect altered the requirement for the national vote spread in the elections, thereby allowing Shagari to be declared elected after the first round.

In each of these cases, the rule-implementing function of FEDECO prevailed because it had the force of the military government behind it. Yet no one pretended that such decisions were being made independently of the regime's wishes. In 1983, however, when there was no longer a theoretically non-partisan military government standing behind FEDECO, two features of this earlier process were to take on decisive importance. The first of these features was the resort to the courts to counter the arbitrary authority of

FEDECO, and the second was the widespread malpractice in the conduct of the elections. Two contestants for the presidency in 1979, Nnamdi Azikiwe and Aminu Kano, obtained court decisions in their local states which reversed their disqualification from competing on the grounds of non-payment of income taxes. FEDECO-FMG (to reflect the Commission's subordination to the Military Government) bowed to this court ruling for what were clearly reasons of political expediency, and not an acknowledgement of the court's review powers in these matters.[6] In 1983, as we shall see, the explosion in appeals to the courts to counter unfavorable FEDECO rulings, as well as the electoral results themselves, was an important factor in the delegitimizing of the entire political process. With regard to electoral irregularities, the 1979 elections could be compared to a planet which appears smooth when looked at from a distance. For those close at hand, however, the seemingly even surface is pockmarked by craters. The critical difference between 1979 and 1983 in this regard is that, in the latter case, the nation's gaze was kept focused on the numerous irregularities taking place, rather than being dazzled by the long-awaited transition from military rule.

There appeared in 1983 two studies of the 1979 elections, each of which, by frankly revealing the variety of malpractices which had occurred, served as a grim forecast of what was in store for the country later that year. The first study was written by a senior official responsible for the conduct of the 1979 elections, and the second was the work of two university academics (one of them a sometime journalist). Ahmadu Kurfi, drawing on FEDECO's own report on the elections, pointed out that in 1979 surplus ballot papers had been sold to the highest bidder, that polling agents had thumb-printed ballots for those who paid them, that ballot boxes stuffed with pre-marked ballots were substituted for the real ones on the way to counting centers, and that the deliberate invalidation of ballots by polling and counting officials had occurred.[7] Ogunsanwo and Adamu similarly demonstrated in copious detail how members of the huge temporary bureaucracy recruited by FEDECO to conduct the elections, as well as police and other security officials assigned to guard against electoral malpractices, and finally the officers, candidates and supporters of the contesting parties, engaged in extensive acts of collusion to manipulate various aspects of the electoral process.[8]

The contention can be made, on the basis of the evidence accumulated by Ogunsanwo and Adamu, that Nigerian elections are principally a competition for control of the electoral machinery and, secondarily, a competition for individual votes. Any party which fails to win control of this machinery in a particular area, or to neutralize the influence of its opponents over the personnel operating the machinery, risks losing elections regardless of the actual support it enjoys among the electorate. As Ogunsanwo and Adamu point out, "political parties are in direct control of the various civil and local government services all over the country and it is from this group that FEDECO 'appoints' its hundreds of thousands of officials."[9] At the polling stations, such local personnel can permit voting by underaged persons,

155

multiple voting, deliberately misleading voters regarding voting procedures, "inadvertently" taking the wrong voting lists to particular polling stations or deliberately failing to sign and stamp the envelopes given to voters.[10] At the counting centers, assuming the actual ballot boxes did arrive safely, votes were deliberately invalidated by counting agents who surreptitiously marked or thumb-printed them a second time.[11] As for the police officers and orderlies assigned to guard against such abuses, they were as likely to be susceptible to acting on the basis of monetary and other inducements as they were to be honest in carrying out their duties. Furthermore, as the above summary illustrates, a properly conducted poll at one level of this complex operation could be nullified by malfeasance at a higher one.

After discussing the role of bribery in the Nigerian political and the electoral system, Adamu Kurfi concludes that "since virtually all contestants at elections, by and large, engage in the practice, the effects seem to cancel each other."[12] A more troubling conclusion suggested by the same evidence, however, is that since the operation of Nigerian elections is so susceptible to manipulation, victory will go to those best able to outperform their opponents in skullduggery. Moreover, once the balance of "manipulative power" shifts from one of relative equality among contestants to another in which a particular party enjoys a definite advantage, the consequent degree of unfairness of the results is likely to be proportionately affected. In 1983, instead of the voting results being flawed yet roughly acceptable to the competing parties, as 1979, they were now so excessively falsified that the electoral system lost the capacity to reflect, even roughly, the relative strength of the parties.

To conclude this review of the weakened electoral basis of the governments of the Second Republic, one can cite both Kurfi and Ogunsanwo and Adamu when they point to the role of the military government in 1979 in giving Nigeria the most peaceful election – despite the malpractices – it had known since the last colonial election of 1959:

> The presence of a military government which rounded up potential party thugs and effectively checked their activities, created a peaceful atmosphere for the elections.[13]

> The calm atmosphere prevalent during the 1979 elections was not brought about by the existence of [a] fine political culture in the Nigerian people but was due to the veiled threat of immediate military retribution should law and order break down – and worse, the possibility of postponement of the date of hand-over of power to the civilians.[14]

On 1 October 1979, therefore, Nigeria stumbled into the Second Republic, with its first President reaching office through a split vote in the Supreme Court which rejected a challenge to his election by his leading opponent, Obafemi Awolowo. For a constitutional democracy to work, to amplify Adamu Kurfi's contention, not only must the elections enjoy "absolute integrity," but elections must at least be elections, i.e. objective procedures for registering and counting votes. The same can be said about other vital aspects of this process, whether they be the compiling of a voters list, the registration of new parties, the review of FEDECO decisions by the judiciary, or the interpretation and implementation of numerous regulations established by the Constitution and the National Assembly. If the rules of the system, and those appointed to interpret them, cannot disinterestedly determine the nature of the electoral arena, but themselves become spoils to be fought over and shifted to favor one person or group rather than another, then the critical step in the transition from a Hobbesian state-of-nature to a constituted political society cannot occur. And that is one difference between military and civilian governments in Nigeria. The former, for all their failings, are able to give the country a political order, even if temporary and authoritarian in nature, while the latter eventually carries the war-of-all-against-all into the legislative chambers, the executive offices of government, the temporary headquarters and sub-offices of the electoral bureaucracy and, most fatally, into the courtrooms of the nation's judiciary.

Liberal democracy, the system attempted by Nigeria from 1975 to 1983, is as much a method of governing a country as a way of deciding who rules. In a 1982 essay, which reflects his unswerving commitment to democratic government, Richard Sklar included Nigeria among the handful of liberal democracies then in existence in Africa.[15] He cautioned that such systems have tended to be "democracies with tears and many reservations." Nevertheless, Sklar believed that a "developmental democracy would evoke fresh and original responses to the problems of economic development, social stratification and political drift." What Nigerians had experienced during the first administration of the Second Republic, however, was a system characterized by a deepening economic crisis, sharpened social conflict and political immobilism. Claude Ake, one of the country's most perceptive social scientists, captured the situation well when the contended in 1981 that "all over Nigeria, the discontent and anxiety are palpable."[16] The blame for this state of affairs Ake placed, in language which parallels much of the analysis of this study, on the nature of the country's social and economic structures and the consequent intense political struggles for control of state power.

Despite this general sense of "discontent and anxiety," the promise of political renewal via the forthcoming elections was also "palpable" in Nigeria in 1983.[17] This hopeful mood was captured by many commentators. Dr T. Akinola Aguda, for example, the Director of the Nigerian institute of Advanced Legal Studies and former federal judge, exclaimed,

> We all do realise our unique position in the continent and indeed among all the so-called Third World countries. We are the largest black democracy in the world today, and in fact throughout human history. We cannot and must not fail for our failure is the failure of all black peoples throughout the world.[18]

Some politicians running for office, especially President Shagari and his running-mate Alex Ekueme, often reminded the electorate of the broader issues at stake in the elections. And Justice Ovie-Whiskey, Chairman of

157

FEDECO, never tired of urging Nigerians "not to damage the reputation of our country for such ephemeral things as elections." "The whole world is watching," he urged, because Nigeria is "the greatest democracy in Africa."[19]

Many Nigerian journalists, who had devoted much effort to reporting on the inadequacies of the pre-electoral arrangements, were encouraged by this upbeat mood when the time for the elections arrived:

> true victory will go to the Nigerian people, as we prove to the world that we have a capacity for democracy ... our elections come against a backdrop of a sustained Nigerian claim, especially in the last four years, that we are the biggest black democracy on earth ... we will be setting the tone for the way the world looks at the Black and African world.[20]

Some private commentators, however, refused to see these blandishments as providing any more than a camouflage for a failing political system. For Ifeanyi A. Azuka, the behavior of Nigerian politicians, so lacking in "restraint, tolerance, morality and modesty," had exposed the country "to outside ridicule."[21] Wole Soyinka, the country's premier dramatist, took to the airwaves during the 1983 electoral period with a long-playing album entitled "Unlimited Liability Company," in which he satirized the politicians and the policies which had brought such unprecedented levels of corruption, inefficiency, and cynicism to the public life of Nigeria. Ola Balogun, a writer and film-maker, dismissed the existing political system as incapable of giving Nigeria "a truly representative form of government."[22] For him, the "major preoccupation of the contending parties seemed to be the accession to power and nothing else; winning has become an end in itself." In words which echoed General Murtala Muhammed's cautionary remarks at the launching of the transitional process in October 1975, Balogun wrote,

> Unfortunately for our nation ... the subversion of true democracy by the politics of party patronage and ethnic jingoism has considerably eroded the basis for the emergence of genuinely representative government within our present political framework. It is a paradox indeed that the ideals of democratic government seem further from our grasp than ever, in spite of the outward semblance of democracy enshrined in the constitution of the Second Republic.

In an article published at a point when the 1983 elections seemed to be lurching from one crisis to another, B. Olusegun Babalola wrote with passion of the dishonesty, the numerous acts of embezzlement, that now characterized the country's governmental as well as social institutions.[23] Without needing to mention his name, Babalola repeated the somber words of Major Nzeogwu, at the time of the first Nigerian military coup of January 1966, castigating

> the political profiteers, the swindlers, the men (and women too!) in high and low places who seek bribes and demand ten percent... those that make the country look big for nothing in international circles; those that have corrupted the Nigerian society and put its political calendar back by their words and deeds.

Against the mounting evidence of corruption and abuse of power, Babalola's reiteration of Nzeogwu's words could not have been more apposite.

Democracy in Nigeria appeared to have been subverted into its opposite. Its legitimacy was increasingly questioned, and open appeals were being made to the soldiers to spare the Nigerian people further suffering at the hands of their elected "representatives." Here is Babalola's own *cri de coeur*:

> Democratic rights give legal cover to so many evil things ... Many people have stopped bothering themselves with classifying African regimes as democratic or otherwise. They instead keep asking: how much do the regimes address themselves to the needs and aspirations of the people? I am one, I tell you, all these noises about democracy and democratic are mere luxuries to the sufferers.

After summarizing the main features of the Nigerian system which I have characterized as "prebendal politics," Sylvester Whitaker opined that the "moral incapacity of the state" had become "endemic."[24] Whitaker gave President Shehu Shagari the benefit of the doubt for "perhaps meaning to serve the higher ends of Nigerian unity and/or to preserve the strategic position of his own northern culture and society." Yet, as he concluded, Shagari had "lent himself to the purposes of a rogue government," words almost identical to those cited here from Dr Datti Ahmad (p. 137) to characterize in 1978 the political associates attracted to Shagari's candidacy.

Two of the most frequently used expressions in Nigerian political discourse in 1983 were "austerity" – to describe the severe economic measures imposed by the Shagari government beginning in 1982, to cope with the country's declining wealth and its increasing foreign debt – and "democracy" – to refer to the still viable promise of a government accountable to, and revocable by, the Nigerian people. Unlike "austerity," "democracy" had for many Nigerians a residual positive connotation which reflected the hope of getting something better, through elections, than they had known since 1979. The actual experience of those elections, as will now be shown, destroyed that remaining hope. Fundamental change, if it was to come, seemed to lie no longer at the polls, but in the return to the now universal starting point of military intervention. The politicians, to paraphrase again Chief Fani-Kayode's words from an earlier civilian era, could remain in office whether or not the people actually voted for them. The arrogance of civilian politicians once in power called forth a similar response from a corporate group which was even more arrogant, and more directly in control of the means of compulsion, than the politicians. Each corruptly obtained victory, at the polls or in the courts, between July and September 1983, was one more argument in favor of renewed military rule.

A TIME OF FEAR AND UNCERTAINTY

Anyone with vivid memories of the 1979 elections could not help noticing the change from the mood of optimism, and even joy, which had then characterized the approaching end to thirteen years of military rule, to one of uncertainty and fear as the 1983 elections approached. Elections and violence are woven together in the collective consciousness of Nigerians. The consider-

159

able loss of life and property, particularly in the Western Region during the final general elections of the First Republic in 1965, was still deeply etched in the minds of the populace. Moreover, many of the surviving members of the political class of the First Republic, and their political machines, had moved once again to the fore of the country's politics in 1978–9. The expectation that history was likely to repeat itself in any elections under a civilian party government was therefore a rational and even self-fulfilling one for the Nigerian citizenry.

As we noted from Ogunsanwo and Adamu, the 1979 elections had been relatively peaceful because the military government had rounded up "potential party thugs and effectively checked their activities." Such actions were carried out without fanfare, perhaps because of the military's extraconstitutional powers of detention. Ifeanyi Izuka, whom I cited earlier (p. 158), contends that "it [is] difficult to identify any political party that does not run an army of thugs . . . Thuggery has become rapidly enthroned in Nigerian politics." Other private commentaries concerning this murky area of Nigerian party politics could also be noted here. Richard Sklar once told me of his personal and traumatic experience of political thuggery in Nigeria while observing political campaigns during the earlier civilian era. And there were boastful comments made to me by certain aspirant Nigerian politicians in 1978–9, about their own "defence squads" to counteract those of their opponents. This is an area of Nigerian "party politics" which should obviously be properly researched and analyzed.[25]

The anxiety that Claude Ake had spoken about in 1981 was succeeded by a palpable fear and a sense of increasing intimidation by mid-1983. The newspapers regularly reported the flight of Nigerians from the major urban areas to their rural villages or abroad.[26] The lorry parks were jammed by the increased traffic and the airlines were fully booked until after the elections. Foodstuffs disappeared from the shelves of shops as the fearful prepared for any eventuality. Individuals were quoted as preferring "not to vote to being a victim of [the] election. . . We don't want trouble to start before running."[27] What contributed to the sense of uncertainty and fear that mounted as the first election of 6 August 1983 approached was the behavior and comments of those individuals in command of the coercive armory of the state.

On 4 August, Alhaji Umaru Dikko, the cabinet minister who had played such a critical role in obtaining the presidential nomination for Shehu Shagari and had been subsequently appointed Minister of Transport in the NPN government, held a conference for foreign journalists who had come to report on the elections. Although Dikko had been defeated by his PRP opponent in his home state, Kaduna, in the senatorial elections of 1979, he still was given a position of high visibility, and even centrality, in the Shagari Administration.[28] By 1983, his seemingly modest ministerial position of Minister of Transport was bolstered by his other party and government positions: Director-General of the Presidential Campaign Organization and Chairman of the Presidential Task-Force on Rice. Dikko's political brief therefore covered a wide swath. His remarks on this occasion, just two days before the presidential elections, heightened the sense of calculated intimidation.[29] He proclaimed, in seemingly vague language, that "the enemies of our country will find it a little tougher next time." "While democracy and freedom should flourish, at the same time people who are enemies of our country cannot be allowed... They don't have to be foreigners, they could be sons of the soil." Alhaji Dikko went ahead on this occasion to make other declarations such as the likely personnel changes in the anticipated second Shagari administration and the correct interpretation of technical issues regarding the new federal capital as an electoral entity under the 1979 Constitution. He also castigated those newsmen who had failed to produce evidence to back up their claims of austerity in the country: "Outside of Lagos," according to Dikko, "there were no shortages."[30]

Dikko's comments were not appreciated by the media in Nigeria, which was not under the control of the central government. In a sober editorial, the country's leading independent newspaper reminded the nation of Dikko's statement a year earlier that "there was no hunger in the country because Nigerians had not reached a situation where they feed from dustbins."[31] This remark, taken together with the minister's new threat to "deal with" journalists who released unauthorized election results, suggested to *The Guardian* that "Mr. Dikko holds in contempt not only our system, which insists on due process and the rule of law, but also our people whose hardships are audible, visible and real." The editorial concluded with a statement which is worth fully citing because it reflects the depth of opposition within Nigeria to arbitrary and irresponsible government:

> Mr. Shagari has a duty to call Umaru Dikko to order even as he and his party toil to get re-elected. These are delicate times and everyone, big and small, needs to watch his language more carefully... This sinister threat to an amorphous nameless group of "enemies" must not be allowed to give credence to the widely circulated view that it was designed as a signal of things to come in the next four years. Nigerians are capable, and will, as they have done in the past, resist any region of terror unleashed on them by any administration – repeat, any administration.[32]

The militarization of civilian government was a very noticeable feature of the Second Republic. Nigerians are not an easy people to govern. Here I am referring not only to the kind of social conflicts whose extent and bases were explored in earlier chapters, but also to Nigerian behavioral dispositions on a more individual and unreflective level. The country's military rulers often use the general term "indiscipline" to cover the lack of respect for order and regulations in many walks of Nigerian life. Such dispositions often provoke arbitrary measures to keep them in check. They can also, conversely, serve to hinder attempts to impose systems of authoritarian political control. There is a strong vigilante tradition in Nigerian social life. For example, a thief who is apprehended in public is more likely to be summarily lynched – often by being battered with sticks and stones before being set on fire – than he is to be turned over to the police. After 1979, as a consequence of the Armed Forces being confined to their barracks except for times of mass upheaval (as in the two "Maitatsine" religious uprisings in the Islamic north, or border conflicts with neighboring countries), the civil police – entirely under the control of the central government – were permitted to establish a unit that could be described as a militarized gendarmerie.

Nigerians are accustomed to the use of whips and batons by police and paramilitary personnel to inflict summary punishment on individuals caught up in some local instance of public disorder. In January 1983, international television showed viewers throughout the world how callously Nigerian police and soldiers were allowed to treat the West African immigrants expelled on short notice from their country. This general set of practices took on particular significance with the militarization of units within the Nigerian police, to fill the vacuum left by the withdrawal of the soldiers to their barracks. It also took concrete shape in the recruitment and training of an anti-riot squad, popularly known as "the mobile police," whose rough appearance, low educational qualifications, and exaggerated combat outfits gave the central government new instruments of political and social control. As the country reached the week of the presidential elections, Nigerians could read, listen to on the radio, or see on daily television, broadcasts by their Inspector-General of Police. Sunday Adewusi projected himself as a no-nonsense defender of the country's peace, order and democracy. Like Dikko's, Adewusi's governmental reponsibilities seemed to grow with each of his public pronouncements. On 4 August, he not only gave details of the ways in which the Armed Forces would be used to back up police personnel assigned to security duties in the polling stations and FEDECO offices, he also went on to inform the country that "the police would ensure that Nigeria, the 3rd largest democracy in the world, holds a peaceful and hitchfree election to the admiration of all other countries."[33] Adewusi warned party thugs to stay away from the polling booths because the new special squad in the police had been given orders to meet "force with force" and to shoot on sight if necessary.

If the Inspector-General had confined his threats to party thugs, his interventions might have merely added to "the mounting doubts that the elections will not be violence free."[34] Instead, he proceeded a few days later to reiterate the warning issued by Alhaji Dikko to those individuals, particularly journalists, who announced "unverified and unauthorized electoral results." In a broadcast which was regularly repeated on the airwaves, the Police Chief took on the unusual role of explaining the relevant provisions of the Constitution and the Electoral Law and, moreover, branding any alleged violation of them as a

> calculated and deliberate attempt to confuse members of the public with the intention of creating uncertainties leading to the disturbance of the public peace. All those news media concerned in this mischievous and diabolical act are therefore warned in their own interest to desist forthwith as serious and firm measures will be taken against them in accordance with the law... Once again

we advise these mischievous groups to desist from anything which will disturb the peace of the ordinary man.[35]

Later in this chapter, I shall discuss why the publication of electoral results became so central to the struggle for control of the electoral process. Adewusi's strong language, and what was seen as a deliberate attempt to intimidate the Nigerian press, was greeted by a barrage of criticism. An injunction was obtained in the Lagos High Court by the Nigerian Union of Journalists, restraining Adewusi from harassing reporters. Editorials appeared questioning the tone and message of the Inspector-General's broadcast. And opposition party leaders, who had a vested interest in not seeing the media cowed as they reached the final stage of their campaign to unseat the NPN government, also responded vigorously to this unusual development (in Nigeria) of an Inspector-General of Police making pronouncements on constitutional issues and openly threatening the non-governmental media. Here was Chief Awolowo's riposte:

> The Inspector-General of Police, Mr. Adewusi, has just issued a statement threatening the mass media, under the pain of punishment, not to publish results of the Presidential election unless confirmed by FEDECO. The police chief cited the Constitution to support his view. The Constitution, as far as I know, makes no provision about counting but section 65 of the Electoral Act does. The correct legal position is that, after the appropriate returning officer in each case has announced the results at the polling station, at the constituency headquarters or at the state capital, anyone who hears it is perfectly free under the law and by natural rights to publish it. Adewusi's threat is, therefore, outrageous and totally untenable.[36]

The NPN government, through these senior officials, seemed to be taking steps not only to forestall trouble during the elections, but also to issue warnings in language which seemed to threaten the freedom of expression of the country's citizens and the mass media. The repeated interventions of Dikko and Adewusi suggested that they spoke with the approval of the President, while allowing him to keep to a higher level of political discourse. One commentator suggested that Shagari's "silence often leads Nigerians to conclude that he is not truly in charge or that he subscribes to such dangerous pronouncements."[37] Moreover, underlying the verbal exchanges were reminders that there was a deeper basis to these conflicts, namely, the mounting indignation that the Second Republic had been corrupted in its philosophy and practices into a system of misrule and callous exploitation of the Nigerian people. The question frequently asked was who, in effect, were "the enemies of Nigeria" – the persons threatened by Dikko and Adewusi as the elections approached or these very men and their associates firmly entrenched in power?

> The enemies of Nigeria are indeed many. Ministers, party officials and governors, commissioners, who pre-1979 could not afford a bicycle or a flat but who now are suspected of owning jets and mansions... Legislators and top government functionaries who maintain bulging bank accounts and real estate abroad are some of them. The currency racketeers who export so many millions

of Naira and sell them at disgraceful rates are also part of them. But these are probably not the men Umaru Dikko has in mind, given the manifest government capitulation in dealing with those powerful elements of our society.[38]

THE NPN AND ITS OPPONENTS

Despite the solid one-third of legislative seats in the two Houses of the National Assembly which the NPN held after the 1979 elections, its control of seven of nineteen gubernatorial offices, and its substantial share of legislative seats in most of the state governments, it did not behave as a confident governing party between 1979 and 1983. In fact, the major states in the three territorial angles of the Nigerian triangle, had been won by the opposition parties: Kano and Kaduna in the North, Oyo and Lagos in the West and Anambra and Imo in the East.[39] Moreover, the NPN was accused of having won the presidency on the first round in 1979 not just with some strategic electoral rigging in the states under the party's operational control but also, as mentioned earlier, by a last minute re-interpreting of the electoral rules in its favor by FEDECO-FMG. The period 1979–83 therefore witnessed a continuous struggle to achieve enhanced political control on the part of the NPN, as well as the other four registered political parties.

In Chapter 7, I showed how much the NPN had sought to obtain access to the bloc of Igbo voters in the East to offset the expected appeal of the UPN to Yoruba voters in the West. On the eve of the handing-over of power on 1 October 1979, an announcement was made that the NPN and NPP had agreed to an Accord under whose terms the NPP would collaborate with the NPN in the National Assembly in return for ministerial positions and other political appointments, as well as sympathetic treatment of the major items on the NPP's platform such as the "abandoned property" issue. The Accord appointments, as well as sympathetic treatment of the major items on the National Assembly and therefore to guarantee it greater success in obtaining passage of its legislative proposals. The Accord lasted less than two years and became the basis for the almost continuous acrimony between leaders of the two parties. I shall not discuss the specifics of these squabbles in any detail, but will simply try to relate them to what was occurring in the general context of party politics in 1979–83. These developments could be discussed in terms of four sets of dynamics: the attempt by the NPN to widen its control over the political system by neutralizing and undermining its opponents; the maneuvering for advantage by individuals and factions within each party; attempts among the "opposition" parties to create a common front or even a new party committed to unseating the NPN; and the failure of FEDECO to exercise its statutory independence of the new NPN party-government.

If one examined each of the major party disputes of 1979–83, one would be likely to find reflected two or more of the above sets of dynamics. In the NPN-NPP dispute, for example, tensions arose between those Igbo politicians who

164

had won office as a result of their early affiliation with the NPN, and others who had opposed the NPN but still obtained positions in the central government as a result of the NPN-NPP Accord. In the first half of 1981, NPP leaders found themselves pulled in two directions: towards increasing collaboration with the NPN and, conversely, towards co-operation with the other three "progressive" parties as they termed themselves – the GNPP, PRP and UPN – in a program designed to provide a co-ordinated and broad-based opposition to the "conservative" NPN.

Leaving aside the personality conflicts, and the accusations of NPN betrayal in the allocation of patronage appointments to NPP members, the area where the NPN-NPP Accord came up against a sharp contradiction concerned the NPP's main base of support in the three state governments it controlled (Anambra, Imo and Plateau), and the general attempt by the NPN to weaken its opponents in all the non-NPN states. A bitter struggle over the NPN's new revenue allocation policy, which retained an excessive share of national income for the central government, was one issue which sharply divided the two allied parties. Similarly, the insistence by President Shagari and his advisers on the appointment of Presidential Liaison Officers to represent the central government in the states – with particular implications for those states under "opposition" governors – also placed these two parties at odds. Finally, the participation of the three NPP governors in meetings of the "Twelve progressive governors" convened to co-ordinate their policies, and their opposition to the NPN, also added to the widening gulf between the NPN and NPP.[40]

The PRP, which had also entered into negotiations with the NPN on the eve of the Second Republic, but which did not obtain a formal power-sharing arrangement, also found itself increasingly rent by divergent opinions which eventually split the party. Nigerian parties had had such a short period to organize themselves between the lifting of the ban on politics in September 1978 and the first elections of July 1979, that some of them entered the Second Republic with internal divisions that had been papered over for the elections. In the case of the PRP, the major rift was between those leaders who wished to enter into an arrangement with the NPN in Lagos, principally Aminu Kano and S. G. Ikoku, and those more rigorously socialist party members who saw the PRP as the vanguard of a class struggle against a "bankrupt and corrupt political class" of Nigeria, represented by the NPN, and an entrenched "feudal system" which the NPN was seen as protecting in the emirate North.[41] In 1981 the PRP underwent the most complete schism of any of the existing parties, perhaps because its internal disagreements were most clearly ideological. An Aminu Kano faction, which was recognized by FEDECO as entitled to the use of the PRP name, and an Imoudu faction (named after a veteran Nigerian trade unionist active among its leaders), became bitter opponents. The two PRP governors in Kano and Kaduna, who were prominent advocates of the state-based strategy of opposition to the NPN, as well as a substantial number of elected PRP federal and state legislators, sided with the Imoudu faction of the party. Yet, as I shall soon discuss, these and other divisions within the opposition parties became complicated, and rendered more far-reaching, by the fact that they took place within the general context of efforts by NPN leaders to exploit such opportunities to widen the overt and covert bases of their party.

The case of the GNPP is more ambiguous because of the personalist nature of this party's organization. Claims by people other than Waziri Ibrahim to speak on behalf of the party can never be adequately assessed. Nevertheless, the GNPP did experience a serious rift within its ranks when, in 1982, Waziri Ibrahim made public his disagreement with the majority of his party's National Excutive Committee over the latter's wish to enter into a Progressive Peoples Alliance, formed in March of that year by the four opposition parties (including, on the PRP side, the Imoudu faction). Waziri was duly dismissed from the party in May and June in meetings called by other leading members of his party, and was replaced by Dr Shettima Mustafa. This dissident faction within the GNPP pushed ahead in the latter part of 1982 to bring about the merger of three parties – the GNPP organization they controlled, the NPP, and the PRP (Imoudu faction) – into a Progressive People's Party (PPP). However, all these moves came up against a series of unfavorable decisions by FEDECO.[42]

Despite the significant number of PRP legislators who sided with the PRP governors in the Imoudu faction, FEDECO decided to accord recognition to the Aminu Kano wing of the party which, because of the defections, was no longer a radical force within Nigerian politics. The removal by his colleagues of Waziri Ibrahim as the GNPP leader was also not recognized by FEDECO. More inexplicable, however, if collusion between FEDECO and the NPN government is to be ruled out, were FEDECO's decisions in 1982–3, to refuse registration to the PPP party, which reflected a national spread of support which drew on the NPP, as well as major factions of the GNPP and PRP, and the Commission's subsequent refusal to permit the NPP to change its name to the PPP and alter its constitution and slogan to reflect its status as a new party. Finally, what dissolved any lingering hope among the NPN opposition that FEDECO would act impartially, and independently of NPN's political strategists, was the granting of registration to one additional party for the 1983 elections, the Nigerian Advance Party (NAP) led by Mr Tunji Brathwaite, a politically active lawyer of Lagos. This party received derisory electoral support in the 1983 elections, reflecting its superficial basis and weak leadership structure and often comic posturing. Its registration was regarded by those who put together the broad-based PPP, with its numerous elected officials in the federal and state governments, as indicative of the fact that they were now in competition not only with the NPN itself but also with the theoretically non-partisan institutions such as the police, the government-owned media and the electoral commission.[43]

Chief Obafemi Awolowo often pointed out that his party was the most disciplined in Nigeria, and had not experienced the same divisions as the others. However, by the time of the 1983 elections the UPN found itself deeply divided in specific localities. In most cases, the cause of these rifts was not ideological in nature, nor did it involve conflicting attitudes towards collaboration with the NPN.[44] Instead, what tore apart some state branches of the UPN – minimally in the case of Ogun, Kwara and Oyo, but disastrously in the case of Ondo – were battles over the party's nominations, especially to run for the offices of state governor and senator. Such battles usually pitted long-standing associates of Awolowo, such as Governor Michael Ajasin of Ondo, against younger aspirants, such as Ajasin's former deputy, Akin Omoboriowo. The UPN was further stymied in its ability to work co-operatively with the other opposition parties for two reasons: the Igbo-Yoruba conflicts which had entrenched what could be called an NPP-UPN "incompatibility," and more personalist concerns regarding the presidential ambitions of Awolowo. So, although the UPN was actively engaged in meetings of the "progressive governors," and although it participated in the negotiations which led to the creation of the Progressive People's Alliance (PPA) in March 1982, it did not enter into the subsequent arrangements to have a new party, the PPP, absorb the opposition parties and party-factions. Despite their shared wish to unseat the NPN from power, what divided the UPN and the NPP could not, in other words, be papered over in the promotional literature of a new party organization.[45]

In the following chapter I shall discuss various instruments of control which were available to the NPN, and the ways in which the use of them added to the uncertainties of the 1983 election period. Of these, most crucial was probably FEDECO, first because of the extent of its powers and responsibilities under the 1979 Constitution and the Electoral Act, and second-ly because it was constitutionally accorded such a high degree of power and authority that it became a formidable instrument of control when captured, or brought under the sway, of any one of the country's party organizations. In the final chapter, I shall review the crucial issue of institutional integrity in the governance of Nigeria. Here we can look at the specific case of how the electoral commission, which was meant to stand above the competing political parties, came to be perceived as being under the control of one of them, the NPN, and how it was consequently hampered in playing its critical role in the relegitimizing of the personnel and institutions of the Second Republic. As one commentator aptly summed up this vacuum within the Nigerian polity in 1983: "We are once again going to try our hands with no Leviathan in supervision."[46]

One action by FEDECO which seemed to demonstrate more than any other that it had been "captured" by the ruling party, was the quite unnecessary change in the order of the elections from 1979. Instead of the crucial election of the president coming last of the five, as in 1979, it was shifted by the FEDECO Chairman, Ovie-Whiskey and his associates, to first in 1983. According to one account, of the many controversial decisions of FEDECO in the run-up to the 1983 elections, "the one that spectacularly stands out is the decision on the order of the elections."[47] As it turned out, not only did all the parties except the NPN call for a retention of the 1979 order of elections, a committee set up by FEDECO to examine the issue also supported such a policy. Some constitutional reasons were advanced for having the presidential elections first, but these were not convincing.[48] From the standpoint of the NPN's opponents, the original order of the elections would have enabled their parties to establish their relative strength in various constituencies as in 1979 and thus have allowed them to implement what seemed the best strategy to compete against the NPN in the subsequent elections and, most importantly, in the race for the presidency.

In addition to other important considerations, such as getting a smoother running of the electoral machinery by the time the crucial presidential contest was held, a different order of the election might have forestalled the massive irregularities of the presidential election in 1983 which rendered the subsequent elections an increasing free-for-all in which the NPN's opponents felt they had everything to lose, and little to gain, by continuing to play by any of the rules. It can be argued, though space cannot be allocated to such a purpose here, that the maintenance of a viable multi-party system in Nigeria in 1983 depended squarely on the NPN's opponents continuing to believe that their parties had a fair chance, individually or in some combination, of voting Shehu Shagari out of office. Moreover, a less complete change in the order of the elections might have enabled these parties, as in 1979, to acquire a definite share of governmental power after the first few rounds of voting which, whatever their misgivings about the complete fairness of the electoral process, would have been worth protecting even if they lost, once again, the plum of the Presidency.

By contrast, the 1983 order seemed designed to erode just such a belief, since it was likely to ensure, for reasons of Nigerian electoral and party dynamics, that the five elections would in effect be settled by the results of the first one. An NPN victory in the first vote of 6 August – giving it the next Presidency, and thus the central government – would enable it to go on and rack up landslide votes in the other elections, because of the discouragement of opposition party supporters, the willingness of electoral and police officers to serve the wishes of what was already going to be the next government, and the desire of many candidates to be part of the bandwagon rather than risk being cut off from the largesse of the central government for another four years. The complete reversal in the order of the elections gave NPN strategists the opportunity to use their control of the various instruments of government, in a concentrated way, to keep their opponents off-balance, and to arrange a massive vote total for Shehu Shagari by a combination of legitimate and illegitimate means.

The decisions of FEDECO – so crucial as it was to the gaining of strategic advantage by one party over another, and to the defence of acquired governmental power – should have been made, wherever possible, on the basis of established precedents, and on what was in the best interest of the *political system.* Until Nigerians find a way to create institutions which, like the electoral bureaucracy of India and other multi-cultural, multi-party democracies, can remain part of the state, or polity, itself, and not become instruments susceptible to being captured by factions of civil society which win (temporary) control of the state, any hope for a constitutional democracy is certain to be regularly frustrated.

11

Electoral fraud and violence: the Republic's demise

From the standpoint of this study, the demise of the Second Republic cannot be simply attributed to any particular act of omission or commission on the part of the politicians who took control of the offices to which they had been elected or appointed after 1 October 1979. The social terrain needed to sustain the system of competitive party politics carefully devised between 1975 and 1978, a system which drew on ideas and proposals that were advanced throughout the previous thirteen years of military rule, did not exist in Nigeria. This is the reason why, after closely studying the formation of political parties and their electoral campaigns in 1978–9, I turned my attention to exploring the nature of Nigeria's fundamental socio-political dynamics, that is, to seeking to understand what were the social processes which shaped political behavior and how such behavior was likely to affect the functioning of the new institutions and practices of constitutional democracy.

To argue as I have done that the requisite social terrain for competitive party politics did not exist in Nigeria, is not to make claims for the unsuitability of constitutional democracy for this or any other African nation. It is, rather, to suggest that other processes must be introduced, or allowed to operate, which would carry Nigerian society across the bridge from what I have characterized as prebendal politics to an alternate mode of group representation and competition for public resources. The military is always quick to claim that its system of governance can serve as such a bridge. The evidence, unfortunately, often suggests otherwise. The motives, outlook, and preferred governing structures of military regimes are profoundly counter-democratic. For this reason, most renewed experiments with civilian democracies usually take place as a consequence of the delegitimizing of military rule as a result of the Armed Forces' failure to govern, over the long term, any more effectively than the civilians they overthrew.

The Nigerian soldiers who intervened on 31 December 1983, cannot be held responsible, merely by that act, for the collapse of the Second Republic, nor can the thousands of politicians and government officials detained and brought to trial since then. Change the names of these Nigerian politicians – many of whom were discussed in Part III, and who, five years later, could be found in detention, sentenced to long terms of imprisonment, or chased into exile abroad – and the performance of the Second Republic is not likely to have been much different. The individuals who emerged to win control of the machinery of the political parties which were able to gain registration, and subsequently to win offices at the state or federal level in Nigeria, displayed the range of skills that competitive party politics calls for in any country. However, the Nigerian social context which I have analyzed ensures that such individuals carry into the legislative halls and ministerial offices certain attitudes and priorities which eventually convert democratic politics into a system characterized by greed, sectionalism and disregard for stipulated procedures. Instead of democracy being a mode of collective self-representation, a way of harmoniously pursuing divergent interests within the bounds of the law, it becomes a mere ordeal, a tragedy in which government leaders and the masses of the people are increasingly trapped until rescued by military officers eager once again to extend the walls of their barracks to the nation's boundaries.

ELECTION BY ORDEAL

The conduct of elections in countries with a functioning liberal democracy is usually a matter that occupies a low profile in the political process. There are occasional disagreements over the kind of ballots to be used, on the introduction of new procedures such as voting machines, and about the times at which the results of the voting in particular localities should be announced. In Nigeria, however, virtually all aspects of the electoral process become, at some moment or another, subject to disagreement. When the degree of trust sinks to a low level, as in 1983, the controversies accumulate faster than they can be resolved. It would probably take a few electoral cycles before the mere practical business of casting and counting votes in Nigeria achieved general acceptance and became a routinized aspect of the political process. One significant barrier in the way of the normalization of electoral procedures, however, is the folk or collective knowledge dating from the pre-1966 period, which has been handed down to successive generations of party militants. Stories about the concoction of non-existent voting figures in remote communities of northern Nigeria, or about the change in the identity of the winners of particular contests in the West between the announcement at the counting centers and the radio broadcasts, or about the arrest on bogus charges of party agents at polling stations, and so on, abound in the oral history of Nigerian elections. In short, it took very little – given the intensity of party conflict in 1983 – for individuals involved in the elections, at all levels, to revert to the socialized methods of offense and defense in the arena of electoral competition.

This "political culture" of electoral behavior is appropriately captured by the following remark: "Rigging elections has for a long time been as Nigerian as pounded yam or millet."[1] When interviewed for an overseas article on the

171

state of affairs in Nigeria in mid-1983, Wole Soyinka's comment about the probable behavior of the ruling party, the NPN, can be applied broadly to all the parties, depending upon the leverage they already enjoyed based on their share of political and economic power: "They'll steal it... Sure, they might not take the whole thing. But they'll steal enough to stay in power."[2] What threw the entire process into a rapid downward spiral is the fact that, in the context of the 1983 party competition, it was difficult to carry out such precise operations suggested by the phrase "steal enough to stay in power." Indeed, as political actors, from party headquarters in Lagos down to offices in remote localities, obeyed the precept of prebendal politics – i.e., that their entitlement to governmental office would be based on their ability to appear representative of a distinguishable client-group, now manifested in the "hard" form of electoral ballots – the "stealing enough," when nationally aggregated, turned into the generating of a vote total for the NPN which was so massive as to be finally unconvincing.[3]

One overseas commentator, who was steadfast in her publicized exhortations on behalf of "Nigerian democracy" throughout the first Shagari administration, came up with a way of seeing some virtue in this feature of the 1983 exercises:

> The elections, although marred by fraud and violent incidents, were a victory for democracy – a victory that surprised many skeptics... Paradoxically, the fraud can be interpreted as evidence of Nigeria's commitment to democracy. Local party members often did their rigging with an eye to the 1987 elections, positioning themselves to stake claims based on what they "delivered" this time.[4]

For me, on the contrary, prebendal politics is a barrier to the achievement of a stable constitutional democracy in Nigeria. Electoral fraud is not evidence of a "commitment to democracy" but rather belongs to a general social practice deeply embedded in the culture of party politics in that country, which justifies all attempts to defeat one's opponents whatever the means. Such individual and group actions constantly re-establish, in Kantian terms, a universal law of electoral behavior which is deeply at odds with the minimum requirement for a stable democracy. Indeed, the hundreds of clauses of Nigeria's Electoral Law can be read as invariably unsuccessful attempts to override the unwritten laws of electoral brigandage.

In 1979, all close observers of the transitional process were immediately aware of the inaccuracy of the register of 48,499,091 voters.[5] In 1983, a few weeks before the first election, a revised register, compiled at great financial cost to the nation, was published with a list of 65,304,818 voters, which reflected an increase of 18 per cent over the 1979 total. As the *Economist* coolly commented: "The elections were in effect over before they began with the publication of the new register."[6] Any calculation based on the largest estimates of the country's population, its age pyramid, and the highest possible proportion of registered to eligible voters, showed that the new total belonged even more to the realm of fantasy than that of 1979.[7] Not only did these figures suggest that there were going to be many phantom voters, bogus polling booths, and arbitrarily expanded constituencies, their analysis further suggested that, once again, any population census in Nigeria will reflect the balance of power among the various party organizations and, in the case of military governments, among the various regions of the country. The new electoral register provided moments of tragicomic relief, as commentators immediately made calculations of which states and regions seemed to have undergone the most implausible jumps in their potential voting population since 1979. The northern states showed a 33 per cent increase over 1979, the eastern states 25 per cent, and the western states 12.3 per cent, figures which accurately reflected the regional strength and prospects of the ruling NPN in 1983. A state like Sokoto, home of President Shagari, seemed to have a population density quite out of proportion to the neighboring sovereign state of Niger, which it resembled in many economic, ecological and social respects.[8] In some cases, particular communities, which were strongholds within states controlled by an opposition party, were found to have multiplied their voting strength by as much as tenfold in four years.[9]

Against such a background, the reports of malfeasance which flowed from constituencies throughout the nation as the elections commenced – underage voters, the distribution of already thumb-printed ballots, unauthorized possession of electoral materials, forged voting cards, impersonation, etc. – could not be kept in any reasonable perspective, because each documented instance suggested that there were others that did not, or could not, come to light. Within FEDECO, which swelled within a matter of months into an organization of a million employees to superintend an electoral machinery with, at its base, 160,000 voting booths, the reassuring voice of its Chairman, Ovie-Whiskey, was sometimes out of harmony with the frank and revealing statements of its commissioners at the state level. One of these, Colonel Ayo Ariyo of Bendel State, made it a point to warn the nation how unprepared FEDECO was for the awesome task before it a mere month before the first election. When the elections began, Ariyo would make well-publicized sweeps of particular localities, seizing false voting registers, closing down unauthorized voting booths, and revealing how tenuous was the Commission's control of the thousands who acted in its name: "We could not vouchsafe for the conduct of the officials themselves... these 29,000 people [in Bendel], recruited on paper, became FEDECO officials just like that – there are so many of them who are not quite honest."[10]

What should we call a process in which electoral officials are just as likely to be arrested for misconduct as the party supporters seeking dishonest ways to inflate their parties' vote? In some cases, for instance that of the Idoma area of Benue State, the revelation that more people had voted than there were names on the electoral register led to a cancellation of the results and a new vote being held the following day.[11] In other communities, similar revelations were just as likely to have been taken care of by a salutary adjustment of the figures, the use of police to detain on grounds of disturbing the peace people making vigorous protests, or a dismissal of any complaints by a FEDECO presiding official by citing the relevant provisions of the Electoral Law that appeals should be made to High Court tribunals. Even without the predilection for spontaneous, vigilante-style violence within Nigerian society, the intensity of electoral conflict, and the widespread belief that elections would not fairly reflect the voting strength of parties, would have been enough to make the outbreak of violence inevitable. Put all these together, however, and elections "without a Leviathan in supervision" quickly become a clear and present danger to life and property throughout the nation.

Nigeria had just one relatively peaceful election in 1983, that for the President on 6 August. By the time of the gubernatorial elections on 13 August, the struggles in the streets, on the airwaves, and in the compounds where FEDECO headquarters are located, had begun to supplant the actual voting itself as arenas of competition for, or resistance to, political power. [12] Overt appeals to the populace to resist the NPN's fraudulent electoral conduct were made with increasing frequency, especially by UPN militants in the western states. The UPN major newspaper made the following cautionary-cum-threatening remark: "No party should allow the NPN to monopolise violence to rig the elections. Men of brawn are not only in the NPN. So let's watch."[13] Chief Bisi Akande, UPN candidate for deputy-governor in Oyo, declared that if his party lost as a result of electoral rigging in the state, there were two lines of action open to it: "the court of law or the people's judgment."[14] In fact, both lines of action were eventually invoked. Throughout the state, vigilante groups went around beating individuals suspected of belonging to the NPN or to any organs of the media controlled by this party. Woe to anyone caught with electoral materials, especially ballot boxes or papers, in a vehicle or a private residence. It will never be known how many FEDECO and police personnel tragically lost their lives while legitimately transporting such materials.[15]

Some FEDECO headquarters were placed under virtual state of siege. In Oyo State, UPN and NPN officials kept a vigil, watching each other and the FEDECO representatives, to forestall what each believed would be an attempt by the other to command a doctoring of the voting results.[16] In Imo state, NPP supporters barricaded the FEDECO offices, while in Anambra the police chief eventually had to clear the FEDECO compound of opposing party members and then place a ban on all public assemblies.[17] In Ondo State, where the carnage reached levels of public mayhem similar to those in 1964–5, entire families of politicians were wiped out, and hundreds of houses were set on fire including the state headquarters of FEDECO. I myself listened as a UPN supporter from this state chillingly informed FEDECO and NPN officials, in a television broadcast from a station owned by the Lagos state government, that they should either announce the correct results in the gubernatorial election in Ondo or face the consequences to themselves and their families.[18]

The peculiar Nigerian practice of multi-party democracy was exacting a huge price in a country already buffeted by economic austerity. In Abeokuta, capital of Ogun State, the transmitter of the federal television station was attacked and set on fire. In those states such as Oyo, Ondo and Niger, where the electoral contest had suddenly become intense after a landslide victory of a particular party in 1979, the bloodletting and arson were greatest. In Niger State, on the south-western fringe of the Northern Region, the failure of the NPN to satisfy the majority group of the population, the Nupes, in appointments to the party and state leadership, brought to that state a level of electoral violence usually associated with their southern neighbors, the Yoruba. Similarly, the physical battles in the East between supporters of Emeka Ojukwu, and NPN senatorial candidate in Anambra State, and his NPP opponents, as well as other conflicts in Bendel and Plateau States (all placed under emergency restrictions after the gubernatorial elections), suggested that the tradition of political violence of the "wild, wild west" was becoming, like other aspects of political competition in Nigeria, a national phenomenon. For the first time in many years, military checkpoints and close searches of vehicles and automobiles were imposed in many regions of the country – with three of the five elections still to be held. Nigeria, by mid-August 1983, was therefore descending to a deeper level of political incapacity: from the inability to set limits to prebendal politics in the drive for, and utilization of, public offices, to the failure to keep elections a peaceful, non-violent registration of the preferences of the populace. Here is a graphic statement of the level of social pathology to which the electoral process had dropped in Western Nigeria after the first two elections:

> According to the Nigerian News Agency, more than 60 people have died during the electoral campaign. Most of the dead over the last two weeks were burned alive, following a fairly common practice in Nigeria of pouring petrol over and setting alight the victim. In the last few days, several members of the NPN and at least two policemen accused of having "stolen" votes have been lynched by this method, which is generally reserved for thieves caught red-handed. After being soaked in petrol, an old tyre is put over the victim, whose body then burns for several hours after being ignited. The burning of thieves in this way, "operation wet", is also known as "the bonfire".[19]

The politicians who accused their opponents and FEDECO officials of stealing the election knew exactly what the appeal to the "people's judgment" would entail. The complicity of all categories of political actors in the new "descent into chaos" – from educated lawyer-politicians to illiterate common folk, from ruling party bosses to their determined opponents, from party-paid journalists to unpaid hooligans – could hardly have been more complete.

ELECTION RESULTS AND JUDICIARY

Throughout thirteen years of military rule, from 1966 to 1979, Nigeria had been able to maintain some semblance of being a nation based on the rule of law because of the insistence by the courts and the legal profession on as much

175

adherence to the unsuspended sections of the 1963 Constitution, and established legal practices in the country, as the military governments would allow. The 1983 elections, however, unlike those of four years earlier, threatened to tarnish the reputation of the judiciary to the same extent as it did that of FEDECO and of the security agencies. According to section 119(1) of the 1982 Electoral Act

> No election and no return to the Senate, the House of Representatives, or any State Assembly or to any elective office shall be questioned in any other manner except by a petition complaining about the election or the return and presented to the competent High Court in accordance with the provisions of this Act.

By assigning the adjudicating of electoral disputes wholly to the Nigerian judiciary, the drafters of these provisions assumed that such an arrangement would contribute to political stability in Nigeria and provide a way for the expeditious and impartial settlement of conflicting claims. As it turned out, many of the elections were so controversial, and the range of evidence opposing sides brought before the court so different and of such questionable reliability, that the judiciary found its own integrity placed at risk by its mere involvement in this process.

At 1.30 a.m. on the morning of 11 August 1983, a long five days after the first elections were held, Alhaji Shehu Shagari was declared re-elected President of Nigeria by a vote of 12,037,648 to 7,885,434 (for his nearest rival Obafemi Awolowo). Shagari's vote had doubled from his 1979 total, that of Awolowo had increased by approximately 40 per cent. Of equal importance is the fact that Shagari obtained a minimum of 25 per cent in 16 states of the Federation, compared with 12 states in 1979 (which had then provoked the re-interpretation of his required vote-spread as discussed earlier). The three states which remained outside Shagari's 25-per-cent-plus column were all in the West: Ogun, Ondo and Lagos. In Oyo, the scene of such bitter conflict in mid-August, Shagari and the NPN registered an increase from 12.75 per cent in 1979 to 37 per cent in 1983. The importance for each state branch of the ruling party, and its leaders, to show that they could deliver their state, either massively where the NPN was already predominant, or in the 25-per-cent-plus column where an opposition party ruled, encouraged the doctoring of votes. For example, Chief Ogunsanya of the NPP charged, with detailed lists published in the national newspapers, that an extra 24,300 votes had been added to the NPN's total in Imo State to move its share from the 23.92 per cent recorded by party agents to the 25.07 per cent officially announced.[20]

Chief Awolowo refused to initiate legal action to challenge Shagari's vote totals. However, Waziri Ibrahim persisted with such a challenge all the way to the Supreme Court, only to have his petition rejected on the grounds "that he had failed to prove beyond a reasonable doubt that malpractices had occurred in the election."[21] The dismissal of the strong 1979 legal challenge by Chief Awolowo had created a definite precedent for the next Supreme Court regarding the election of the Nigerian President.[22] If there was a feeling in

1979 that Shagari had substantially, if not wholly, satisfied the constitutional requirements to be elected President, in 1983 there was even more reason to believe that his greatly increased share of the votes, and their broad regional distribution could not be rejected by the courts without bringing the whole political system into question. It would be left to others, and other challenges, to perform that task.

Politics in Nigeria, as Claude Ake has so effectively put it, is an all-consuming business.[23] Not only does it consume the energies of all too many Nigerians because it is the gateway to wealth, as Ake explains, it is also all-consuming because of the ways in which it affects the operations of the major institutions of the nation. The judiciary in Nigeria, like FEDECO and the security agencies, comes under considerable pressure to relinquish its independent stance and adopt a partisan one. When the UPN discovered the fraudulent nature of the voting register for Modakeke (Oranmiyan II constituency), it obtained a court injunction prohibiting its use by FEDECO in the elections. Similarly, as part of the tug-of-war in Anambra State between a resurgent NPN organization and a defiant NPP, the latter moved to get a court injunction enjoining FEDECO from announcing the gubernatorial results until the court had been able to look into allegations of electoral misconduct. In both cases, a judge could be found to provide a provisional ruling which enabled one party or the other to shift the appearance of "illegality" onto its opponents or FEDECO itself. In both of these cases, however, the court's ruling was simply disregarded or circumvented by FEDECO.

Let us try to get closer to the fundamental concern here, namely, that any institution given the responsibility to assist and oversee the process of party competition in Nigeria is, to that same extent, put at risk in terms of its own functioning and legitimacy. In Anambra State, Judge Emmanuel Araka had already demonstrated his willingness to issue rulings having considerable political implications, such as his upholding in 1978 of Dr Azikiwe's qualification to contest for the presidency. In 1983, Justice Araka once again demonstrated a high level of judicial intervention, even involving the moving of cases from other jurisdictions to his own for hearing. When Jim Nwobodo (NPP) challenged the election of C. C. Onoh (NPN) as Governor, Judge Araka's tribunal acted on the basis of highly conflicting testimony from party agents, policemen, FEDECO officials and members of the Nigerian Security Organization (NSO), all of which revealed that massive falsifications had occurred in the election. After deducting a particular sum of false votes from each contestant's total, the Araka tribunal declared Jim Nwobodo the winner.[24]

Mr Justice Araka, for his pains, found that his harsh criticism of FEDECO officials for their dishonesty was subsequently turned against him at the Federal Court of Appeal, when Mr Justice Mamman Nassir, in reversing the lower court's ruling and restoring Onoh to the governorship, rebuked Araka for his failure to accord primary status to the submissions of FEDECO

177

officials over those of other witnesses.[25] What could the public make of such proceedings? Since the courts were obliged to make subjective judgments about comparative degrees of electoral misconduct, about which set of faulty documents were more reliable, and so on, it was not long before the political and personal biases of judges, not to mention material inducements, were cited by critics as the basis of their rulings.

To protect the courts, and prevent drawn-out proceedings, the Electoral Act had stipulated stringent procedures for the lodging of election appeals. It also set firm, and short, periods, in which appeals at all levels could be entertained. To discourage "frivolous" challenges, there were even *ad hoc* requirements imposed by the bench regarding the deposits that had to accompany appeals in the various elections. Yet these procedural hurdles often enabled some judges to dismiss tens of cases in a peremptory manner. The over-eagerness of these courts to find the easiest way to reduce the pressure of appeals at times led to their own rebuke by higher courts, as in the case of the challenge of Paul Unongo (NPP) to the re-election of Aper Aku (NPN) in Benue State. In other instances, the judges simply overruled the electoral law because the procedural hurdles were held to contravene "natural justice."

One major cause of the electoral disorder of 1983, as earlier advanced, was the effort by the NPN to move from being a ruling party whose strength exceeded that of other parties, to one which enjoyed a monopoly of power within the political system. To achieve this objective, it was necessary for the party to increase the size of its vote in the states it already controlled, through its control of the voter registration and voting process, and to pry away from the opposition the heart of their political bases. Three states were of strategic importance in this latter strategy: Kano, Anambra and Oyo. In Kano, the most populous state in the nation, and the economic mainstay of the former "north," the defeat of the opposition involved, to a large extent, the effort to deepen the rift within the PRP and to block moves by the radical wing of the party (in control of the Kano government) to obtain a new party registration with which it could contest the 1983 elections. The forcing of Abubakar Rimi and his associates to campaign under the NPP label (i.e. as a "southern" party with a Christian presidential candidate, Azikiwe), rather than under that of the PRP or the PPP, drastically reduced their voting strength in that state and enabled the NPN to increase its vote total enough to allow the recognized PRP (the tacit ally of the NPN) to take the state government away from the radicals.

In Anambra State, the return of the Biafran leader Emeka Ojukwu, and of Michael Okpara, the former regional Premier, from 13 years of exile – both of whom subsequently declared for the NPN – gave the NPN the ethnic patrons it lacked in 1978–9 to counter Dr Azikiwe's appeal. C. C. Onoh, whose political strategies were discussed in Chapter 7, was once again the NPN gubernatorial candidate with his running-mate being A. A. O. Ezenwa, the PRP candidate for governor in 1979. To bolster this line-up, the NPN was able to rely on the Vice-President of the nation, Alex Ekueme, to use his political influence and powerful financial resources to wrest the heart of the NPP, the state of Anambra, away from this party. As a consequence of this struggle, the gubernatorial battle in this state approximated not politics as war by other means, but war *simpliciter*. The courts followed behind the security agencies and FEDECO in getting drawn into the electoral quagmire in this state, as I discussed. The restoration of Onoh's victory by the Federal Court of Appeal, and its subsequent confirmation by the Supreme Court, brought to the NPN strategic victory number two.

In Oyo, as previously pointed out, the battle involved as much bloodletting as exchanging of vituperative words. Here the NPN achieved strategic victory number three, with the declaration of Omololu Olunloyo of the NPN as governor in place of Bola Ige of the UPN. In Anambra, the NPN had reversed an NPP majority of 76 per cent to 18 per cent in 1979, by a 48.22 per cent to 47.46 per cent victory in 1983. In Oyo, an even wider gap of 84 per cent (UPN) to 14 per cent (NPN) in 1979 had been replaced by a more decisive NPN "victory" of 58 per cent to 39 per cent in 1983. Such a reversal in the very heartland of Yoruba politics cannot be made without the mobilization of a wide range of institutions, resources and "informal" means by the victorious party. Bola Ige went to court confident that the revelation of the many irregularities in the election would swing the governorship back to him or, at least, result in the cancellation of the poll and the call for a new vote.

Hundreds of thousands of voters in the key towns of Ilesha and Ibadan had not been able to exercise their voting rights on 13 April because of a variety of impediments. And then there was the case of Modakeke, in which the injunction obtained against the use of the fraudulent electoral register had been disregarded by FEDECO officials. Bola Ige, a veteran of many legal battles in Nigeria, came to court armed with an array of documents showing how FEDECO's figures differed from those noted by party agents in many constituencies. Ige's appeal did not, however, succeed. The fact that these conflicting results had been registered on forms printed by Ige's agents, because of a shortage of forms in the constituencies in question, led to their rejection by the courts. This ruling was sustained on appeal. The NPN had thereby completed the removal of the three key states from control by opposition governors, in the three angles of Nigeria's ethno-regional triangle. The geographical basis for the transition from the balanced multi-party system of 1979–83 to a single or at least one-party dominant system in 1983–7 had therefore theoretically been achieved.

A final comparison of the court's action in the case of Oyo with that of a different tribunal in the neighboring – and brutalized – case of Ondo, is instructive. There, Judge Orojo, relying on what he called "probabilities," reduced the FEDECO figure of 1,650,531 for Omoboriowo of the NPN by almost a million votes (!) to 703,592, allowing Michael Ajasin (UPN) to regain his governorship without the need to alter his evidently short-counted FEDECO total of 1,150,383.[26] Yet, if FEDECO could not be the Leviathan

179

needed to supervise the 1983 elections, the Nigerian judiciary was even less able to fill this role. The courts could not operate in any salutary way when drawn into this process of vote adjusting, of having to decide which of conflicting, and questionable, sets of results were most "improbable," which impromptu solutions by overwhelmed election officials were most acceptable, which degree of malfeasance was excessive and which excusable. In the context of Nigeria in 1983, every decision of the judiciary could be made to appear, to some extent, to be the wrong one. Truth and fairness had become subordinate to political partisanship.

On balance, the courts gave the NPN what it sought. In addition to Shagari's re-election, the NPN was able to hold on to the near doubling of its number of governorships from seven to thirteen, with a fourteenth, Kano, shifted to the more accommodating hands of the PRP (Aminu Kano). In the final three elections, the NPN victories became a landslide. In the heartland of the West, Oyo State, in whose regional assembly, private homes, and streets the First Republic had met its Waterloo in 1965, the NPN added to its dethronement of Bola Ige as governor the taking of four of the five senatorial seats the UPN had won in 1979, and also sent 36 of the 38 Representatives to the Federal House. No wonder Chief Awolowo would choose to turn his back on his party's humiliating defeat and assert prophetically that the NPN's victory "will only last for a short time."[27] By September 1983, politics had nearly completed its decay into a state of war in Nigeria. Judges cannot adjudicate wars; they can, if they choose, acknowledge the victors and vanquished. For the judiciary to reverse, to any significant degree, positions achieved on an electoral battlefield which contained the media, the polling booths, and the offices of FEDECO, would have meant that it enjoyed a sovereign status, above party and social faction. On the evidence of the 1983 electoral experience, neither the Nigerian state itself, nor any of its major constituent parts, could lay claim to such a status after a quarter-century of independence from colonial rule.

A SYSTEM IN DISARRAY

The 1983 elections, as I have shown, were not only a set of difficult hurdles that the Second Republic needed to get over, but a process which brought into sharp relief the fundamental problems of the new political system itself. A constitutional democracy such as Nigeria attempted to establish between 1975 and 1979, and which had its first trial in 1979–83, depends for its maintenance on governmental institutions, such as the judiciary and the electoral bureaucracy, as much as it does on the responsible operation of a variety of other public and private services. Moreover, one of the major premises of this study has been that even more fundamental than the inability to operate a competitive party system in Nigeria has been the failure to maintain the integrity of the state in relation to the multifarious groups and organizations in civil society. Indeed, between July and September 1983, the boundary

180

between state and civil society seemed to have dissolved: public institutions had become as much party to the struggle for gaining decisive partisan advantage as were the registered party organizations themselves.

I earlier discussed the ways in which the decisions of FEDECO seemed to take on a partisan cast. Indeed, Abubakar Rimi, the radical PRP governor of Kano State, resigned his office in April 1983 on the grounds that since his party had split and all attempts to obtain registration for a new combination of parties and party factions had been rejected by FEDECO, the latter, under the control of the NPN, was certain to do everything possible to prevent him from contesting the election.[28] The substance of Rimi's concerns was borne out by the lengths to which FEDECO went to prevent another governor, Mohammed Goni of Borno State, from competing. Goni had remained in office despite the split in his party, the GNPP, and sought to campaign for re-election on the ticket of another party, the UPN. Using the services of Nigeria's foremost trial lawyer, F. R. A. Williams, FEDECO contested Goni's candidacy all the way to the Nigerian Supreme Court where a unanimous decision of the seven judges ruled in Goni's favor on 3 August 1983, just ten days before the gubernatorial elections.

Why should FEDECO have relied on a slight linguistic ambiguity in a provision of the 1979 Constitution to seek to disqualify an "opposition" governor when the spirit of the provision was not at all at issue, namely, to prevent the "cross-carpeting" which had bedevilled the First Republic?[29] In dismissing the case, the Supreme Court showed its exasperation with the trivial nature of FEDECO's challenge:

> As we are gentlemen here in Nigeria, the derogatory meaning of the word "FACTION" given in the Concise Oxford Dictionary is NOT what is intended by the use of the same word in section 64, sub-section (1) (g) of the Constitution of the Federal Republic of Nigeria 1979.[30]

The fact that the body charged with the daunting task of supervising five sequential elections should seek to overturn a Federal Appeal Court ruling based on technicalities of language quite divorced from the purpose of the constitutional provision in question, is symbolic of the ways in which the major institutions of government had become as much parties to the political competition as were the recognized political organizations taking advantage of every opportunity to harass their opponents.

In each of the states in which an "opposition" party was in control, this dimension of the political struggle was very much in evidence. In Anambra, for example, highly vituperative, one-sided and insulting language was used on regular news broadcasts, especially on the television. All normal restraints were abandoned in this war of words. The state branches of the federal television and radio stations became engaged in vicious tirades against their counterparts controlled by the NPP state government.[31] This brings us to the unsuccessful attempt made via the Electoral Act of 1982 and the Electoral (Amendment) Act of July 1983 to establish a National Advisory Council on the Mass Media. According to these laws, representatives of the registered political parties and FEDECO were to be appointed to a Council which would have powers to ensure the impartiality of government-owned media during the electoral period, equal access to their facilities by all registered parties, and the responsibility for announcing the election results. On 21 July 1983, President Shagari vetoed this Amendment Act citing its incompatibility with the Constitution in several regards as well as the injunction early obtained against the Council's establishment in the High Court of Kwara State.[32]

What is significant about this particular episode, however, is that it stemmed from a recognition by a majority of Nigerian federal legislators that two of the principal means of ensuring a fair election – the free and balanced dissemination of party views and positions, and an impartial electoral bureaucracy – required the creation of an extraordinary body in 1983 whose rules, if contravened, would lead to the imposition of terms of imprisonment "without option of a fine." In other words, whenever the existing Leviathan cannot be trusted, the appropriate solution was to establish another one with temporary powers. The Nigerian polity was therefore being transformed into a rule-making, institution-establishing entity which sought to compensate for the ineffectiveness and/or corruptibility of each set of its institutions by creating *ad hoc* ones to supervise them. Each solution becomes in turn a new source of problems to be resolved. The self-undermining nature of the whole system eventually cannot be postponed by these gambits. As the disarray spreads throughout the polity, the only possible exit from this situation becomes an exit from the political system altogether.

I mentioned earlier the militarization of the security apparatus of the Second Republic which was already in evidence in the form of the mobile police of Inspector-General Adewusi, ordered "to shoot on sight" in handling disturbances of the peace during the elections, and with the use of military units to conduct intensive search operations of individuals and vehicles at the time of the gubernatorial elections. What was also noticeable during the elections were the exceptional outspokenness and autonomous actions of Resident Electoral Officers (the highest authority in each state) who were also retired military officers. Brigadier Ignatius Obeya of Anambra, for example, disregarded a decision announced by Mr Justice Ovie-Whiskey that copies of the voting results should be handed to the police and to personnel of the Nigerian Security Organization. According to Obeya, the order was a decision of the "Chairman alone" not of the "whole Commission."[33] In Bendel State, as earlier pointed out, Colonel Ayo Ariyo had openly criticized the inadequacy of FEDECO's preparations for the elections, contradicting the stream of reassuring words from his superiors. During the elections, Ariyo acted in ways which were not only decisive and authoritative but which were sometimes at odds with the public announcements of FEDECO's Chairman. For example, whereas Ovie-Whiskey had declared that parties which were dissatisfied with particular results could not impede the counting by refusing to sign the results sheets, Colonel Ariyo proclaimed that he would not accept "any dubious result or any not signed by two party agents."[34]

182

Quite fundamentally, therefore, Nigeria in mid-1983 was faced with the delegitimizing of its competitive party system as well as with the more threatening situation, that officials of the state itself were losing the capacity to compel compliance with their dictates. A different kind of authority – embryonically present in the midst of the civilian rulers in the form of the militarized police, armed forces personnel assigned to peace-keeping duties, and retired officers given bureaucratic supervisory tasks – was obviously available with its alternative set of governing norms, practices, personnel and institutions.[35] In short, constitutional democracy in Nigeria was not just overthrown three months after the general elections of 1983, it had also by then been substantially eroded from within.

12

Conclusion: democracy and prebendal politics in Nigeria

The political predicament of Nigeria as a nation-state, and of Nigerians as a people, has deepened during the decade which has elapsed since the military government of Murtala Muhammed acknowledged that the soldiers had to return to soldiering and popularly elected representatives to governing the country. In this conclusion, I shall not presume to have a blueprint for escaping from this predicament. On a less ambitious level, I shall summarize certain aspects of my analysis and indicate the pathways which seem to hold some promise, in contrast to those which this study has revealed to be fraught with difficulties. The preliminary observation to be made about Nigeria's political dilemma is that the country has yet to free itself from Obafemi Awolowo's designation of it as being a mere "geographical expression." Of course, since Awolowo's published remarks in 1947, Nigeria has taken on many of the attributes of a modern nation-state, both internally and externally. Just a short step away from the daily assertion of sovereignty and nationhood, however, is a world of political jostling which, by its very nature and its internal ideological conflicts, indicates that the nation of Nigeria is still a problematic entity even for its highly educated and politically active citizens.

In the course of an interview conducted in 1979, Turi Muhammadu, then Managing Director of the *New Nigerian* newspaper and a former member of the Constituent Assembly of 1977–8, stated that Nigeria is a cultural as well as a political federation.[1] He meant more than the obvious fact that Nigeria is a culturally heterogenous nation. If a federation is composed of political units which enjoy a certain measure of autonomy, the Nigerian Federation referred to by Turi Muhammadu also consists of cultural units which, in some abstruse and fundamental fashion, possess authoritative qualities. Five years later, in a most insightful essay written following the collapse of the Second Republic, C. Sylvester Whitaker wrote: "Despite the dreams of dedicated Nigerian nationalists, national institutions and identity today exercise less of a hold on popular sentiment than at any time since the nation's founding."[2]

The fact that a nation of 100 million people, which includes a few hundred linguistic groups and several major ethnic communities larger than some African nations, has failed to establish a full sense of nationhood a quarter-

184

century after independence, does not in itself represent a significant failing. The problem, however, as Whitaker recognizes and as I have contended throughout this study, is that the distrust which characterizes relations among these communities renders democracy "attractive to most Nigerians and even essential to them."[3] Since a democratic route to nationhood, in the context of Nigeria's social pluralism, is a parlous one, and an authoritarian route has not – at the quarter-century mark after independence – been seriously attempted, Nigerian society is left to oscillate between the broadening of democratic participation and the freezing of such practices with the reimposition of military rule.

At the Aburi Conference in Ghana in January 1967, Colonel Odumegwu Ojukwu, leader of Eastern Nigeria, proposed one option which, had it been adopted, might have suspended this oscillation and its destructive consequences:

> I, in all sincerity, in order to avoid further friction and further killing, do submit that the only realistic form of Government today until tempers can cool is such that will move people slightly apart and a Government that controls the various entities through people of their areas. It is better that we move slightly apart and survive, it is much worse that we move closer and perish in the collision. Therefore, I say no single one person today in Nigeria can command loyalties of various groups and, therefore, to save the suspicion, to enable us to settle down, it is essential that whatever form of Government we have in the centre must be limited and controlled by a consensus to which we all agree.[4]

Biafra lost the war to the Federation and with its defeat was lost any prospect of Nigeria becoming a confederation of self-governing states linked by a weak central government. Much to the contrary, it was the federal government which emerged greatly strengthened from the civil war in its economic, political, and police powers, while the sub-federal units (regions then states) were subdivided and rendered dependent and subordinate. The legitimacy of this arrangement fifteen years after the civil war is, as Whitaker recognizes, still in question: the Nigerian government bristles with power that lacks an ethical or normative girding.[5]

Thus, the question is raised ever anew among articulate Nigerians: Was the 1914 decision of the colonial power to amalgamate the northern and southern communities into one political unit – the predominantly Muslim with the predominantly Christian areas – a good thing? And when is added to this north-south divide, the inter-ethnic conflicts and competition along other geographical axes, the question becomes even more acute: How can a thoroughgoing multi-party democracy be sustained in Nigeria when full political competition only generates patterns of political mobilization and conflict which threaten the very integrity of the nation itself? It would appear that three main courses of action are open to the country in the light of this dilemma: (1) it could continue to search for a fully pluralistic democracy, only to find that the vessel of the nation-state cannot sustain the pressures, and thus that temporary rescue must be provided by the armed forces; or (2) an acknowledgement could be made of the need for a provisional semi-authoritarian governing framework, modified as much as possible by conciliar institutions of representation and by the entrenching of procedures to ensure accountability; or (3) one of the more thoroughgoing authoritarian twentieth-century ideologies, e.g. Leninist or corporatist, could be implemented, with all the travails that customarily follow in their train.

STATE AND CIVIL SOCIETY

Implicit in much of my analysis has been an attempt to understand the nature of the social dynamics of Nigeria and their political consequences or, from the reverse perspective, the nature of the Nigerian state and its relationship to civil society. In carrying out this study, I have moved closer to a Weberian framework for analyzing these dynamics and relationships in post-colonial Africa. In a thoughtful essay based on Weber's works, Randall Collins notes the primacy Weber accorded "the material and ideal interests of individuals, and the group and organizational structures developed by individuals to further these interests."[6] The state is "an apparatus of domination" but it is also a sphere in which "one individual or group is placed in a position to enforce his [or its] will on the others."[7] All viable polities must solve or contain the contradiction between the state as an instrument representing the corporate power of the whole society – as manifested particularly in its monopoly powers of compulsion – and the state as an arena of struggle between individuals, groups and classes to defend or advance their interests.

In Chapter 1, I discussed W. Arthur Lewis's enunciation of the need to modify the prescriptions of liberal democracy in light of what he called the "plural nature" of African countries. Since parties inevitably become identified with sectional groups, the winning of power by any party tends to be perceived as facilitating the domination of the unsuccessful by the successful ones, and this perception is usually reinforced by the misuse of state power. Even in the absence of a multi-party system, offices of the state in Africa are often captured by individuals and their support groups and exploited to favor their interests within the marketplace of civil society as well as in the appropriation of the resources of the state itself. Such on observation makes relevant another perspective in contemporary political analysis, which also draws on Weber.

Alfred Stepan and Theda Skocpol have both expanded on Weber's conception of the state as being capable, in certain circumstances, of structuring relations between the public authority and civil society as well as those within civil society itself.[8] From such an understanding, the democratic option can be seen to be highly problematic in Nigeria. The opening up of the public authority to individuals and groups in civil society via democratic processes and institutions renders it susceptible to being fragmented and drained of its resources. It thus appears that some corporate group is needed to maintain the integrity of the state/civil society boundaries and contain this problem by extending the distance between rent-seeking individuals and groups and those officials with direct control of public expenditures. The Nigerian political scientist, Billy Dudley, following Hegel, advanced the claims of the higher civil bureaucracy to play this role; the military officers who periodically seize power from the civilians increasingly promote themselves. Whichever set of "guardians" of the public weal possess this authority, such solutions are merely temporary, for, as I have discussed, the pressures exerted on those in government offices to use their power for private or sectional ends are so great and unremitting that the state/civil society boundaries are eventually undermined anew.

Hence the crux of the failure of Shehu Shagari, according to Whitaker, is that he "placed his government in virtual receivership to a broad coalition of sectional interests within his party."[9] The very strategies that led to the triumph of the NPN rendered the Nigerian state hostage to the depredations of Shagari's cohorts. Clearly, the advance of democracy and the consolidation of public authority must be reconceptualized in Nigeria, so that progress in the former does not entail the enfeeblement of the latter. What renders this process even more problematic is the fact that the majority of liberal democratic nations in the world – which provide most of the prevailing models – followed a path of democratizing this public authority over centuries of struggle. Nigeria, and other ex-colonial polities, must seek to replicate this process within decades, experimenting with what Edmund Burke would have called "arithmetical and geometrical constitutions," i.e. ones that do not emerge in a natural way out of the country's social practices and institutions.

DEMOCRACY AND THE SELF-REGULATING SOCIETY

Students of Western liberal democracy since de Tocqueville have often recognized that constitutional democracies rest on something more diffuse, yet no less significant, than the laws, institutions and procedural principles which govern the conduct of public affairs. "If I have hitherto failed," de Tocqueville stated, "in making the reader feel the important influence of the practical experience, the habits, the opinions, in short of the customs of the Americans upon the maintenance of their institutions, I have failed in the principal object of my work."[10] Liberal democracy, for de Tocqueville, carries into the public arena particular social practices that are to be found "in all details of daily life." And hence we may follow Michael Burrage and refer to a democratic society as one in which there prevails "a distinctive set of norms" governing actions in the private as well as public domain.[11]

From such a perspective, one can go on to the idea of democracy as a "self-regulating society." Of course, the state, as I discussed earlier, is susceptible to having its powers shifted to favor now one, now another, set of class and social forces. But some of these victories cannot be absolute if the system is to remain a liberal democracy. Liberal democracy is not only limited government, it is

187

often a system of government of limited or provisional victories. Social actors and forces know not to carry their successes to their fullest conclusion, i.e. to the political elimination of their opponents and of the latter's ability to mount new challenges. The practices of "judicial review," "recall and referendum," "checks and balances," can thus be seen as the institutionalization of more generalized norms of social conduct. Thus, Michael Burrage can speak of democracy as "the primary notion of right. Among the various notions of right which together constitute the moral order of contemporary society, democracy is pre-eminent. Every other good is conditional, limited and subordinate to democracy."[12]

When one returns with these insights to one's study of Nigerian society and politics, it can be observed that the nation is made up of numerous communities which have evolved their own moral orders, their own notions of right, their own ways of practising "limited victories" among the clanic or lineage groups which constitute them. Yet, as I shall discuss below, the amalgamation of such social systems to form the states, regions and federation of Nigeria, carries into these wider arenas the pursuit of "material and ideal interests" and ways of aggregating such interests but not the institutions and procedures for regulating, balancing and adjudicating them at the community or traditional political level. From time to time, the designated representatives of these sub-national units are brought together – as in the Constitution-making bodies of 1975–8 – and charged with devising a new constitutional system that will give legitimacy to particular forms of interest-representation, conciliation and implementation. Long before these constitutional edicts can become rooted in the society, however, the absence of a public ethic renders political life increasingly Hobbesian in character. What Whitaker has appropriately referred to as "the moral incapacity of the Nigerian state" is the consequence of this gap between the self-interested activities of individuals, classes and social groups and the formal institutions and laws of the Republic.[13] It is no wonder that the Shagari administration found itself advocating the need for an "ethical revolution" in Nigeria while presiding over the looting by its high officials of the state's treasury, or that its military successor has devoted much energy to a "War Against Indiscipline," the WAI, with which it hopes to alter radically all aspects of Nigerian social behavior, from the unwillingness to form peaceful queues at bus-stops to the diversion of public monies in governmental offices. In short, de Tocqueville's "habits of the heart," the customs, opinions, and forms of social intercourse which sustain a democratic political order, are advocated in Nigeria, with usually disappointing results, by directive from above.

Bertrand Badie and Pierre Birnbaum, who examine some of the implications of a democracy as a self-regulating society, advanced the following contention:

> The ability of civil society to govern itself not only fostered the development of the market, but also encouraged reliance on representative forms of government, thereby making a strong state unnecessary.[14]

I would question the precise causal sequence implied in this remark, and would not want to obscure the dialectical interplay among these social, economic and political factors. However, when combined with de Tocqueville's insights, it embodies a perspective which directs us to ask which political forms are fostered, and which hindered, by the entrenched, as well as evolving, social practices of the communities which were corralled together by the British colonial powers to constitute the Nigerian nation-state.

SOCIAL SCIENCE AND PREBENDAL POLITICS

The realization that the conduct of Nigerian politics could be conceived as a general system of social and political behavior which was not fully accounted for in the available literature led to the formulation of the concept of prebendal politics. I shall not rehearse in this section all the dimensions of this conceptual framework outlined in Chapter 6, nor the many factual illustrations given throughout the book of its mode of operation. Rather, I shall briefly indicate some of its implications for social science analysis in Africa and elsewhere. Eric Wolf, in his discussion of three types of landed domains – patrimonial, prebendal and mercantile – identified in a precise manner the distinguishing aspects of each of these categories.[15] A "patrimonial domain" involves an inheritable right, a patrimony, granted to an individual (and his kinship group and lineage), to receive tribute from those occupying the area it covers. A "mercantile domain" is regarded as the private property of its owner, and can be bought and sold and generally used as a commodity to generate profit. A "prebendal domain," however, involves not land but income: a state official is given the right to attach a certain portion of the tribute due to the state and use it for his or her own purposes. Although many writers on the politics of Third World countries have been attracted to the notion of patrimonialism, in many instances the idea of prebendalism would have been even more appropriate for their analyses. An extremely suggestive contention of Wolf is that the particular "mix" of these three forms of domain is likely to determine "the organizational profile of a particular social order."[16]

I. Clientelism and corruption

Prebendalism carries us a step forward in the discussion of clientelism and corruption which feature so prominently in nearly all peripheral capitalist societies. Morris Szeftel, in his writings on Zambia, touches on many of the observations which I have integrated into my model of prebendal politics: the nature of the state as the main reservoir of financial resources; the existence of patronage networks which are sustained by corrupt practices; and the pervasive governmental inefficiencies which result from the foregoing.[17] Writers on patron-client systems have refined their perspective to the point where their discussions of the basic social exchange relationships, of the importance of affective identities and group solidarities, and of the inequalities which are contained and rendered advantageous to some classes of people within clientelistic networks, cannot be left out of the study of most Third World nations. Of particular relevance here is the recognition, in a general essay by Eisenstadt and Roniger, of "the combination of emphasis on these obligations and solidarity with the somewhat illegal or semi-legal aspect of these relations."[18] As fundamental as patron-client relations may have become in the acquisition of political power, in the maintenance of public support for government office-holders, and in the distribution of material resources, such relations usually remain in the penumbra between legality and illegality and sometimes, as in the case of Nigeria, can slide decidedly into the latter domain.

One text which incorporates the many insights from the study of clientelism and carries them forward in a broad conceptualization of state and society is Christopher Clapham's *Private Patronage and Public Power*.[19] Clapham explains the two-stage historical process by which patron-client bonds, first forged in peasant societies between cultivators and local notables or landowners, are replicated during the incorporation of such societies into national political systems. One can appreciate from Clapham's discussion the compelling nature of this process: "this incorporation almost invariably takes place through the co-option of local notables whose principal political resource, from central government's point of view, lay in their control of their local peasantries."[20] Clapham adds weight to our recognition that the clientelistic pattern of political mobilization in Nigeria emerges in a natural way from the pre-national social dynamics of the country's constituent communities. Of equal importance, also, is the suggestion that class and clientelistic models of analysis have an additional point of overlap to the one described in Chapter 5 concerning bourgeois class action, namely the fact that the traditional mode of improving the personal security of peasant cultivators is through the forging by them of vertical ties which are "encapsulated within a set of moral obligations."[21] In short, there is more than ethnic identity to explain why political mobilization in Nigeria involves the subordination of class action, even among subordinate rural and urban dwellers, to the establishment of the vertical structures of sectional parties and party-factions.

Clientelistic behavior, Clapham emphasizes, must be seen as "a form of behavior which it becomes rational for people to pursue, given specified external conditions,"[22] a point which echoes the recognition here that while such practices present hurdles to the consolidation of a multi-party democracy in Nigeria, they also reflect a deep understanding of the most efficacious way in which individuals, at all levels of the society, can act to acquire goods, services and other desired resources. When such clientelistic modes of behavior become intertwined with ethnic group identities, the periodic debate concerning the entrenchment of a constitutional democracy based on parties which transcend ethnicity becomes a debate between an abstract rationality, conducted in the language of Western political thought, and an experiential rationality voiced in the language of the daily struggle for material well-being.

The four conditions which Clapham sees as favoring the emergence of a clientelistic system – all of which are reflected in my analysis – also suggest additional reasons why corruption is greatly fostered in such a system. One of these conditions is the control over critical resources by one particular group and the fact that lack of access to such resources generates a sense of "vulnerability, insecurity and the inability to achieve other goals."[23] In Nigeria, this sense of insecurity is felt as much by those who temporarily win control of critical resources as by those who feel excluded from them. When this situation is combined with another of Clapham's conditions, namely the absence of a system of public allocation based on "universalistic criteria rather than private and personalist ones," we are brought to the crux of Nigeria's political dilemma. The history of all countries which have now established multi-party democracies would reveal periods in which patronage systems based on "private and personalist criteria" predominated. Clearly, the exit from such systems took place primarily as a consequence of economic processes rather than purely political ones. Of course, reformers emerged who succeeded in getting legislation passed which replaced some of the monopoly exercised by party machines with the application of universalistic criteria in the appointment of civil servants and in the allocation of public goods. Yet such successes facilitated the expansion of the private sectors of the economy, which reduced the relative importance of the patronage systems. The problem confronting Nigeria and other peripheral capitalist nations is that the external constraints on their economic dynamism often make it necessary to emphasize ineffective political – as well as moralizing – routes to breaking the hold of clientelism and its "extra-legal" consequences on public life.

A final reference can be made here to a work which includes many parallel insights from the study of another continent. Robert R. Kaufman, in an overview article on Latin American politics, constructs his argument in a manner which overlaps with this one in several respects.[24] For Kaufman, the capacity to win votes becomes a political resource in Latin American countries, resulting in the predominance of the *politico* who is able to manipulate symbols and produce benefits for individuals and groups:

> clientelistic ties constitute mechanisms whereby a relatively large number of individuals can make demands upon the state, manipulate the political game, and acquire some degree of resources and security. Finally, through personal attachments to higher-status patrons and brokers, many unincorporated and otherwise atomized peasants and "urban marginals" are linked into the larger sociopolitical order in ways that preserve the essentially elitist character of that order.[25]

Kaufman therefore presents, as I have done, a complex process of competition for resources and security in which patrons, brokers and individuals at the base of the social hierarchy become linked in ways that sustain a dominant class. What my analysis adds to this model – perhaps reflecting the greater fragility of the state in Africa as compared to that in Latin America – is that individuals do not just "make demands upon the state" and "manipulate the political game" but go on to *appropriate* parts of the state which are then exploited and utilized to provide resources for self and group consumption.

There must surely be cases within Latin America in which the extent of the privatization, and group control, of offices or sectors of the state warrant the application of this notion of prebendalism. Interestingly, Clapham contends that when the state machinery is used to provide "private benefits to groups and individuals, in the process giving them a vested – and purely instrumental – interest in the maintenance of the state itself," this tendency "in states where there is no conception of public interest...may be the next best thing to it."[26] Unfortunately, this process in Africa contributes more often than not to the undermining rather than the "maintenance of the state itself." The missing ingredient that might enable representatives of social groups and electoral constituencies to undertake these fundamental and universal tasks without prebendalizing the state, is one that Nigerians must discover through trial and error, that is, as an indirect consequence of the succession of autocratic and democratized systems and the accompanying reflection and debate about these experiences. It is unlikely that the solution will be found by undertaking a new constitution-making exercise, of a comprehensive nature, as was tried in 1975–8.

II. Social closure and the two publics

Another line of social analysis derived from Weber, which has considerable relevance for the formulation of an appropriate paradigm for the study of Nigerian and other African societies, is Frank Parkin's discussion of social closure:

> By social closure, Weber means the process by which social collectivities seek to maximize rewards by restricting access to resources and opportunities to a limited circle of eligibles. This entails the singling out of certain physical attributes as the justificatory basis of exclusion. Weber suggests that virtually any group attribute – race, language, social origin, religion – may be seized upon provided it can be used for 'the monopolization of specific, usually economic opportunities' ... its purpose is always the closure of social and economic opportunities to *outsiders.*[27]

The attractiveness of Parkin's essay is that it helps us move beyond the kind of interpretive disagreements, usually between class and ethnic models of African politics, which – as I have argued – have stymied rather than aided the discipline in recent decades. According to Parkin, the practice of social closure is as fundamental to the functioning of human societies as is the maximizing of individual interests through collective action. The various modes of effecting closure differ according to the circumstances; they can be said to represent "different means of mobilizing power for the purpose of engaging in the distributive struggle."[28] Such a perspective is "consistent with the analysis of class relations"[29] while not being bound by it. Whether the process of exclusion and subordination of outsiders will be based on physical, ascriptive or class criteria – some combination of them – will vary according to the nature of the society and especially the stage of its economic development. Since the ultimate goals of social closure are the achievement of "exclusion and subordination," the more this process has evolved based on physical and ascriptive attributes, the more widely the stratification order will differ from a "Marxist model of class polarization."[30]

The idea of social closure also has implications for the study of the general political predicament of Nigeria. The logic of social closure involves the tendency for social collectivities within the political arena to be monopolistic, to be exclusionary in nature: it is, according to Parkin, "the attempt by one group to secure for itself a privileged position at the expense of some other group through a process of subordination."[31] By contrast, liberal democracy, as I have argued, is a system in which, on most issues, the vanquished are not barred from legitimately continuing the struggle at another time. Party politics in Nigeria is driven as much by a desire to participate effectively in "the distribution struggle" as it is by a fear of being excluded from this process. Moreover, if social closure can lead to the usurpation of public power and the subordination of those excluded, then a significant gap exists between the norms of a socio-political system which permits "exclusionary closure" and those which make liberal democracy feasible. Parkin's interpretation therefore complements very forcefully the reflections in Part II on the politics of distrust in Nigeria and on the persistent fear among its citizens of all regions and ethno-linguistic groups that the country might be governed as if it were a "plural society," i.e. with one cultural section dominating the others and monopolizing access to "resources and opportunities."

One of the most cogent attempts to explain the fundamental social dynamics in Nigeria, which underlie and bedevil the political process, will be found in a 1975 article by Peter Ekeh.[32] By showing the insights as well as limitations of Ekeh's analysis, I hope to make even clearer the interpretation of Nigerian socio-political dynamics which has been advanced in this study. Ekeh divides the social and normative universe of Nigeria into three realms, one private and two public. The main focus of his analysis is on the two public realms, one of which he calls "primordial" and the other "civic." By "primordial," Ekeh understands what can be called "communal" or "sectional" and, from his perspective, usually involves "emergent ethnic groups." His choice of the term "primordial" is unfortunate because he does not accept the "primordialism" of such ethnic groups, seeing many of them as having been "created by modern politics" and as reflecting "the ideology-creating achievements of the emergent African bourgeoisie."[33]

Ekeh advances a highly dichotomous view of the two public realms in Nigeria. The primordial realm is a moral one, the civic is for the main part amoral. The primordial involves a sense of membership in a community, a sense of citizenship, while the civic derives from the colonial administration and its imposed military, civil service and police institutions. The private individual has a sense of being morally linked with his primordial group: "he sees his duties as moral obligations to benefit and sustain a primordial public of which he is a member."[34] His attitude towards the civic realm, conversely, is purely materialistic and exploitative. The individual experiences "no moral urge on him to give back to the civic public in return for his benefits."[35] Indeed, he is driven to exploit that civic realm for the benefit of his primordial group. Ekeh is therefore able to explain the unending and crippling corruption in civic life in post-colonial African nations by contending that "the civic public is starved of badly needed morality ... the destructive results of African politics in the post-colonial era owes something to the amorality in the civic public."[36]

Ekeh's analysis is an important one, and it embodies insights which are essential to the study of post-colonial Africa. Yet his approach is too rigidly dichotomous, and it tends to squeeze out important aspects of the social process he is examining. First, the communal realm (a term more appropriate than Ekeh's "primordial") is not the non-economic universe he idealizes: "A good citizen of the primordial public gives out and asks for nothing in return."[37] Indeed, as I shall demonstrate, the communal world is an arena as much characterized by the active, and legitimate, pursuit of material interests as is the wider civic realm. Secondly, it is not the case that individuals "seize largesse from the civic public to benefit the primordial public" as if these were two distinct domains growing up "side by side."[38] Instead, as was noted from Richard Sandbrook in Chapter 5, mercenary relations in the civic realm in post-colonial Africa are strengthened by the fact that they are often combined with a moral tie. It is not that individuals accept bribes within the civic public which they then turn over, in part, to their communal group. Rather, the very persons with whom they are likely to be corruptly involved in the civic realm are their kinfolk. The two realms therefore overlap and interpenetrate in Nigeria; it is a mere abstraction to regard them as existing side by side, linked only by the transfer of resources from one to the other.

Finally, the crucial factor which is left out of Ekeh's scheme is that the civic realm is not just an artificial creation which derived from the superimposed colonial administration; it also has its historical roots within African societies. From our perspective, the ultimately destructive patterns of behavior in the public life of Nigeria, which in Chapter 11 were contended also to characterize the functioning of many social organizations, must be primarily explained on the basis of the carry-over into the wider civic realm of interest-seeking efforts unaccompanied by the normative and conciliar controls that usually keep such efforts functional to the stability and harmony of the community. This perspective therefore merges with that of Ekeh at a number of important points but diverges at others. Moreover, the two perspectives differ significantly in the causal explanations advanced. For me, there is a continuum in the creation of civic realms, from those which exist in the villages, clans or indigenous states – the designation varying according to the region and community concerned – to the sub-national political units (regions or constitutional states) and, finally, to the Federation. The communal realm, with its dominant ideologies and norms, political and economic structures, and languages of communication, is a public realm as Ekeh rightly observes. It also has the attributes, however, of a civic realm which is stronger in certain respects than the wider civic realm in which citizenship is based on universalistic criteria. In countries which achieve a settled socio-political order, this national civic realm eventually subsumes or subordinates all others.

The study of any region of Nigeria, or of Africa for that matter, will demonstrate how much the defining criteria of inclusion within its constitutive communities have changed over time. Once a multi-ethnic system gets underway, however, as discussed in Chapter 4, cultural sections of the population become consolidated and reified in the language and dynamics of political action. The creation of a national polity subsequently becomes hostage to the consolidation of such units at all levels of the society. Even situations of relative amity can be transformed into arenas of bitter conflict along new lines of sectional identity, as happened between communities which found themselves included in the same Nigerian states after the state-creation exercises of 1967 and 1976. The amorality of the public domain in Nigeria, and the destructive consequences of individual and group action, are as dire as Ekeh outlined them before the transition to the Second Republic. However, the social dynamics which underlie them are more complex and multi-causal than he suggests. Whether such an interpretation has more optimistic than pessimistic implications is a question that might be fruitfully explored by other scholars.

III. Elementary social behavior: the case of Yoruba society

Ever since I became aware that Nigerian politics and society reflected a correspondence between everyday social conduct and the pattern of political mobilization and conflict, one question which remained unaddressed was: What are the sources or origins (as opposed to bases) of this pattern of behavior? Put another way: Are there forms of "elementary social behavior" from which that of Nigerian "society at large" is derived?[39] Part II of this book set forward the ways in which the major facets of this wider universe of thought, identity and action are interwoven. In this final chapter I began by reiterating some of those arguments and now seek to relate them to broader theoretical models or perspectives in contemporary social science. In this concluding section, I shall attempt to demonstrate a further dimension of the "rootedness" of the phenomena I have analyzed within the conceptual framework of prebendal politics.

The following exercise, drawing primarily on the work of students of Yoruba society and culture, will be largely illustrative in nature. It would take a comprehensive study to explore the degree to which the society and culture of Nigeria's constitutive groups contribute to prebendal politics on a national scale. There is evidently some all-embracing mechanism, suggested by the work of Christopher Clapham and other students of clientelism, by which the pattern of vertical exchange relationships in societies which are largely composed of peasant cultivators generates particular attitudes to the use of state power which are then either transformed by economic changes on a national scale or are preserved by the slow pace or unevenness of those economic processes.

A reader of drafts of earlier chapters of this book suggested that there were parallels to what I was discussing in the struggles within ethnic groups, as reflected in the continuing salience of chieftaincy titles and in the drive by individuals to advance within the ranks of ethnic or other sectional groupings.[40] Such a suggestion was reinforced by the discussion by P. C. Lloyd, in one of his many articles on the Yoruba, of the pattern of conflict between descent groups, with their respective chiefs and elders vying to assert and defend corporate claims to land, chieftaincy titles and jural rights over people.[41] The town of Ibadan in Oyo State seemed to represent a society whose pattern of internal politics was similar to the one which prevailed in the trans-ethnic arena, most likely reflecting its origins as a military encampment during the pre-colonial nineteenth-century Yoruba wars:

> to an extent greater than in any other Yoruba town...the interests of the individual were represented through his descent group. This fact accounts for the heightened competition between descent groups in Ibadan, competition which is even further increased by the struggle for high titled office which itself brings further wealth and personal following to the successful chiefs and their groups.[42]

It appeared, therefore, that the internal political universe of this closely studied Nigerian people reflected some of the features of the wider political process I had outlined.

The appearance in 1983 of J. D. Y. Peel's masterly study of the Ijesha people of the Yoruba, made it unambiguous that the political sociology of Nigeria should be seen as a continuum from communal to trans-communal arenas, rather than as the two separate "publics" Ekeh and others had hypothesized.[43] Contemporary African states had their origins in the arbitrary national boundaries drawn around existing social collectivities by the imperial powers. These encapsulated societies expanded or contracted, aggregated or underwent fission, all the while maintaining or altering a dynamic balance between the interest-advancing practices of their inhabitants and their normative imperatives and conciliar institutions. In other words, when we peer within the socio-political universe of certain Nigerian peoples, such as the Yoruba, we are likely to find sub-systems of prebendal politics which have long operated in ways that do not leave the political order exhausted and fragmented.

One has only to present some of Peel's contentions about the politics and society of the Ijesha to illustrate the considerable congruence between his mode of analysis and the one advanced in this book:

196

Virtually all Ijesha are interested in what they consider to be 'development' (*idagbasoke*)... Politics, as a collective activity is about securing it, and about managing the distribution of advantages that political success brings between individuals and groups within the community. What is so striking is that, while the material ends of politics are so contemporary, the framework of action within which they are sought show such continuity with the past. The Ijesha have, as it were, chosen to make their history relevant to their politics.[44]

The basis of modern political competition was presaged in the nineteenth-century activities of the Ijesha. The success of states depended on the control of trade routes which generated revenues from the levies imposed. Such revenues "put resources in the hands of leaders who, through redistribution, could ensure the loyalty and increase the size of their following."[45] Competition among rival communities depended on the success of political actors in increasing their following.[46]

Peel describes a highly developed clientelistic system in late nineteenth-century Ilesha. Chiefs had their constituencies which consisted of members of their own lineages or quarters, as well as of subordinate chiefs with their own following.[47] He goes on to speak of a "pyramid of interest groups" maintained, not automatically by customary ties, but by the regular "distribution of patronage."[48] Peel speaks of Ilesha politics as having always involved "two faces": "an 'interior' face, concerned with the allocation of rewards and access within the local system, and an 'exterior' face, concerned with maximizing Ilesha gains from the regional system and latterly, the Nigerian state."[49] Once one views the communal world as an arena of active struggle for self and group advancement, one should expect that these elementary forms of social behavior will not be simply abandoned and entirely new ways of acting acquired for the trans-communal political realm. Peel is able to use explanatory language from the study of party and interest-group politics because the processes he discusses differ in extent but not in kind from those of the wider arena: "The resources of a chief came partly from 'below', from his dependants, and partly from 'above', by virtue of his being an effective titleholder, that is of his having acknowledged dependants."[50] This observation is virtually identical to the explanation of the two-way legitimization and maintenance of prebendal politics in Chapter 5: a public post was "a client-creating resource... it should also be seen that the support of a set of clients can be used to give legitimacy to the pursuit and appropriation of such posts."

An important aspect of the predicament of African states can thus be seen to be the fact that the conduct of public affairs has deep historical and social roots, which reflect a rationality of thought and action which becomes distorted and destructive in the wider political arenas. David Apter made this essential observation quite some time ago using the terminology of the time:

Nepotism, for example, is considered a grave offense in Western bureaucratic practice, yet in African practice providing jobs for the members of one's own family is socially compulsory. It is one of the normal forms of social security and

197

job recruitment in traditional society and one of the crucial elements in the satisfactory maintenance of tribal social structure. When such practices are carried over into the administrative service, they break down into favoritism, corruption, and graft, in a Western-type of bureaucratic setup.[51]

Similarly, Peel discusses the need for Ijesha chiefs to attract resources sufficient to maintain a luxurious life-style and a large household, and also for redistribution to their followers.[52] By the late nineteenth century, he points out, some chiefs had acquired so much money in the form of bags of cowries that a small room in the recesses of their houses had to be set aside as a treasury.[53] Those Nigerian politicians a century later who acquire fabulous houses at home and abroad, private airplanes and large foreign bank accounts, are therefore not exclusively a modern phenomenon. Of course, this argument should not be overdone: one can certainly find quite different sets of practices in the pre-colonial dynamics of other Nigerian peoples. The reason why some of these practices were transferred, in a distorted form, to the contemporary political arena and others left behind, is a question that warrants further and fuller investigation. What I have sought to demonstrate here is that prebendal politics, and especially its major features involving the mobilization of sectional support groups, the exploitation of public office, and the resulting encouragement of corrupt practices, should not be regarded as just a form of social pathology which has emerged in contemporary Africa. Instead, these processes should be seen as embodying a political rationality or logic which is ill-suited to the creation of the national political order that Africans, from the time of their anti-colonial struggles, have seen as indispensable to their rapid social and economic development.

The major political challenge which confronts Africa in the next quarter-century of independent rule is to evolve forms of political order in which history is made relevant to the present in a positive way. As indicated throughout this concluding chapter, such a process is likely to occur less by prescription from above than by the maturing of modern economic and political processes in the towns and villages of African nations. The real test of African governments, from this standpoint, is how much their system of rule facilitates, by creative action as much as by "positive inaction," the forging by their peoples of appropriate norms, modes of action and institutions that will not sacrifice the emergence of an effective political authority for the transient claim to being included among the "democratic" nations of the twentieth century. Consensual politics, governmental efficiency, economic resiliency and public ethics must evolve via a process of dynamic interaction. Such a process requires of political actors and commentators a long view of the contemporary historical period. There are no "quick fixes" for Africa's post-colonial predicament in all its ramifications. This study of the political travails and temporary triumphs of Africa's most populous nation ends, therefore, on a note of moderate optimism. After the completion of the current cycle of political rule by military officers, perhaps some author will have good reason to write of the political triumphs and temporary travails of the Third Republic.

Notes

1. Introduction

1 Alan Cowell, "In Nigerian vote, old leaders come out fighting," *The New York Times*, 3 May 1982, p. 2.
2 Crawford Young, "Patterns of Social Conflict: State, Class, and Ethnicity," *Daedalus*, Vol. III, No. 2 (Spring 1982), p. 92.
3 David Parkin, *The Cultural Definition of Political Response: Lineal Destiny Among the Luo* (London, etc.: Academic Press, 1978), p. 4.
4 Ibid., p. 5.
5 Ibid., p. 2.
6 Abner Cohen, *Two-Dimensional Man: An essay on the anthropology of power and symbolism in complex society* (Berkeley and Los Angeles: University of California Press, 1974), pp. 96–7.
7 Young, "Patterns of Social Conflict," p. 89.
8 Cohen, *Two-Dimensional Man*, p. 96.
9 David Parkin, "Congregational and Interpersonal Ideologies in Political Ethnicity," in Abner Cohen, ed., *Urban Ethnicity* (London: Tavistock Publications, Ltd., 1974), p. 119.
10 Cohen, *Two-Dimensional Man*, p. 87.
11 Parkin, "Congregational and Interpersonal Ideologies," p. 120.
12 Daniel Bell, cited by Young in "Patterns of Social Conflict," p. 93.
13 Young, "Patterns of Social Conflict," p. 85.
14 Douglas Rimmer, "Development in Nigeria: An Overview," in Henry Bienen and V.P. Diejomaoh, ed., *The Political Economy of Income Distribution in Nigeria* (New York and London: Holmes and Meier Publishers, Inc., 1981), pp. 29–87.
15 Ibid., p. 35.
16 Ibid., p. 41
17 Ibid., p. 45.
18 Ibid., p. 46.
19 Ibid., p. 48.
20 Terisa Turner, "Multinational Corporations and the Instability of the Nigerian State," *Review of African Political Economy*, No. 5 (1976), pp. 63–79.
21 Chinua Achebe, *A Man of the People* (New York: Doubleday and Co. Inc., 1969), p. 2.
22 Ibid., p. 11.

2. A democracy that works

1 See, in particular, Robert A. Dahl, *Polyarchy: Participation and Opposition* (New Haven and London: Yale University Press, 1971).

199

2 Ibid., p. 1. This definition refers to Delhi's "ideal" democracy, or what he regards as the "theoretical limit."

3 J. Roland Pennock, *Democratic Political Theory* (Princeton, N. J.: Princeton University Press, 1979), p. 265.

4 Ibid., p. 263.

5 Lane Davis, "The Cost of Realism: Contemporary Restatements of Democracy," in *Apolitical Politics: A Critique of Behavioralism* (New York: Thomas Y. Crowell Co., 1967), p. 187.

6 Dennis G. Sullivan, Robert T. Nakamura and Richard F. Winters, *How America Is Ruled* (New York: John Wiley and Sons, 1980), p. 22.

7 Ibid., pp. 33–8.

8 Ibid., p. 26.

9 Ibid., p. 22.

10 C. B. Macpherson, *The Real World of Democracy* (Oxford: The Clarendon Press, 1966), p. 5.

11 Lane Davis, "The Cost of Realism," p. 186, and Jack L. Walker, "A Critique of the Elitist Theory of Democracy," in *Apolitical Politics*, p. 204.

12 James Madison, "Federalist Paper No. 10," in Charles A. Beard, ed., *The Enduring Federalist* (New York: Doubleday and Co., Inc., 1984), p. 72.

13 Ibid., p. 73.

14 Thomas Hodgkin, "The Relevance of 'Western' Ideas for the New African States," in J. Roland Pennock, ed., *Self-Government in Modernizing Nations* (Englewood Cliffs, N. J.: Prentice Hall, Inc., 1964), p. 71.

15 Ibid.

16 Ibid., pp. 71–2.

17 W. Arthur Lewis, *Politics in West Africa* (Toronto and New York: Oxford University Press 1965), p. 65.

18 Julius Nyerere, "Democracy and the Party System," in *Freedom and Unity: A Selection of Writings and Speeches, 1952–65* (Dar es Salaam, etc.: Oxford University Press, 1966), p. 196.

19 Cited in Benn and Peters, *Social Principles and the Democratic State* (London: Allen and Unwin, Ltd., 1959), pp. 333–4.

20 J. A. Schumpeter, *Capitalism, Socialism and Democracy* (New York: Harper and Brothers, 1942), p. 269.

21 Max Weber, "Bureaucracy," in H. H. Gerth and C. Wright Mills, ed. and trans., *From Max Weber: Essays in Sociology* (London: Routledge and Kegan Paul, Ltd., 1948), pp. 225–6.

22 *Apolitical Politics*, passim.

23 Robert A. Dahl, *Polyarchy: Participation and Opposition* (New Haven and London: Yale University Press, 1973), p. 42.

24 Richard L. Sklar, "The Nature of Class Domination in Africa," *Journal of Modern African Studies*, 17, 4 (1979), p. 541. The restoration of competitive party politics in Senegal in 1983 represents a significant breakthrough in francophone Africa. However, the coups of December 1981 and December 1983 in Ghana and Nigeria keep the "democratic" picture in Africa as bleak as ever.

25 Schumpeter, *Capitalism, Socialism and Democracy*, pp. 265–8.

26 Juan Linz, "The Future of an Authoritarian Situation or the Institutionalization of an Authoritarian Regime: The Case of Brazil," in Alfred Stepan, ed., *Authoritarian Brazil: Origins, Policies and Future* (New Haven and London: Yale University Press, 1973). Linz, therefore, in considering the degree of adequacy of various legitimacy formulas, points out that "in the modern world, all legitimacy formulas refer in some way to the authority coming from the *demos*, the people." Ibid., p. 240.

27 Ibid., p. 251.

28 Ibid., p. 253. For the notion of institutionalization, see Samuel P. Huntington's *Political Order in Changing Societies* (New Haven and London: Yale University Press, 1968), *passim*.

29 Linz, "The Future of an Authoritarian Situation..." p. 251.
30 Ibid., pp. 251–2.
31 Dahl, *Polyarchy: Participation and Opposition*, pp. 57, 60.
32 Macpherson, *The Real World of Democracy*, pp. 7–9, 35–45. See also Macpherson's *The Political Theory of Possessive Individualism: Hobbes to Locke* (Oxford: The Clarendon Press, 1962), and *Democratic Theory: Essays in Retrieval* (Oxford: The Clarendon Press, 1973).
33 Macpherson, *The Real World of Democracy*, p. 9. Dahl similarly recognizes that "polyarchy" is unlikely to persist in the contrary situation, "a highly centralized economy." Dahl, *Polyarchy: Participation and Opposition*, p. 61.
34 Macpherson, *The Real World of Democracy*, p. 10.
35 Arend Lijphart, *Democracy in Plural Societies: A Comparative Exploration* (New Haven and London: Yale University Press, 1977), p. 1. The notion of a "plural society" will be discussed in Chapter 3.
36 Ibid., p. 3. Indeed, the subtitle of that section of his book is entitled "A Challenge to Democratic Pessimists."
37 Ibid., p. 18. For a discussion of the concern expressed by M. G. Smith, see Ian Lustick, "Stability in Deeply Divided Societies: Consociationalism versus Control," *World Politics*, Vol. 31, No. 3 (April 1979), pp. 325–44.
38 Granville Austen, *The Indian Constitution: Cornerstone of a Nation* (Oxford and Bombay: Oxford University Press, 1966), p. 308.
39 Lewis, *Politics in West Africa*, pp. 89–90.
40 Robert A. Dahl, ed., *Regimes and Oppositions* (New Haven and London: Yale University Press, 1973), p. 23.
41 Huntington, *Political Order in Changing Societies*, p. 194.
42 Ibid., p. 196.
43 Ibid., p. 243.
44 Ibid., p. 198.
45 Ibid.
46 These are indeed some of the key features of "institutionalization."
47 Samuel P. Huntington and Joan M. Nelson, *No Easy Choice: Political Participation in Developing Societies* (Cambridge: Harvard University Press, 1976), p. 26.
48 Huntington, *Political Order in Changing Societies*, p. 261.
49 Ibid.
50 John Locke, *The Second Treatise of Government: An Essay Concerning the True Original, Extent and End of Civil Government* (New York: The Liberal Press, Inc., 1952), p. 55.
51 Jean Jacques Rousseau, *The Social Contract*, trans. G.-D. H. Cole (New York: E. P. Dutton and Co., Inc., 1950), p. 106.
52 Schumpeter, *Capitalism, Socialism and Democracy*, p. 272.
53 James Mill, *An Essay on Government* (Indianapolis and New York: The Bobbs-Merrill Company, Inc., 1955).
54 Benn and Peters, *Social Principles and the Democratic State*, p. 348. A pertinent comment by these authors is that Madison "glimpsed...the way in which a democratic government would operate in a 'plural' society."
55 Madison, "Federalist Paper No. 10," *The Enduring Federalist*, p. 74.
56 John C. Calhoun, *A Disquisition on Government* (New York: The Liberal Arts Press, Inc., 1953), p. 21.
57 Ibid., p. 20.
58 Lewis, *Politics in West Africa*, passim.
59 Ibid., pp. 65–6.
60 Ibid., p. 74.
61 Ibid., p. 76.
62 Ibid., p. 67.

63 Ibid., p. 68.
64 Ibid., pp. 83–4.
65 Apter's comments were made in his book on Uganda, *The Political Kingdom in Uganda: A Study in Bureaucratic Nationalism* (Princeton: Princeton University Press, 1961), pp. 24–5. Apter's cursory remarks, however, contain statements which are perceptive as well as others that are inaccurate regarding the pre-independence and transitional coalition government in Nigeria.
66 One of the assumptions that the primary consociational theorist, Arend Lijphart, seeks to dislodge is that "plural" societies and their special problems are to be found in the "Third World," while "First World" societies are generally more homogeneous. Indeed, he defines consociational democracies as "fragmented but stable democracies" – *Democracy in Plural Societies*, p. 142, and "Consociational Democracy," *World Politics*, Vol. 21, No. 2 (January 1969), p. 211. For a useful collection of articles, see K. D. McRae, *Consociational Democracy: Political Accommodation in Segmented Societies* (Toronto: McClelland and Stewart Ltd., 1974).
67 Cited in Eric A. Nordlinger, *Conflict Regulation in Divided Societies*, Occasional Papers in International Affairs, No. 29 (Cambridge, Mass.: Center for International Affairs, 1972), p. 34.
68 Ibid., p. 94. See, for reference to a similar argument in the work of Gabriel Almond, Hans Daalder, "The Consociational Democracy Theme," *World Politics*, Vol. 26, No. 4 (July 1964), pp. 606–7.
69 Lijphart, "Typologies of Democratic Systems," *Comparative Political Studies*, Vol. 1, No. 1 (1968), p. 28.
70 Nordlinger, *Conflict Regulation in Divided Societies*, p. 22.
71 Ibid., p. 33. This is a much stronger statement than the other theorists are prepared to make, since the task of conflict regulation (Nordlinger's concern) does not necessarily require the search for a democratic system.
72 Lijphart, "Typologies of Democratic Systems," p. 28. Elsewhere Lijphart contends that consociationalism "does not deviate much from normative democratic theory." He does not elaborate on this apparent distinction between democratic theory on the one hand and normative and empirical models of democracy on the other.
73 Nordlinger, *Conflict Regulation in Divided Societies*, pp. 21–9. Briefly, proportionality refers to the distribution of elected and appointive government positions as well as to the allocation of public resources. Depoliticization would be applied to issues that impinge on the values and interests of particular segments. Unilateral concessions take place from the stronger to the weaker groups.
74 Lijphart, *Democracy in Plural Societies*, p. 28.
75 Ibid., p. 25.
76 Lijphart, "Consociational Democracy," p. 26.
77 Hans Daalder, "On Building Consociational Nations: The Cases of the Netherlands and Switzerland," *International Social Science Journal*, Vol. 23, No. 3 (1971), p. 355.
78 Nordlinger, *Conflict Regulation in Divided Societies*, p. 73.
79 Daalder, "On Building Consociational Nations," *passim*.
80 Daalder, "The Consociational Democracy Theme," p. 618. For a review of some of these criticisms and suggestions for adjusting the theory to avoid them, see Jürg Steiner, "The Consociational Theory and Beyond: Review Article," *Comparative Politics*, Vol. 13, No. 3 (1981), pp. 339–54.
81 Brian Barry, "Political Accommodation and Consociational Democracy: Review Article," *British Journal of Political Science*, 5, 4 (1975), p. 501. Barry's seemingly damaging critique is itself open to some criticism. See Jürg Steiner, "The Consociational Theory and Beyond," p. 340, and Arend Lijphart, "Consociational Politics: Problems and Prospects," *Comparative Politics*, Vol. 13, No. 3 (1981), p. 357.

82 Lijphart, "Consociational Democracy," p. 216.
83 Lijphart, *Democracy in Plural Societies*, p. 163. One of the least convincing arguments in Nordlinger's work is his rejection of federalism as a "conflict-regulating practice" – *Conflict Regulation in Divided Societies*, pp. 30–3.
84 Barry, "Political Accommodation and Consociational Democracy," p. 502.
85 Lijphart, *Democracy in Plural Societies*, p. 48.
86 Ibid., p. 45.
87 Nordlinger, *Conflict Regulation in Divided Societies*, p. 64.
88 Daalder, "On Building Consociational Nations," p. 369.
89 Lijphart, *Democracy in Plural Societies*, p. 51. It is often remarked that contemporary Nigeria is a country for which consociational theory might have some relevance, yet such comments are usually quite fleeting. See Steiner, "The Consociational Theory and Beyond," p. 344, and Lijphart, "Consociational Theory: Problems and Prospects," p. 357.

3. Dilemmas of Nigerian democracy

1 Huntington and Nelson, *No Easy Choice: Political Participation in Developing Societies*, p. 166. I can think of no compelling reason why Nigeria should be such an exception. An unintended development might shift a country back onto a democratic path (e.g., Greece after the 1974 conflict with Turkey in Cyprus) but this still leaves open the question of why that path and not another.
2 Linz, "The Future of an Authoritarian Situation," p. 246.
3 Dahl, Introduction to *Regimes and Oppositions*, p. 15.
4 Ibid., p. 18.
5 For a relevant discussion, see the review article by Paul R. Brass, "Class, Ethnic Group and Party in Indian Politics," *World Politics*, Vol. 33, No. 3 (April 1981), pp. 449–67. Brass is impatient with scholars who seek to examine Indian politics through the prism of a model of democracy, and rejects using the notion of participation "as an ethic – rather than as most Indian voters probably see it, namely, as a way of pursuing their personal and group interests" (p. 461). I do not, however, regard these two perspectives as mutually exclusive. Central to this study will be the interplay between models of democracy and the pursuit of personal and group interests by Nigerians.
6 K. W. J. Post and Michael Vickers, *Structure and Conflict in Nigeria, 1960–1966* (London: Heinemann, 1973), p. 1.
7 K. W. J. Post, "The National Council of Nigeria and The Cameroons, The decision of December 1959," in John P. Mackintosh, ed., *Nigerian Government and Politics* (London: George Allen and Unwin, Ltd., 1966), p. 406.
8 "NCNC" stood for the National Convention of Nigerian Citizens. Before 1961, it was the National Council of Nigeria and the Cameroons.
9 It was the lot of a colorful politician in the former Western Region, Chief Fani-Kayode, to convey the fine cynicism of Nigerian politics: "Whether you vote for us or not, we will remain in power." Mackintosh, *Nigerian Government and Politics*, p. 42.
10 A. H. M. Kirk-Greene, *Crisis and Conflict in Nigeria: A Documentary Sourcebook 1966–1969*, Vol. 1 (London: Oxford University Press, 1971), p. 23.
11 Ibid.
12 It is difficult to state this phenomenon in a way that does not sound trite or even projected. Yet it is fundamental to the pattern of socio-political behavior in Nigeria as will be discussed later.
13 From J. S. Furnivall's classic *Colonial Policy and Practice* (1948), cited in Leo Kuper, "Plural Societies: Perspectives and Problems," in Leo Kuper and M. G. Smith, *Pluralism in Africa* (Berkeley and Los Angeles: University of California Press, 1969), pp. 10–11. The following summary of the main positions in this debate are drawn directly from Kuper's chapter.

14 Ibid., p. 13.
15 Ibid. An important theme of Nigerian politics has been the unwillingness of cultural sections to accept just this "subordinate" status relative to others.
16 Obafemi Awolowo, *Path to Nigerian Freedom* (London: Faber, 1947), p. 47.
17 In 1968, he argued on the basis of his own detailed criteria the feasibility of creating 17 states in the near future (Nigeria had been declared the previous year, by decree of the Gowon military government, to have 12 states, in place of the four regions of 1963–6). In the future, Awolowo saw as many as 51 states being desirable for Nigeria. Since 1976, again by military decree, the Federation has been divided into 19 states, with great pressure still being exerted for the creation of several more. See Awolowo's *The People's Republic* (Ibadan: Oxford University Press, 1968), pp. 235–53.
18 The Action Group never dominated its region, however, as much as the two other major parties did theirs.
19 The third major party up to 1966, along with the Action Group and the NCNC, was the Northern People's Congress (NPC).
20 The overlap between ideology and instrumental politics in Nigeria is one of the more intractable problems encountered in any attempt to apply the basic consociational model. This model usually requires the separating and even downplaying of ideological concerns.
21 For a full discussion of these stages, see Richard L. Sklar, *Nigerian Political Parties: Power in an Emergent Nation* (Princeton: Princeton University Press, 1963).
22 According to James Coleman, one of the important ways in which the Action Group differed from other Nigerian political organizations was in the collegial nature of its leadership "and this at Awolowo's insistence." See "The Ibo and Yoruba Strands in Nigerian Nationalism," in *Nigeria: Modernization and the Politics of Communalism* (East Lansing: Michigan State University Press, 1971), p. 87. On the overruling of Awolowo by his colleagues on this occasion, see J. P. Mackintosh, "The Action Group: The Crisis of 1962 and its Aftermath," in *Nigerian Government and Politics*, p. 439.
23 Mackintosh, "The Action Group: The Crisis of 1962," p. 442.
24 Ibid., p. 445.
25 For analyses of the election results, see Keith Panter-Brick, "Nigeria: The 1979 Elections," *Afrika Spectrum*, 14, 3 (1979), and Richard A. Joseph, "Democratization under Military Tutelage: Crisis and Consensus in the Nigerian 1979 Elections," *Comparative Politics*, Vol. 14, No. 1 (1981). See also the special volume on Nigeria edited by C. S. Whitaker, *Issue*, Vol. 11, Nos. 1/2 (1981).
26 NEPU, the Northern Elements Progressive Union, was the chief opposition party in Northern Nigeria during the pre-military period.
27 Obafemi Awolowo, "Advice to new Federal Government," *Daily Sketch* (Ibadan, Nigeria), 21 August 1975, p. 3. He also counselled postponing the introduction of a new revenue allocation formula, another basic item of governmental business which in Nigeria can never be undertaken without provoking sharp conflicts.
28 Ibid.
29 These structures were reinstated after the military coup of 31 December 1983. The Supreme Military Council (SMC) was the sovereign body in the military government, with the FEC serving as a subordinate cabinet with wide decision-making powers. After the palace coup of August 1985, the SMC became the Armed Forces Ruling Council and the FEC the Council of Ministers.
30 With the relinquishing of political authority by the military in 1979, the major Nigerian political figures such as Chief Awolowo, Malam Aminu Kano and Alhaji Shehu Shagari (elected President in 1979) reverted to their former political affiliations.
31 Mackintosh, *Nigerian Government and Politics*, pp. 99–100.
32 Richard L. Sklar, "Nigerian Politics: The Ordeal of Chief Awolowo, 1960–65," in Gwendolyn M. Carter, ed., *Politics in Africa: Seven Cases* (New York: Harcourt, Brace and

World, Inc.), pp. 119–66. On NEPU and the NPC, see B. J. Dudley, *Parties and Politics in Northern Nigeria* (London: Frank Cass, 1968).

33 This was Alhaji Waziri Ibrahim, leader of the Great Nigerian People's Party (GNPP). His slogan soon appeared trite and even naive as the political campaign became increasingly acrimonious.

34 Mackintosh, "Nigerian Democracy," in *Nigerian Government and Politics*, p. 620.

35 Ibid.

36 Of course, Nigerian advocates of a one-party state do rely as elsewhere on the argument that it is the only way to have politics without strife in their country.

37 Post and Vickers, *Structure and Conflict in Nigeria, passim.*

38 Ibid., p. 64.

39 Mackintosh, *Nigerian Government and Politics*, p. 105.

40 B. J. Dudley, *Instability and Political Order: Politics and Crisis in Nigeria* (Ibadan: Ibadan University Press, 1973), p. 35.

41 Ibid., p. 50.

42 *Report of the Constitution Drafting Committee Containing the Draft Constitution*, Volume I (Lagos: Federal Ministry of Information, 1976), p. xli.

43 Ibid., p. xli.

44 Ibid., p. xlii. "Public accountability" features prominently in Nigerian political discourse, and is the element I have indicated is so absent in the writing of the consociationalists. It has the special sense in Nigeria of referring to political corruption, as well as the more general democratic sense of government officials being accountable representatives of the community.

45 Ibid.

46 These hopes did turn out, in the light of the shortcomings of the Second Republic and its eventual demise, to have been "pious" ones. (I feel it appropriate to leave my original wording here.)

4. Politics in a multi-ethnic society

1 *Report of the Constitution Drafting Committee*, Volume I, pp. viii–x.

2 Ibid., p. viii, and *The Constitution of the Federal Republic of Nigeria 1979* (Lagos: Federal Ministry of Information, 1979), p. 8.

3 See Gabriel A. Almond and Sidney Verba, *The Civic Culture: Political Attitudes and Democracy in Five Nations* (Princeton: Princeton University Press, 1963); Samuel H. Beer *et al.*, *Patterns of Government: The Major Political Systems of Europe* (New York: Random House, 1958); and Harry Eckstein, *Division and Cohesion in Democracy: A Study of Norway* (Princeton: Princeton University Press, 1966).

4 For detailed discussions, see the works cited in Chapter 3, note 25, and Richard A. Joseph, "Political Parties and Ideology in Nigeria," *Review of African Political Economy*, 13 (1979).

5 The full names of the parties were: the Great Nigerian People's Party (GNPP), the National Party of Nigeria (NPN), the Nigerian People's Party (NPP), the People's Redemption Party (PRP), and the Unity Party of Nigeria (UPN).

6 Joseph, "Political Parties and Ideology in Nigeria," p. 84.

7 Richard A. Joseph, "The Ethnic Trap: Notes on the Nigerian Campaign and Elections, 1978–79," *Issue*, Vol. 11, Nos. 1/2 (1981), p. 20. An interesting topic for further inquiry concerns the changes the UPN and other opposition parties introduced in 1983 in the light of the success of the NPN's approach to recruitment.

8 Alvin Rabushka and Kenneth A. Shepsle, *Politics in Plural Societies: A Theory of Democratic Instability* (Columbus, Ohio: Charles E. Merrill Publishing Co., 1972), pp. 20, 21.

9 Steiner, "The Consociational Theory and Beyond," p. 340.

10 Ibid., p. 341.

11 Frederick Barth, *Ethnic Groups and Boundaries: The Social Organization of Culture Difference* (Boston: Little, Brown and Co., 1969), p. 17.

12 Elliot Skinner, "Competition within Ethnic Systems in Africa," in Leo A. Despres, ed., *Ethnicity and Resource Competition in Plural Societies* (The Hague and Paris: Mouton Publishers, 1975), p. 152.

13 Cited in M. G. Smith, "Institutional and Political Conditions of Pluralism," *Pluralism in Africa*, p. 29.

14 Ibid. pp. 33, 36. The examples Smith has in mind include Rwanda-Burundi, South Africa and, to a certain extent, the Fulani emirates in northern Nigeria.

15 Leo Kuper, "Ethnic and Racial Pluralism: Some Aspects of Polarization and Depluralization," *Pluralism in Africa*, p. 14.

16 Ibid., p. 18.

17 Since political leaders and political formations from the North have dominated national politics in much of the modern era, opposition to that domination is often phrased in terms of cultural domination in a plural society.

18 *Report of the Constitution Drafting Committee*, pp. viii, ix.

19 After three decades of careful presentation of this point, it is with some exasperation that one can still read statements such as the following in the general political science literature: "Civil wars in the Congo and Nigeria illustrate the difficulties that tribal diversity poses for orderly government" (Rabushka and Shepsle, *Politics in Plural Societies*, p. 10). "Tribal diversity" does not account for the civil wars mentioned, nor does it explain "disorderly government" in Africa generally. The point is not simply to recognize the instances of cultural diversity but to explain why such diversity may or may not become politically salient.

20 For a strong presentation of the relevant arguments, see Nelson Kasfir, "Explaining Ethnic Political Participation," *World Politics*, Vol. 31, No. 3 (April 1979), pp. 345–64, as well as his book, *The Shrinking Political Arena: Participation and Ethnicity in African Politics with a Case Study of Uganda* (Berkeley and Los Angeles: University of California Press, 1976).

21 The classic statement of these processes remains Barth, *Ethnic Groups and Boundaries*. For a highly informed survey of the interaction between ethnicity, class and politics, see Okwudiba Nnoli, *Ethnic Politics in Nigeria* (Enugu: Fourth Dimension Publishers, 1978).

22 This process has gained even greater visibility in contemporary Nigeria with the pressure to carve new states out of existing ones, or regroup peoples from neighboring states to create new entities. The basic justification for such demands remains "cultural similarity," a term which could be defined loosely or rigidly according to the circumstances.

23 Richard Sklar, "Political Science and National Integration – A Radical Approach," *Journal of Modern African Studies*, Vol. 5, No. 1 (1967), p. 6.

24 Ibid., and *Nigerian Political Parties, passim.*

25 Richard Sklar, "Contradictions in the Nigerian Political System," *Journal of Modern African Studies*, Vol. 3, No. 2 (August 1965), p. 203.

26 "Modernization and the Politics of Communalism: A Theoretical Perspective," in Melson and Wolpe, ed., *Nigeria: Modernization and the Politics of Communalism* (East Lansing, Michigan: Michigan State University Press, 1971), pp. 1–38. Both these authors, and Richard Sklar, often use the term "communalism" to refer to, or include, ethnicity.

27 Ibid., p. 2 and *passim.*

28 Ibid., pp. 25, 29.

29 Ibid., p. 19. For a relevant set of observations by Crawford Young regarding the celebratory nature of elections in Africa which encourages the resort to cultural symbols, see *The Politics of Cultural Pluralism* (Madison, Wisconsin: University of Wisconsin Press, 1976), p. 516.

30 Skinner, "Competition within Ethnic Systems in Africa," p. 131.

31 Ibid.

32 Richard Sklar makes much of this expectation in his resort to Tönnies' distinction between

Gemeinschaft (community) and *Gesellshaft* (society), with the latter applied to class-based associations. See *Nigerian Political Parties*, pp. 474–7.

33 On the cultural dimension of social classes, see Barth's comment based on Edmund Leach, *Ethnic Groups and Boundaries*, p. 27, and a review article by Richard Cobb in *The New York Review of Books*, Vol. 28, No. 20 (1980).

34 Young, *The Politics of Cultural Pluralism*, p. 277.

35 For an interesting parallel to the usual writings on such group oppositions in the urban context, see the discussion of conflicts within an agricultural community in Onigu Otite, "Resource Competition and Inter-Ethnic Relations in Nigeria," in Despres, *Ethnicity and Resource Competition in Plural Societies*, pp. 119–30.

36 Barth, *Ethnic Groups and Boundaries*, p. 17.

37 Kirk-Greene, *Crisis and Conflict in Nigeria*, Vol. 1, p. 5.

38 Pierre L. van den Berghe, *Power and Privilege in an African University* (London: Routledge and Kegan Paul, 1973), pp. 222, 252. Van den Berghe coined a fictitious name for the university in his study, but the disguise was left very thin.

39 Young, *The Politics of Cultural Pluralism*, p. 464. One of the best introductions to the contribution of urbanization to ethnicity is Immanuel Wallerstein, "Ethnicity and National Integration in West Africa," in P. L. van den Berghe, *Africa: Social Problems of Change and Conflict* (San Francisco: Chandler Publishing Co., 1965).

40 Skinner, "Competition within Ethnic Systems in Africa," p. 131. A classic case-study of cultural consolidation and the forging of an advantageous group strategy is Abner Cohen's examination of the Hausa community in Ibadan, Nigeria: *Custom and Politics in Urban Africa* (London: Routledge and Kegan Paul, 1969).

41 Barth, *Ethnic Groups and Boundaries*, p. 16.

42 B. J. Dudley, *Instability and Political Order: Politics and Crisis in Nigeria* (Ibadan: University of Ibadan Press, 1973), pp. 41, 51. This argument is also taken up by Peter Ekeh in "Colonialism and the Two Publics in Africa: A Theoretical Statement," *Comparative Studies in Society and History*, Vol. 17, No. 1 (January 1975). Ekeh's theoretical framework will be discussed in the concluding chapter.

43 Cited in van den Berghe, *Power and Privilege in an African University*, p. 224. The fact that the last four scholars cited wrote primarily with the University of Ibadan in mind reflects the "premier" status of that university within Nigeria. Several of these arguments could certainly be applied more generally today to Nigeria's other universities.

44 R. Cohen, *Labour and Politics in Nigeria* (London: Heinemann, 1974), p. 28.

45 Post and Vickers, *Structure and Conflict in Nigeria*, pp. 58, 59.

46 Richard A. Joseph, "Political Parties and Ideology in Nigeria," p. 90.

47 Nelson Kasfir, personal communication.

48 Mancur Olson, *The Logic of Collective Action* (Cambridge: Harvard University Press, 1971), p. 126.

5. Clientelism and prebendal politics

1 Weber, "Bureaucracy," in Gerth and Wright Mills, *From Max Weber: Essays in Sociology*, p. 207.

2 The term *oga* in Yoruba refers to a male adult. It takes on a special sense of respect and dependence when used to reflect a patron-client tie. Similarly, in common parlance, "god-fatherism" is the process by which an individual establishes links with a senior within a given institutional hierarchy in the expectation of favored treatment. Even more evocative is the use of such pidgin English terms as "chop," meaning to eat when applied to the sharing of the "national cake." The military government was not amused when a group of individuals

sought registration as a political party in late 1978 with the name of the "I Chop You Chop Party."

3 For a full discussion of these state-provided instruments, see Sayre P. Schatz, *Nigerian Capitalism* (Berkeley and Los Angeles: University of California Press, 1977), *passim*.

4 James C. Scott, "Patron-Client Politics and Political Change in Southeast Asia," *American Political Science Review*, 66 (1972), p. 92.

5 Peter Flynn, "Class, Clientelism, and Coercion: Some Mechanisms of Internal Dependency and Control," *Journal of Commonwealth and Comparative Politics*, 12, 2 (July 1974), p. 133.

6 Alex Weingrod, "Patrons, Patronage and Political Parties," *Comparative Studies in Society and History*, 10 (July 1978), p. 379. For a useful collection which includes this and other pertinent essays, see Steffen W. Schmidt *et al.*, *Friends, Followers, and Factions: A Reader in Political Clientelism* (Berkeley and Los Angeles: University of California Press, 1977).

7 René Lemarchand, "Political Clientelism and Ethnicity in Tropical Africa: Competing Solidarities in Nation-Building," *American Political Science Review*, 66, 1 (1972), p. 76.

8 Ibid., p. 76.

9 C. S. Whitaker, *The Politics of Tradition: Continuity and Change in Northern Nigeria, 1946–1966* (Princeton: Princeton University Press, 1970).

10 Lemarchand, "Political Clientelism and Ethnicity," p. 72.

11 Scott, "Patron-Client Politics and Political Change," p. 91. For an application of such an argument to contemporary Africa, see Richard Sandbrook, "Patrons, Clients, and Factions: New Dimensions of Conflict Analysis in Africa," *Canadian Journal of Political Science*, 5, 1 (1972), p. 104.

12 Flynn, "Class, Clientelism, and Coercion," pp. 42, 46.

13 Lemarchand, "Comparative Political Clientelism: Structure, Process, and Optic," in S. N. Eisenstadt and René Lemarchand, *Political Clientelism, Patronage and Development* (Beverly Hills and London: Sage Publications, 1981), p. 10.

14 Sydel Silverman, "Patronage as Myth," in Ernest Gellner and John Waterbury, ed., *Patrons and Clients in Mediterranean Societies* (London: Gerald Duckworth and Co., Ltd., 1977), p. 8.

15 Judith Chubb, "The Social Bases of an Urban Political Machine: The Christian Democratic Party in Palermo," in *Political Clientelism, Patronage and Development*, p. 71.

16 Lemarchand, "Political Clientelism and Ethnicity," p. 83.

17 Chubb, "The Social Bases of an Urban Political Machine," p. 81.

18 Sandbrook, "Patrons, Clients and Factions," p. 106.

19 See Judith Chubb's acknowledgement in "The Social Bases of an Urban Political Machine," p. 58.

20 Scott, "Patron-Client Politics and Political Change," p. 99*n*.

21 Ibid., p. 97. Scott also goes on to claim that patron-client ties are different from what he calls the "categorical ties" of ethnicity, religion and caste.

22 Sandbrook, "Patrons, Clients and Factions," p. 111.

23 Lemarchand, "Political Clientelism and Ethnicity," p. 70.

24 Chubb, "The Social Bases of an Urban Political Machine," p. 66.

25 Lemarchand, "Comparative Political Clientelism," p. 22.

26 See Crawford Young's discussion of these intra- and inter-regional ethnic clientage relationships; *The Politics of Cultural Pluralism*, p. 303.

27 Based on Talcott Parsons, ed., *Max Weber: The Theory of Social and Economic Organization* (London: Collier-Macmillan, Ltd., 1964), pp. 342–5.

28 Ibid., pp. 349, 347.

29 Ibid., p. 351.

30 Ibid., pp. 349–50.

31 See Chapter 3, note 9.

32 Robin Theobald, "Patrimonialism," *World Politics*, Vol. 34, No. 4 (July 1982), pp. 248–59.

33 H. G. Gadamer's cogent phrase, cited by Lemarchand, in *Political Clientelism, Patronage and Development*, p. 10.
34 *Sunday Times* (Lagos), June 1977.
35 Lemarchand, "Political Clientelism and Ethnicity," p. 73.
36 Ibid., p. 85.
37 Sandbrook, "Patrons, Clients and Factions," p. 108. For a fuller discussion of this point, see Scott, "Patron-Client Politics and Political Change," pp. 101–3.
38 Scott, "Patron-Client Politics and Political Change," p. 96*n*.
39 John Waterbury, "An attempt to put patrons and clients in their place," *Patrons and Clients in Mediterranean Societies*, p. 336.
40 Ibid., p. 337.

6. Military rule and economic statism

1 Amos Perlmutter, "The Comparative Analysis of Military Regimes: Formations, Aspirations, and Achievement," *World Politics*, 33, No. 1 (October 1980), p. 99. I will be extending this idea to include the civil bureaucracy, as well as the military, as discussed by Perlmutter.
2 For full discussions of these points – the ethnic composition of the army and especially the pivotal role played by Nigerian military officers from the Christianized Middle Belt (i.e., lower North) – see Robin Luckham, *The Nigerian Military: A Sociological Analysis of Authority and Revolt, 1960–67* (Cambridge: Cambridge University Press, 1971); B. J. Dudley, *Instability and Political Order* (Ibadan: Ibadan University Press, 1973); and John J. Stremlau, *The International Politics of the Nigerian Civil War, 1967–1970* (Princeton: Princeton University Press, 1977). Typical of the Nigerian higher civil servants, to whom much credit must be given for seeing the country through the civil war crisis and then managing the burgeoning state apparatus and post-war economy, is Allison Ayida of Bendel State (former Mid-West). Ayida served as Permanent Secretary in each of the economic ministries, as a key participant in wartime diplomatic meetings, and then as Secretary to the Federal Military Government and Head of the Public Service under both Gowon and his successor Murtala.
3 David M. Jemibewon, *A Combatant in Government* (Ibadan, Nigeria: Heinemann Educational Books, Ltd., 1978), pp. 91–2.
4 The words quoted again here are from Haroun Adamu's article (*Sunday Times* (Lagos), June 1977).
5 A state which was meant fully to satisfy such demands would exactly duplicate civil society and thus would be no state at all.
6 B. J. Dudley, "The Military and Development," *The Nigerian Journal of Economic and Social Studies*, 13, No. 2 (July 1971), p. 171.
7 Cited in S. K. Panter-Brick, "From Military Rule to Civil War," p. 82.
8 Jemibewon, *A Combatant in Government*, p. 12.
9 Kirk-Greene, *Crisis and Conflict in Nigeria*, Vol. 1, p. 284.
10 Ibid., p. 455.
11 Jemibewon, *A Combatant in Government*, p. 31. Nelson Kasfir points out that some of the governors – for example, Joseph Gomwalk of Benue-Plateau State – who were the targets persistent and often substantiated accusations, "had appeared incorruptible when originally appointed. But the temptations of illicit wealth sooner or later became too much to resist." "Soldiers as Policymakers in Nigeria," *American Universities Field Staff, West African Series*, 17, 3 (October 1977).
12 Ibid.
13 Terisa Turner, "Multinational Corporations and the Instability of the Nigerian State," *Review of African Political Economy*, No. 5 (1976), p. 76.

14 Adapted from Tom Forrest, "State Capital in Nigeria," table 4, p. 9. Paper presented at the Conference on "The African Bourgeoisie: The Development of Capitalism in Nigeria, Kenya and the Ivory Coast," 2–4 December 1980, Dakar, Senegal, sponsored by the Social Science Research Council and the American Council of Learned Societies.

15 It also meant that individuals would be encouraged to leave their occupations, whether as civil servants or even junior professionals, and become "contractors," since such an occupation was a uniquely political one involving contacts within the state bureaucracy and the capacity to delegate the actual filling of the contracts to subcontractors.

16 The euphoric attitude was reflected in government statements of the day, including the text of the Third National Development Plan (1975–80): "there will be no savings and foreign exchange constraints during the Third Plan period and beyond." Cited in Joseph, "Affluence and Underdevelopment: The Nigerian Experience," p. 236. Two years before the end of the "Third Plan period," the Nigerian government was forced to negotiate large Eurodollar loans to compensate for the rapid drop in reserves.

17 These comments are based on interviews with high officials of the government, military and civil. The sense of the argument here should not be overlooked: Obasanjo was both attentive to the relative weight of political opinion in the country, while being able to follow his own line of action within the military government once he had decided upon it.

18 The relative weight assigned to each of these initial concerns can be seen in the National Day Broadcast of Head-of-State Murtala Muhammed on 1 October 1975 (and reprinted in Nigerian newspapers the following day), and his opening address to the CDC, 18 October 1975. See *Report of the Constitution Drafting Committee*, Vol. I, pp. xli–xliii.

19 Excerpts from the Presidential Address to the annual conference of the Nigerian Political Science Association, 1981, printed in *West Africa*, 25 May 1981, pp. 1162–3. By using the term "overpoliticisation," Ake leaves himself open to the charge of rephrasing Huntington's ideas on praetorian societies and the need for "depoliticisation" in such societies. What I find most perceptive in Ake's argument is that "the desperate struggle to win control of state power" – which I have argued characterizes modern Nigeria – underwent a "stifled" intensification with the expansion of the state's capacity during the military era, only to be unleashed in the political arena with the return of the soldiers to the barracks.

20 *Report of the CDC*, Vol. I, p. xli.

21 See Obasanjo's Inaugural Address at the National Institute for Policy and Strategic Studies, *New Nigerian* (6 September 1979).

22 P. Chiedo Asiodu (one of the most powerful, and equally controversial, civil servants during the period of military rule) has defined the term "higher civil service" as referring to "the most senior corps of administrative and professional officers." Among them he includes "permanent secretaries, deputy permanent secretaries and administrative officers of equivalent grade, directors of professional departments and their deputies." Also, from the numerous government statutory bodies and corporations, he adds the "chief executives, general managers and assistant general managers." "The Civil Service: an insider's view," in O. Oyediran, ed., *Nigerian Government and Politics under Military Rule* (London and Lagos: Macmillan, 1979), p. 75.

23 The respective titles in Nigeria were Permanent Secretary, and the Head of Service and Secretary to the Federal Military Government.

24 In the case of Britain, the topmost position was held by the Joint Permanent Secretary of the Treasury, whereas in colonial Nigeria it was the Chief Secretary, either in the Regions or the capital. Such a "monocratic type," where the "administration came to an apex under a single chief or head," represented for Max Weber "the culmination of bureaucratic development." David Beetham, *Max Weber and the Theory of Modern Politics* (London: George Allen & Unwin, Ltd., 1974), p. 69.

25 See Dudley, *Instability and Political Order*, pp. 119–25. Interestingly, the coup leader, Major Nzeogwu, who deferred to his superior Ironsi, had quickly set up an executive council of top

civil servants in the Northern Region after seizing power there. See Stephen O. Olugbemi, "The Civil Service: an outsider's view," in O. Oyediran, ed., *Nigerian Government and Politics under Military Rule*, p. 98.

26 Ironsi had appointed Francis Nwokedi, a Permanent Secretary in the Ministry of Foreign Affairs, to serve as Sole Commissioner "charged with the responsibility for putting forward proposals for the unification of the regional and federal public service." Dudley, *Instability and Political Order*, p. 119.

27 P. Asiodu, "The Civil Service: an insider's view," pp. 87–8.

28 Ibid., p. 81; A. A. Ayida, "The Nigerian Revolution, 1966–1976," Presidential Address, Annual Conference of the Nigerian Economic Society, Enugu, April 1973, p. 11.

29 J. Isawa Elaigwu contends that the permanent secretaries became "*de facto* political executives." See "The Political Trio in Nigeria's Military Government: The Dynamics of Inter-Elite Relations in a Military Regime, 1967–75," *The Nigerian Journal of Public Affairs*, Vol. 6, No. 2 (October 1976), p. 102.

30 The choice of the term "commissioners" rather than "ministers" was specifically made to avoid controversy, although Gowon assured the appointees that they would have "full responsibilities for Ministries and Departments." See his "Address to the First Civilian Members of the Federal Executive Council," in Kirk-Greene, ed., *Crisis and Conflict in Nigeria*, Vol. 1, p. 454.

31 Ayida, "The Nigerian Revolution, 1966–1976," p. 14.

32 Asiodu expressed this point quite crisply – namely, that the higher civil servants became drawn into the policy-making process in a new way in 1966–7 because "the federal argument was going by default." One significant reflection of the strong "pro-unity" stance of Nigeria's federal civil servants after July 1966, and the threatened secession by the East, was the strong opposition by Colonel Ojukwu to their participation in meetings of government leaders. At one point, according to Ayida, he and some of his colleagues made a "pilgrimage" to Enugu to to urge Ojukwu not to secede. "The Nigerian Revolution, 1966–1976," p. 15.

33 Personal interview with Allison Ayida, Lagos, December 1978.

34 Ayida has argued that Ojukwu, however, took along "about nine Permanent Secretaries and other senior official advisers" with him to Aburi to argue the anti-federal case. "The Nigerian Revolution, 1966–1976," p. 15.

35 For the secret memorandum of 20 January 1967, see "Comments by the Federal Permanent Secretaries on the Decisions Reached at Aburi," in Kirk-Greene, *Crisis and Conflict in Nigeria*, Vol. 1, pp. 340–5.

36 The mutual accusations of "misinterpreting" the Aburi Accords can be found in ibid., pp. 345–72. It is clear that Gowon's resolve was stiffened after Aburi, and he was convinced by his advisers to revert to earlier policy statements rather than fulfill the concessions extracted at Aburi.

37 For details, see Stremlau, *The International Politics of the Nigerian Civil War*, pp. 142–214.

38 Ibid., pp. 145–61.

39 See Ayida, "The Nigerian Revolution, 1966–1976," p. 11, and J. I. Elaigwu, "The Political Trio in Nigeria's Military Government," pp. 112, 114.

40 This summary is based in part on Elaigwu's report of his interviews with some of the principals involved. Ibid., pp. 112–16.

41 Paul Collins, "Current Issues of Administrative Reform in the Nigerian Public Services. The Case of the Udoji Review Commission," in *Administration for Development in Nigeria*, p. 311. For the same practice during the civil war, see Stremlau, *The International Politics of the Nigerian Civil War*, pp. 26–7.

42 The Nigerian experience has therefore confirmed Ruth First's recognition of the importance of the "civil-service military axis" in such regimes, as effective rule is exercised by "bureaucrats of the civil service and army." *The Barrel of a Gun: Political Power in Africa* (London: Allen Lane, 1970), pp. 432–5. See also Henry Bienen, *Armies and Parties in Africa* (New York and

London: Africana Publishing Company, 1978), pp. 232–3. Elaigwu points out that there was little military interference in civil service matters as such – "The Political Trio in Nigeria's Military Government," p. 104. By insisting on adherence to their General Orders, the civil service hierarchy was able (until the sweeping purge of their ranks after July 1975) to match the corporate autonomy of the soldiers-in-power with their own.

43 For Alfred Stepan's notion of a "strategic elite", see *The State and Society: Peru in Comparative Perspective* (Princeton: Princeton University Press, 1978), p. xiv and *passim*.

44 Theda Skocpol, *States and Social Revolutions: A Comparative Analysis of France, Russia, and China* (Cambridge: Cambridge University Press, 1979), p. 164.

45 The initial intention of the military after it seized power in 1966 was to establish a government which formally included members from each of these constituent groups. See Ayida, "The Nigerian Revolution, 1966–1976," p. 11. Such an arrangement did informally emerge, however, during the formulating of economic policy and especially the Second Development Plan for post-war reconstruction and the Indigenization Program.

46 For the recognition of how the military's interest in a strong state becomes harmonized with certain nationalist economic strategies, see Ellen Trimberger, *Revolutionaries from Above: Military Bureaucrats and Development in Japan, Turkey, Egypt and Peru* (New Brunswick, NJ: Transaction Books, 1978), p. 53. For Nigeria, see O. Aboyade, "Nigerian Public Enterprises as an Organizational Dilemma," in Paul Collins, ed., *Administration for Development in Nigeria* (Lagos: African Education Press, 1980), p. 89.

47 P. N. C. Okigbo, "Ideological Perspectives of Public Sector Role in the Nigerian Economy," *Public Sector Role in Nigerian Development*, Proceedings of the Nigerian Economic Society Annual Conference, Lagos, 8–11 February 1979, p. 12.

48 Turner, "The Working of the Nigerian Oil Corporation," *Administration for Development in Nigeria*, p. 124.

49 Sayre P. Schatz, *Nigerian Capitalism*, p. 2.

50 Peter Kilby, "What Oil Wealth Did to Nigeria," *The Wall Street Journal*, 25 November 1981.

51 Sani, "An Ex-Insider's Overview of the Civil Service," p. 87.

52 Ibid.

53 Mahmud Tukur, *Reform of the Nigerian Public Service*, Report of a Conference held at the Institute of Administration, Ahmadu Bello University, Zaria, October 1971, p. 36.

54 Sani, "An Ex-Insider's Overview," p. 89.

55 Y. Abubakar, "The Role of the Public Service in a Plural Society," p. 5.

56 This summary is based on Turner's "Multinational Corporations and the Instability of the Nigerian State," *Review of African Political Economy*, No. 5 (1976), pp. 63–79.

57 Schatz, *Nigerian Capitalism*, pp. 235–53.

58 Ibid., *passim*.

59 Ayida, "The Contribution of politicians and administrators to Nigeria's national economic planning," in Adebayo Adedeji, ed., *Nigerian Administration and Its Policy Setting* (London: Hutchinson Educational for Institute of Administration, University of Ife, 1968), p. 50.

60 Akeredolu-Ale, "Some Thoughts on the Indigenization Process and the Quality of Nigerian Capitalism," *Nigeria's Indigenization Policy*, p. 70.

61 On the widespread defaulting on loans, see Schatz, *Nigerian Capitalism*, pp. 230–3.

62 This perspective could be used to explain the peculiar combination of financial strength with political/administrative weakness found in a number of developing countries in the modern period with access to vast revenues from mineral export.

63 P. Chiedo Asiodu, "The Civil Service: an insider's view," pp. 89–90. Asiodu was himself, as we shall see, one of its more illustrious casualties.

64 There was the additional consideration that the purge became the occasion for the "settling of accounts" based on private grievances. Revelations about the true motivation behind many accusations, as well as low morale in the civil service, induced the government to apply the brakes to the whole process.

212

65 After the attempted coup in February 1976, which resulted in the death of General Muhammed but the survival of the regime, reprisals within the military were possibly more far-reaching than has been publicized.

66 Bienen, *Armies and Parties in Africa*, p. 29.

67 See Ladipo Adamolekun, "Politicisation of the Civil Service under Military Rule," *New Nigerian*, 30 August 1978.

68 "Public Complaints Commission Decree (Decree No. 31)," Ministry of Information, Lagos, 16 October 1975.

69 "Government Views on Second Report of the Federal Assets Investigation Panel," Ministry of Information, Lagos, 1978. The value of the naira during the period in question was approximately $US1.50–$US1.65.

70 Ibid., pp. 5–7.

71 Ibid., p. 12.

72 Ibid., p. 15.

73 Ibid., p. 3. For the corrupt use of the labor of government employees – a widespread practice – see "Federal Military Government's Views on the Investigations of the Farms Owned by S. O. Ogbemudia and Alhaji Audu Bako," Ministry of Information, Lagos, 1976. A thorough and systematic study of the whole retirement exercise is clearly needed.

74 Collins, *Administration for Development in Nigeria*, p. 24.

75 The extraordinary levels of corruption quickly reached during the Second Republic, and the consequent collapse of the legitimacy of the political system, bear out the truth of these remarks.

7. Personality and alignment in Igbo politics

1 Cited in James O. Ijiako, *13 Years of Military Rule, 1966–79 The Daily Times* (Lagos) (n.d.), p. 200.

2 Sam Ifeka, writing in the *Daily Star* (Enugu), 24 October 1978.

3 C. C. Onoh, cited in the *Daily Star*, 14 March 1979, and in N. A. Okpaleke, "Politics of Transition in Aguata Local Government Area, 1978–79," Essay in part-fulfillment of the BSc degree in Political Science, University of Ibadan, June 1979, p. 71.

4 Interviews with Mbazulike Amechi, Enugu, 6 December 1979, and A. A. O. Ezenwa, Enugu, 12 June 1979. This phrase was repeated in various versions by virtually all of the Igbo politicians I interviewed.

5 Alhaji Abubakar Rimi, cited in the *Daily Star*, 28 June 1979.

6 See Robin Horton, "Stateless Societies in the History of West Africa," in J. F. A. Ajayi and Michael Crowder, ed., *History of West Africa*, Vol. 1 (New York: Columbia University Press, 1976), pp. 72–113; Martin Dent, "A Minority Party – The United Middle Belt Congress," in J. P. Mackintosh, ed., *Nigerian Government and Politics*, pp. 461–507.

7 Four of my final-year students at the University of Ibadan, who were writing research papers on the politics of Anambra State, must be thanked for providing me with this background information: O. J. Chukwuike, A. D. Nwankwo, N. A. Okpaleke, and N. Ugolo.

8 Statistical information based on charts in Monyelu Ugolo, "A Case-Study of Anambra State Politics, 1978–79," Essay in part-fulfillment of the BSc degree in Political Science, University of Ibadan, June 1979, pp. 74–5.

9 Interviews with Dr Okwudiba Nnoli and Dr Mazi Ray Ofoegbu, Nsukka, November 1978. Onoh attacked Odenigwe for corruption through petitions to the government and full-page advertisements in the newspapers. He left the government in a manner reported to me as "abrupt" or "dramatic."

10 Sam Mbakwe, *Daily Star*, 15 March 1979, and interview with Sam Mbakwe, Owerri, 31 November 1978.

11 Mbakwe, *Daily Star*, 15 March 1979.

12 Interview with Sam Mbakwe,. Owerri, 31 November 1978.
13 Chief N. N. Anah, cited in the *Daily Star*, 30 October 1978.
14 Interviews with Arthur Nwankwo and A. A. O. Ezenwa, Enugu, 11 and 12 June 1979.
15 Okechukwu Joseph Chukwuike, "Towards 1979: Parties in Awgu Local Government Area of Anambra State," Essay in part-fulfillment of the BSc degree in Political Science, University of Ibadan, June 1979, pp. 45–6. The predominantly Catholic Igbos were resolutely opposed to the attempt to elevate Islamic law in Nigeria by creating a Federal Shari'a Court of Appeal, an attempt with which Aminu Kano became identified when he joined a temporary boycott of the Constituent Assembly.
16 Personal interview with Sam Ekpe, Enugu, 12 June 1979.
17 Interviews with Dr Chuba Okadigbo, Nsukka, 2 November 1978, and with Mbazulike Amechi, Enugu, 12 June 1979.
18 *Daily Star*, 26 February 1979.
19 *Daily Star*, 19 October 1978.
20 Interview with Chuba Okadigbo, Nsukka, 2 November 1978. Several other leading Igbos – for example, A. A. O. Ezenwa – flirted with a few political groupings before deciding which one offered them the best possibility of obtaining a desired nomination.
21 *The Punch* (Lagos), 19 February 1979.
22 Not only must the mechanics of Nwobodo's involvement be elucidated, but also those of retired Colonel Anthony Ochefu, who was also a member of the delegation which brought Azikiwe's letter to the first NPP Congress in December 1978, in which the latter offered to serve the party.
23 Interview with Dr Omo Omoruyi, Benin, 10 June 1979.
24 Interview with M. Amechi, Enugu, 6 December 1978.
25 *Daily Star*, 26 February 1979.
26 Ibid.
27 *Daily Star*, 27 March 1979.
28 Ibid.
29 *The Punch*, 19 February 1979. What O. J. S. Chukwuike reported for his home district would most likely apply to other recipients of Nwobodo's "generosity": "The party's governorship candidate impressed the people tremendously when he made a personal donation of ₦5,000 to the Awgu development fund." "Towards 1979: Political Parties in Awgu Local Government Area of Anambra State," Essay in part-fulfillment of the BSc degree in political Science, University of Ibadan, June 1979, p. 51. This pattern of continuous gift-giving sometimes appeared rather inappropriate as, for example, when candidate Nwobodo promised in a speech in Enugu that the NPP would uphold freedom of the press after the elections. This declaration was immediately followed by Nwobodo's donation of "a giant water cooler to the State's Council of the Nigerian Union of Journalists." *New Nigerian* (Kaduna and Lagos), 24 November 1978.
30 *Daily Star*, 9 January 1979.
31 Interview with Sam Ekpe, Enugu, 12 June 1979.
32 *Daily Times* (Lagos), 13 November 1978.
33 Interview with Chuba Okadigbo, Lagos, 10 March 1979.
34 Interviews with Chuba Okadigbo, Lagos, 10 March 1979, and Ibrahim Tahir, Lagos, 22 July 1979.
35 Interview with Shettima Ali Monguno, Maiduguri, 20 June 1979.
36 Ugolo, "A Case-Study of Anambra State Politics, 1978–79," p. 27.
37 O. J. Chukwuike, "Towards 1979: Political Parties in Awgu Local Government Area of Anambra State," pp. 30, 60. This transition from potential to risk was often made by other commentators: "There is a tendency among Igbos to identify with one leader and then band together and follow him. This leaves them open to being exploited." Interview with Arthur Nwankwo, Enugu, 11 June 1979.

38 Ugolo, "A Case-Study of Anambra State Politics, 1978–79," p. 79. The embodiment by Dr Azikiwe of the political will of the overwhelming majority of the Igbo people in 1979 was succinctly captured by this same writer: "To the Igbos he is more than a leader. When Dr. Azikiwe declared his support for the NPP, the whole politics of the state changed." (p. 77).

39 B. O. Odinamadu, "The Dilemma of the Igbo Political Elite," *Daily Star*, 4 November 1978. These arguments are similar to those Dr Akanu Ibiam advocated in meetings he held with members of this political elite throughout 1978. The problem, according to Dr Ibiam, is that "the politicans are only interested in their own interests," that they are "after jobs and money." He believed that the best course was for Igbos to stand aside "and use their veto power to decide who will get in and who wouldn't." Interview in Enugu, November 1978.

8. Ethnicity, faction and class in Western Nigeria

1 *The Punch* (Lagos), 24 November 1978.

2 The state of Oyo, which dates from 1976, contains a town by the name of Oyo which originated in the nineteenth century after the sacking of the ancestral city, Oyo-Ile or Old Oyo.

3 Akintola's NNDP should not be confused with the first Nigerian nationalist party of the same name formed by Herbert Macaulay in 1923.

4 Despite the even division between Muslims and Christians among those Yoruba who profess a world religion, religion has been largely transcended among them as a politically relevant factor. This intriguing phenomenon is the subject of a pioneering study by David Laitin: *Hegemony and Culture: Politics and Religious Change among the Yoruba* (Chicago: University of Chicago Press, 1986).

5 Personal interview with Chief G. Ajeigbe, Ibadan, October 1978.

6 One possible index of the decay of Nigerian political life is the degree to which such language drives out other forms of communication. At the time of the 1983 campaign and elections in Oyo State, crude sub-ethnic appeals had driven out most other forms of political discourse.

7 Personal interview with Adamu Ciroma, NPN National Secretary, Lagos, 19 March 1979. This discussion also draws on a fine research effort by M. E. Olusegun, "Ogun State and Local Politics: Nigeria 1978–79," BSc thesis, University of Ibadan, 1979.

8 *Daily Sketch*, 26 April 1979.

9 Personal interview with Chief Awolowo, Ikenne, 26 March 1979.

10 Adamu Kurfi, *The Nigerian General Elections 1959 and 1979 and the Aftermath* (Lagos and Ibadan: Macmillan Nigerian Publishers, Ltd., 1983).

11 *Daily Sketch*, 26 February 1979, and *The Daily Times*, 5 March 1979.

12 *The Punch*, 24 November 1978.

13 *The Punch*, 21 February 1979.

14 Personal interview with Bola Ige, Ibadan, 26 October 1978.

15 Personal interview with A. L. Jakande, Lagos, 2 December 1978.

16 All my associated student researchers in 1978–9, who undertook projects in Western Nigeria, stressed the anxiety that the UPN's socialistic program was engendering among affluent chiefs and business people. Yet, only sophisticated survey data would enable us to disaggregate these overlapping motivations.

17 This summary and much of the ensuing discussion is drawn from extensive interviews with Awolowo himself, Bola Ige, Lateef Jakande, Ebenezer Babatope, and Odia Ofeimun (Awolowo's then private secretary), as well as research notes from personal attendance at several UPN political rallies.

18 *The Punch*, 13 March 1979.

19 Awolowo remarked to me how, following a lecture he had delivered, Professor Aboyade of the University of Ibadan, who had been a trenchant critic of his views, admitted in private his indebtedness to the state scholarship he had received as a result of the Action Group's educational program.

20 Personal interview with A. L. Jakande, Lagos, 2 December 1978.
21 Personal interview with Bola Ige, Ibadan, 26 October 1978.
22 In this case, the original Western Region, including what became the Mid-West or Bendel State, is the frame of reference. A strong opponent of the UPN acknowledged the rapid rise in popularity of that party in Bendel State because of the appeal to women of the free education promise and the memory of the Action Group's effective educational program when that state was under the Western Regional government. Personal interview with Dr Omo Omoruyi, Benin, 10 June 1979.
23 *The President* (Lagos), No. 5, November 1978.
24 The fascinating dynamics at work here could be further used as a case-study of the arguments advanced in Chapters 4 and 5. The UPN had a powerful hold on Yoruba ethnic chauvinism through the symbolic presence of Awolowo and the cultural features of party recruitment and identification at the popular level. Yet it was the UPN's opponents, especially the NPN and NPP, which more overtly sought to invoke such efforts; for example, through the public courting of traditional rulers.
25 *Nigerian Tribune*, 11 July 1978.
26 *Drum* (Nigeria), January 1979.
27 Ibid.
28 *The Punch*, 24 November 1978.
29 Personal interview with Femi Okunnu, Lagos, 18 November 1978.
30 *Daily Sketch*, 5 November 1978.
31 Personal interview with Shettima Ali Monguno, Maiduguri, 20 June 1979.
32 *New Nation* (Lagos), Vol. 2, No. 2, July 1979.
33 Nakura was later dropped for "anti-party" activities, and Umeadi had to be muzzled because his caustic remarks about his own people, the Igbos, were hurting the party's already poor showing among them.
34 Such an assessment is based on personal interviews with the UPN's gubernatorial candidates, who were also state chairmen, throughout the North and Middle-belt.

9. Northern primacy and prebendal politics: the making of the NPN

1 The "North" can refer to the area included in the former Northern Region, or the more heavily Islamicized areas which I will often designate with a prefix such as the "far" or "emirate" North. Thus Gowon, a northerner but a Christian, belonged to a small non-Hausa group, the Angas, in the area which is now Plateau State.
2 Personal interview with Alhaji Shettima Ali Monguno, Maiduguri, 20 June 1979.
3 A realignment and regrouping of Nigeria's parties into two broad alliances, the NNA and the United Progressive Grand Alliance (UPGA), took place in time for the federal elections of 1964. The political turbulence of that period, and the fact that civilian rule ended little more than a year later, prevented this process from being fully consummated.
4 Personal interview with Alhaji Shettima Ali Monguno, Maiduguri, 20 June 1979.
5 In extensive discussions about the "Kaduna Mafia," neither Adamu Ciroma, who would be included in it, nor Nuhu Bamalli, who would not, expressed any reservations about the term itself (personal interviews in Lagos and Zaria, 19 March 1979 and 27 January 1979, respectively). For a discussion of the Kaduna Mafia, see Shehu Othman, "Classes, Crises and Coup: The Demise of Shagari's Regime," *African Affairs*, Vol. 83, No. 333 (October 1984).
6 In the case of Kumo, his extreme northern chauvinism prevented him from playing any significant role once party formation moved from creating a northern political core to building a national party. Personal interviews, Zaria, 24 January and 18 May 1979.
7 Personal interview with Alhaji A. Rufai, Makurdi (Benue State), 13 June 1979. In the Constituent Assembly, Alhaji Rufai was given the nickname of "Baba Shari'a" (roughly "Papa Shari'a"), because of his strong commitment to this issue.

8 Personal interview with Alhaji Nuhu Bamalli, Zaria, 27 January 1979. While Alhaji Bamalli was engaged in seeking to settle a strike by employees of a major Lagos hospital of which he was Chairman of the Board, Mahmud Tukrur, a pivotal figure in the Kaduna Mafia, was achieving a quite opposite notoriety for his refusal to accept the position of Vice-Chancellor of the University of Lagos for what were widely perceived as sectionalist reasons.

9 Personal interview with Chief Simeon Adebo, Ikoyi, Lagos, 20 December 1979, and with Alhaji Sule Gaya, Kano, 8 December 1979.

10 Personal interview with Habibu Sani, Zaria, 26 January 1979. Sani was reporting on arguments advanced by these and other individuals during the planning meetings which he attended of the "National Movement" in July and August 1978.

11 Personal interview with Dr Suleiman Kumo, Zaria, 24 January 1979.

12 Personal interview with Haroun Adamu, Zaria, 25 January 1979.

13 Personal interview with Dr Datti Ahmad, Kano, 10 January 1979.

14 Personal interviews with Dr Ibrahim Tahir, Lagos, 17 November 1978 and 22 July 1979.

15 *Daily Times*, 30 November 1978, and *The Punch*, 29 November 1978.

16 *Nigerian Tribune*, 22 January 1979.

17 *The Constitution of the Federal Republic of Nigeria 1979*, section 203(b).

18 This discussion is based on my direct observations during the final stage of the contest for the NPN presidential nomination, at the NPN convention in December 1978.

19 *Africa* (London), No. 92 (April 1979).

20 *Drum* (Nigeria), June 1979.

21 This account is based on information widely disseminated at the time in Nigeria, in addition to a detailed communication to the author from Dr A. D. Yahaya, of 4 March 1981.

22 Aminu Kano provided me with extended and insightful comments on these matters which are of such richness that they will have to be published independently along with other similar first-person accounts from the 1978–9 period.

23 For the most complete information on rigging and other malpractices in the 1979 elections, see Haroun Adamu and Alaba Ogunsanwo, *Nigeria, The Making of the Presidential System: 1979 General Elections* (Kano, Nigeria: Triumph Publishing Co., Ltd., 1983).

24 *Daily Times*, 8 February 1979.

25 Personal interview with Dr Suleiman Kumo, Zaria, 18 May 1979.

26 Ibid., and personal interview with Alhaji Dantsoho, Kaduna, 19 May 1979.

27 For the relevant background, see C. Sylvester Whitaker, *The Politics of Tradition: Continuity and Change in Northern Nigeria, 1946–1966* (Princeton: Princeton University Press, 1970).

28 See H. Adamu and A. Ogunsanwo, *Nigeria, The Making of the Presidential System, passion.*

29 *Nigerian Herald*, 2 March 1979.

30 Personal interviews with Batoure Aga and Simon Shango, Makurdi (Benue State), 13 June 1979.

31 Personal interviews with Dr Idoko Obe (NPP senatorial candidate), and with NPN party activists at their headquarters in Oturkpo (Benue State), 13 June 1979.

32 Personal interviews with Batoure Aga and Simon Shango, Makurdi, 13 June 1979.

33 Personal interview with Dr Idoko Obe, Oturkpo, 13 June 1979.

10. The challenge of the 1983 elections

1 See, in particular, the writings of Larry Diamond: "Social Change and Political Conflict in Nigeria's Second Republic," in I. William Zartman, ed., *The Political Economy of Nigeria* (New York: Praeger Publishers, 1983), pp. 25–84; "Cleavage, Conflict and Anxiety in the Second Nigerian Republic," *The Journal of Modern African Studies*, Vol. 20, No. 4 (1982), pp. 629–68; and "Nigeria in Search of Democracy," *Foreign Affairs*, Vol. 62, No. 14 (Spring 1984), pp. 905–27. Also relevant are M. Watts, "State, oil and accumulation: from boom to

crisis," *Environment and Planning: Society and Space*, Vol. 2 (1984), pp. 403–28; Sayre P. Schatz, "Pirate Capitalism and the Inert Economy of Nigeria," *The Journal of Modern African Studies*, Vol. 22, No. 1 (1984), pp. 45–57; Richard A. Joseph, "The overthrow of Nigeria's Second Republic," *Current History*, Vol. 83, No. 491 (March 1984); and Shehu Othman, "Classes, Crises and Coups: The Demise of Shagari's Regime," *African Affairs* (October 1984).

2 Richard A. Joseph, "Nigeria at the Crossroads," *Harvard International Review*, Vol. 4, No. 3 (1981), pp. 1, 24.

3 Kurfi, *The Nigerian General Elections 1959 and 1979 and the Aftermath*, p. 259.

4 Richard A. Joseph, "Democracy under Military Tutelage: Crisis and Consensus in the Nigerian 1979 Elections," *Comparative Politics*, Vol. 14, No. 1 (1981), pp. 75–100.

5 See the tables on pp. 125–7.

6 Joseph, "Democracy under Military Tutelage," p. 85.

7 Kurfi, *The Nigerian General Elections 1959 and 1979*, pp. 258–63.

8 Adamu and Ogunsanwo, *Nigeria: The Making of the Presidential System: 1979 General Elections, passim.*

9 Ibid., p. 156.

10 Ibid., *passim.*

11 Kurfi, *The Nigerian General Elections 1959 and 1979*, p. 258.

12 Ibid., p. 246.

13 Adamu and Ogunsanwo, *Nigeria: The Making of the Presidential System*, pp. 255–6.

14 Kurfi, *The Nigerian General Elections 1959 and 1979*, p. 243.

15 Richard Sklar, "Democracy in Africa," Presidential Address to the African Studies Association (USA), Washington, DC, 5 November 1982. This talk was reprinted in the *African Studies Review*, Vol. 26, Nos 3/4 (1983).

16 Claude Ake, *West Africa*, 25 May 1981, p. 1162. Reprinted here are excerpts from Ake's 1981 Presidential Address to the Nigerian Political Science Association in Kano.

17 I was present in Nigeria before and during these elections.

18 Dr T. Akinola Aguda, Address at the Nigerian Institute of International Affairs, 1 August 1983.

19 National television broadcast, Lagos, 5 August 1983. Ovie-Whiskey never seemed quite up to the task assigned to him. If democracy was so important how could elections be ephemeral?

20 Sonala Olumhense, "Twenty-four hours to triumph," *The Guardian* (Lagos), 5 August 1983.

21 Ifeanyi A. Azuka, letter to the *New Nigerian*, 16 August 1983.

22 Ola Balogun, "Towards an Alternative Political System," *The Guardian*, 26 July 1983.

23 B. Olusegun Babalola, "Who's 'in love' with 'democracy'?", *The Guardian*, 15 August 1983.

24 Sylvester Whitaker, "The Unfinished State of Nigeria," *Worldview*, Vol. 27, No. 3 (March 1984), p. 7.

25 Another general term occasionally used by interviewees was that of the "underground campaign" being conducted in particular localities which they claimed was sometimes more significant than the publicly visible one. From what could be gathered without probing, such a campaign involved what is referred to in Western countries as "disinformation" activities: the circulation of anonymous pamphlets, incriminating photographs and purloined letters, and perhaps the use of agents placed in the camps of opposition parties or factions.

26 *National Concord*, 5 August 1983.

27 *National Concord*, 11 August 1983. These commentaries should not be over-emphasized. The majority of Nigerians, while experiencing varying degrees of anxiety, were prepared to stay put and vote for their parties or just stay clear of the polls. Travel and several weeks absence, even inland, involved a significant financial outlay and only the affluent, to quote Sonala Olumhense, could avoid getting scalded in our own "soup-pots by jetting to New York, or Florida, or London." *The Guardian*, 5 August 1983.

28 This is an important phenomenon which I alluded to in Part III of this study. NPN politicians

without a popular base in their home states, which were dominated by one of the opposition parties, sometimes achieved power greater than those who defeated them in nomination battles or in the elections, by being awarded strategic positions in the NPN central government. That power was then used to upset the local political balance of power, sometimes with violent consequences.

29 These remarks at the Federal Government Rest House in Lagos on 4 August were widely reported in Nigerian newspapers on the following day.

30 One newspaper, while acknowledging that Alhaji Dikko had often reflected in his public remarks "the administration's thinking on delicate political matters," felt that his 4 August pronouncements raised the question of "whether or not the President has assigned security matters to Alhaji Umaru" along with his other jobs. *National Concord*, 14 August 1983.

31 *The Guardian*, 12 August 1983.

32 Ibid.

33 *Daily Times*, 5 August 1983.

34 *National Concord*, 11 August 1983.

35 National broadcast of 7 August 1983.

36 *The Guardian*, 8 August 1983.

37 *Sunday Concord*, 14 August 1983.

38 Ibid. It might be noticed that these charges are the same as those levied by the leaders of the military coup which overthrew the Second Republic on 31 December 1983, and which also served as the basis for the prosecution of politicians and government officials by the military tribunals they subsequently established.

39 Although the PRP won the governorship in Kaduna, this state was in the unique situation of having the state assembly controlled by a different party from that of the governor. The NPN was able to use its majority in the Kaduna Assembly to resist the policies of the radical PRP governor, Balarabe Musa, and eventually to remove him from office by impeachment.

40 Eukora Joe Okoli, "Causes of NPN and NPP Discord," *West Africa*, 16 March 1981, pp. 539–40; and Alan Cowell, "Conflicts Emerging in Nigeria's 21-month Civil Regime," *New York Times*, 31 July 1981.

41 Ali Yahaya, "PRP Crisis: the Truth of the Matter," *West Africa*, 15 June 1981, pp. 1349–50.

42 Report, News Agency of Nigeria, Maiduguri, 13 March 1982; radio broadcast, Kaduna, 12 June 1982; Dr Basil Nnanna Ukegbu, "My Political Stand," personal advertisement, *National Concord*, 25 July 1983, pp. 10–11.

43 In 1978–9, it was felt that the NAP had been unfairly treated by the preference shown by FEDECO for the registration of only those party organizations led by a major politician of the First Republic. NAP's promise, at that time, to eradicate all rats and mosquitoes in Nigeria, was broadened in inventiveness, and in its ability to provoke hilarity, by its program rendered in the following acronyms in 1983: YES – Youniversal Electrification System; FLOW – Full Level of Water; READ – Revolutionary Education for Development; and HIP – Health Insurance Policy. The leader of the NAP adopted a speaking style in 1983 which was reminiscent of the Black Panthers of the United States in the 1960s, and the NAP designed striking paramilitary outfits for its supporters, complete with sporty berets.

44 As discussed in Chapter 8, those persons likely to favor collaboration with the NPN would not have allied with Awolowo in 1978–83, in the light of his three decades of consistent opposition to such a policy (i.e. "playing second-fiddle to the northern establishment"), and the fact that the Yoruba had long divided into two entrenched political families based, partly, on disagreements over this strategy.

45 This discussion is not based on any specific text but rather on my general reading of accounts of party alliances and disagreements during the 1981–3 period and my understanding of the internal dynamics of these Nigerian parties and their social bases.

46 *National Concord*, 5 August 1983.

47 *West Africa*, 6 June 1983.

48 In an extended discussion, Dr T. Akinola Aguda, Director of the Nigerian Institute of Advanced Legal Studies, convinced me that the presidential election could not have been held last as in 1979. However, our review of the constitutional provisions also showed that it did not have to be moved all the way to becoming the first election in the sequence (personal interview, Cambridge, Mass., 20 April 1984). Ovie-Whiskey's attempt to give additional reasons for the change only added to suspicion about this action. According to the FEDECO Chairman, with the new order the size of constituencies would diminish with each succeeding election, thereby encouraging party field workers "to work for their respective political parties until the end of election" (radio broadcast, 23 March 1983). The 1979 order was Senators, House of Representatives, State Assemblies, Governors and then the Presidency. In 1983 it was changed to President, Governors, Senators, House of Representatives, State Assemblies. The major offices of the Second Republic, the executive positions of President and State Governors, were therefore moved from last to first in the elections. In 1979, contrary to Ovie-Whiskey's suggestion, the level of general involvement, as reflected in statistics for voter turn-out, increased with each election. In 1983, however, with the elections in a shambles, most voters opted to stay away from the polling booths by the time the final contest for the State Assemblies came up.

11. Electoral fraud and violence

1 *West Africa*, 15 August 1983, p. 1863.
2 Jason Berry, "A voice out of Africa," *New York Times Magazine*, 18 August 1983.
3 See, in particular, Larry Diamond, "A tarnished Victory for the NPN?" An interesting case in point is the dismissal of members of the entire FEDECO staff in Cross River state, as a result of the charges made by Senator Joseph Wayas, President of the Senate, that they had been appointed on a partisan basis. Opposition parties, however, had no such capacity to force the removal of distrusted FEDECO officials within their states.
4 Jean Herskovits, "To Ease Nigeria's Debt Crisis," *New York Times*, 5 October 1983.
5 A door-to-door method of registering voters was used for that election. Individuals with temporary residences away from home, e.g. university students, easily obtained more than one voting card. The efficacy of this system depended on the probity and vigor of the hundreds of thousands of enumerators, among others, temporarily hired for the exercise. In all too many cases, such workers were content to get from one household dweller the relevant information concerning all the "residents" of the household and leave the requisite number of cards for distribution. In 1982, registration centers were set up to eliminate abuses noted from the previous exercise, but this only created new opportunities and challenges for those people bent on beating the system.
6 *Economist*, 6–12 August 1983.
7 Nigerian newspapers and independent commentators had quite a field day exposing the incongruities of the new register, both in absolute terms and with regard to particular regions of the country or states.
8 *Africa Confidential*, Vol. 24, No. 18, 7 September 1983.
9 Modakeke in Oyo State, a traditional rival of Ife and, in the context of the factional rivalries among the Yoruba discussed in Chapter 8, a community strongly opposed to the UPN, became symbolic of the political factors which determine voter-registration, as UPN leaders came up with numerous ways of showing how implausible was its great increase in voting strength since 1979.
10 *West Africa*, 22 August 1983. As a precaution, FEDECO had ordered thousands more ballot boxes than the number required. It has been alleged that many of these were diverted for fraudulent purposes during the elections.
11 Nigerian television broadcast, Lagos, 15 August 1983.

12 Senator Uba Ahmed, the NPN National Secretary, subsequently announced in a radio broadcast of 28 August that the UPN had organized a "militia" in some of the western states with the specific intention of fomenting violence during the elections. This charge was earlier made before the elections and rejected by Chief Awolowo. This dimension of Nigerian party politics should be the subject of serious study. People organized to defend their party's property and personnel could very well interpret such a mission as taking on offensive aspects in the context of the electoral disorder discussed here.

13 *Sunday Tribune*, 14 August 1983.

14 *Daily Times*, 16 August 1983.

15 There was no way for the mobs, or people manning impromptu barricades, to know which FEDECO officials were legitimately pursuing their business and, as is common in Nigeria, using whatever means of transport were available to enable them to fulfill their mission. Subsequently, for example in Niger State, the rage against FEDECO and the police rendered their officials targets for violent retribution whatever their appearance and activity.

16 *Daily Times*, 16 August 1983.

17 *West Africa*, 22 August 1983. In each of the three cases mentioned here, leading party members were involved in the confrontations at FEDECO offices.

18 Television broadcast, Lagos, 15 August 1983. The tendency to regard families as legitimate targets of political violence in western Nigeria is a perverse use of family and communal ties in African society. Chief Akinloye, responding to the deliberate language of incitement used by UPN Governor Bola Ige in Oyo, commented, "his children are safe in England. Why does he send you out to die?"

19 *Afrique France Presse*, Paris, 19 August 1983.

20 *The Guardian*, 12 August 1983.

21 *Nigerian Tribune*, 6 September 1983.

22 Moreover, one oversight in the 1979 Constitution, to which Justice Akintola Aguda has drawn my attention, is that there is no provision for the continuation of a President's term of office, or some other arrangement, pending a settlement of such disputes. The brief time-limit set by the Electoral Law for the adjudication of electoral appeals was insufficient, in the opinion of Chief Awolowo, for all the legal work involved in challenging Shagari's victory in 1983.

23 Presidential address to the Nigerian Political Science Association, *West Africa*, 25 May 1981.

24 Subsequently, to ensure that Judge Araka did not delay the transmission of the court papers needed for his appeal against this decision, C. C. Onoh and his associates had to resort to a clear threat of force at the Judge's chambers.

25 *West Africa*, 30 October 1983.

26 *Africa Confidential*, 21 September 1983.

27 *West Africa*, 12 September 1983.

28 *National Concord*, 9 August 1983.

29 It would require too much space here to give an adequate review of this dispute concerning the relevant clauses of the 1979 Constitution, namely, sections 166 and 64(g). The other governors who were likely targets of "FEDECO-NPN" on the basis of the same constitutional argument were Abba Musa Rimi of Kaduna, who declined to be a candidate in 1983, and Abubakar Barde of Gongola, who resigned like Mohammed Rimi and contested, unsuccessfully, on the UPN ticket.

30 *The Guardian*, 4 August 1983.

31 These comments are based on personal observations. One reporter of NTA Enugu even resigned while "on the air," claiming that he was "tired of dishing out falsehoods." *The Guardian*, 8 August 1983.

32 Shagari referred to the court injunction as "the primary basis presently for withholding assent," a fidelity which contrasts with the several other court injunctions which were simply

221

disregarded by government officials throughout the election period. *New Nigerian*, 22 July 1983.

33 *West Africa*, 12 August 1983, p. 2151.
34 Radio broadcast, Lagos, 15 August 1983.
35 See Richard A. Joseph, "Principles and Practices of Nigerian Military Government," in John Harbeson, ed., *The Military in African Politics* (New York: Praeger, 1987).

12. Conclusion

1 Personal interview with Turi Muhammadu, Kaduna, 17 May 1979.
2 C. Sylvester Whitaker, "The Unfinished State of Nigeria," *Worldview*, Vol. 27, No. 3 (March 1984), p. 6.
3 Ibid.
4 Cited in Kirk-Greene, *Crisis and Conflict in Nigeria*, Vol. 1, p. 335.
5 Whitaker, "The Unfinished State of Nigeria," p. 6.
6 Randall Collins, "A Comparative Approach to Political Sociology," in Reinhard Bendix, *State and Society* (Berkeley and Los Angeles: University of California Press, 1968), p. 48.
7 Ibid.
8 See Stepan, *The State and Society: Peru in Comparative Perspective*, and Skocpol, *States and Social Revolutions*.
9 Whitaker, "The Unfinished State of Nigeria," p. 8.
10 Alexis de Tocqueville, *Democracy in America*, Vol. 1 (New York: Vintage, 1945), p. 334, cited by Michael Burrage, "On Tocqueville's Notion of the Irresistibility of Democracy," *Archives européennes de sociologie*, 13 (1972), p. 160.
11 Burrage, "The Irresistibility of Democracy," p. 161.
12 Ibid., p. 162.
13 Whitaker, "The Unfinished State of Nigeria," p. 7.
14 Badie and Birnbaum, *The Sociology of the State*, p. 124.
15 Eric Wolf, *Peasants* (New York: Prentice Hall, 1966), pp. 51–6.
16 Ibid., p. 53.
17 Morris Szeftel, "Corruption and the spoils system in Zambia," in Michael Clarke, ed., *Corruption: Causes, Consequences and Control* (London: Frances Pinter Publishers, Ltd., 1983).
18 S. N. Eisenstadt and Louis Roniger, "Patron-Client Relations as a model of Structuring Social Exchange," *Comparative Studies in Society and History*, Vol. 22, No. 1 (January 1980), p. 51.
19 Christopher Clapham, *Private Patronage and Public Power* (New York: St. Martin's Press, 1982).
20 Ibid., p. 3.
21 Ibid., p. 2.
22 Ibid., p. 3.
23 Ibid., pp. 7–8.
24 Robert R. Kaufman, "Corporatism, Clientelism, and Partisan Conflict: A Study of Seven Latin American Countries," in James M. Malloy, ed., *Authoritarianism and Corporatism in Latin America* (Pittsburgh: University of Pittsburgh Press, 1977).
25 Ibid., p. 114.
26 Clapham, *Private Patronage and Public Power*, p. 2.
27 Frank Parkin, "Social Closure and Class Formation," in Anthony Giddens and David Held, ed., *Classes, Power, and Conflict: Classical and Contemporary Debates* (Berkeley and Los Angeles: University of California Press, 1982), p. 175.
28 Ibid., p. 177.

29 Ibid.
30 Ibid., p. 176.
31 Ibid.
32 Peter Ekeh, "Colonialism and the Two Publics in Africa: A Theoretical Statement," *Comparative Studies in Society and History*, Vol. 17, No. 1 (January 1975).
33 Ibid., pp. 104–5.
34 Ibid., p. 106.
35 Ibid., p. 107.
36 Ibid., p. 111.
37 Ibid., p. 108.
38 Ibid., pp. 110, 106.
39 These terms, and the general problematic, are taken from George C. Homans, *Social Behavior: Its Elementary Forms* (New York: Harcourt, Brace and World, Inc., 1961), esp. pp. 378–98.
40 Communication from Dr Sara Berry, 6 November 1981.
41 P. C. Lloyd, "Political and Social Structure," in S. O. Biobaku, *Sources of Yoruba History* (Oxford: The Clarendon Press, 1973), pp. 207–11.
42 Ibid., p. 215.
43 J. D. Y. Peel, *Ijeshas and Nigerians: The Incorporation of a Yoruba Kingdom, 1890s–1970s* (Cambridge: Cambridge University Press, 1983).
44 Ibid., p. 16.
45 Ibid., p. 27.
46 The pre-publication manuscripts of Karin Barber's writings on the *oriki*, or praise-songs, of the Yoruba, are replete with insights into the mobilization of support networks by "big men" who compete for positions of wealth, power and esteem.
47 Peel, *Ijeshas and Nigerians*, p. 41. (N.B. The people are "Ijeshas," their community "Ilesha.")
48 Ibid., p. 42.
49 Ibid., p. 16.
50 Ibid., p. 43.
51 David Apter, *Ghana in Transition* (Princeton: Princeton University Press, 1972), p. 6.
52 Peel, *Ijeshas and Nigerians*, p. 44.
53 Ibid.

Select bibliography

Articles

Aboyade, Ojetungi. "Indigenizing Foreign Enterprises: Some Lessons from the Nigerian Enterprises Promotion Decree." O. Teriba/M. O. Kayode, *Industrial Development in Nigeria: Patterns, Problems and Prospects* (1977).
  "Nigerian Public Enterprises as an Organizational Dilemma." Paul Collins. *Administration for Development in Nigeria* (1980).
Abubakar, Yaya. "The Role of the Civil Service in a Plural Society." Mahmud Tukur. *Reform of the Nigerian Public Service.* Zaria: Ahmadu Bello University (1971).
Adamolekun, Ladipo. "Politicisation of the Civil Service under Military Rule." *New Nigerian* (30 August 1978).
Aihe, D. O. "Fundamental Human Rights and the Military Regime in Nigeria: What Did the Courts Say?" *Journal of African Law* 15. 2 (Summer 1971).
Ake, Claude. "Presidential Address to the Nigerian Political Science Association in Kano (Excerpts)." *West Africa* (25 May 1981).
Akeredolu-Ale. "Some Thoughts on the Indigenization Process and the Quality of Nigerian Capitalism." *Nigeria's Indigenization Policy* (1975).
Asiodu, P. Chiedo. "The Civil Service: an Insider's View." O. Oyediran. *Nigerian Government and Politics under Military Rule* (1979).
Awolowo, Obafemi. "Advice to New Federal Government." *Daily Sketch* (21 August 1975).
Awoniyi, Sunday. "Integration within the Bureaucratic Elite." Mahmud Tukur. *Reform of the Nigerian Public Service.* Zaria: Ahmadu Bello University (1971).
Ayida, A. A. "The Contributions of politicians and administrators to Nigeria's national economic planning." Adebayo Adedeji. *Nigerian Administration and Its Policy Setting.* London: Hutchinson Educational for Institute of Administration, University of Ife (1968).
  "Development Objectives." *Proceedings of the Conference on National Reconstruction and Development in Nigeria.* Federal Ministry of Economic Development and NISER (1969).
Babalola, Olusegun. "Who's 'in love' with 'democracy'?" *The Guardian* (15 August 1983).
Balogun, Ola. "Towards an Alternative Political System." *The Guardian* (26 July 1983).
Berry, Jason. "A Voice out of Africa." *New York Times Magazine* (18 August 1983).
Bienen, Henry. "Civil Servants under Military Rule in Nigeria." *Armies and Parties in Africa* (1978).
Brass, Paul R. "Class, Ethnic Group and Party in Indian Politics." *World Politics* 33. 3 (April 1981).
Campbell, Ian. "Army Reorganisation and Military Withdrawal." S. K. Panter-Brick. *Soldiers and Oil* (1978).

224

Cardoso, Fernando Henrique. "Associated-Dependent Development: Theoretical and Practical Implication." A. Stepan. *Authoritarian Brazil* (1973).

Chubb, Judith. "The Social Bases of an Urban Political Machine: The Christian Democratic Party in Palermo." S. N. Eisenstadt/René Lemarchand. *Political Clientelism, Patronage and Development*. Beverly Hills and London: Sage Publications (1981).

Chukwuike, Okechukwu Joseph. "Towards 1979: Parties in Awgu Local Government Area of Anambra State." Unpublished thesis, University of Ibadan (1979).

Coleman, James. "The Ibo and Yoruba Strands in Nigerian Nationalism." Robert Melson / Howard Wolpe. *Nigeria: Modernization and the Politics of Communalism* (1971).

Collins, Paul. "Current Issues of Administrative Reform in the Nigerian Public Services. The Case of the Udoji Review Commission." *Administration for Development in Nigeria* (1980).

"Public Policy and the Development of Indigenous Capitalism: The Nigerian Experience." *Administration for Development in Nigeria* (1980).

Collins, Randall. "A Comparative Approach to Political Sociology." Reinhard Bendix. *State and Society*. Berkeley and Los Angeles: University of California Press (1968).

Cowell, Alan. "Conflicts Emerging in Nigeria's 21-month Civil Regime." *New York Times* (31 July 1981).

"In Nigerian vote, old leaders come out fighting." *New York Times* (3 May 1982).

Davis, Lane. "The Cost of Realism: Contemporary Restatements of Democracy." *Western Political Quarterly* 17. 1 (1964).

Dent, Martin. "A Minority Party – The United Middle Belt Congress." John P. Mackintosh. *Nigerian Government and Politics* (1966).

"Corrective Government: Military Rule in Perspective." S. K. Panter-Brick. *Soldiers and Oil* (1978).

Diamond, Larry. "Cleavage, Conflict and Anxiety in the Second Nigerian Republic." *Journal of Modern African Studies* 20. 4 (1982).

"A Tarnished Victory for the NPN." *Africa Report* (Nov.–Dec. 1983).

"Social Change and Political Conflict in Nigeria's Second Republic." I. William Zartman. *The Political Economy of Nigeria* (1983).

"Nigeria in Search of Democracy." *Foreign Affairs* 62. 14 (Spring 1984).

"The Coup and the Future." *Africa Report* (Mar.–Apr. 1984).

Dudley, B. J. "The Military and Development." *Nigerian Journal of Economic and Social Studies* 13. 2 (July 1971).

Eisenstadt, S. N. / Roniger, Louis. "Patron-Client Relations as a Model of Structuring Social Exchange." *Comparative Studies in Society and History* 22. 1 (January 1980).

Ekeh, Peter. "Colonialism and the Two Publics in Africa: A Theoretical Statement." *Comparative Studies in Society and History* 17. 1 (January 1975).

Elaigwu, J. Isawa. "The Political Trio in Nigeria's Military Government: The Dynamics of Inter-Elite Relations in a Military Regime, 1967–75." *Nigerian Journal of Public Affairs* 6. 2 (October 1976).

Flynn, Peter. "Class, Clientelism, and Coercion: Some Mechanisms of Internal Dependency and Control." *Journal of Commonwealth and Comparative Politics* 12. 2 (July 1974).

Forrest, Tom. "State Capital in Nigeria." Paul Lubeck. *The African Bourgeoisie: The Development of Capitalism in Nigeria, Kenya and the Ivory Coast* (1987).

Gowon, Yakubu. "Address to the First Civilian Members of the Federal Executive Council." A. H. M. Kirk-Greene. *Crisis and Conflict in Nigeria* 1 (1971).

Herskovits, Jean. "Democracy in Nigeria." *Foreign Affairs* 58. 2 (Winter 1979/80).

"To Ease Nigeria's Debt Crisis." *New York Times* (5 October 1983).

"Dateline Nigeria: Democracy Down But Not Out." *Foreign Policy* 54 (Spring 1984).

Hodgkin, Thomas. "The Relevance of 'Western' Ideas for the New African States." J. Roland Pennock. *Self-Government in Modernizing Nations* (1964).

Horton, Robin. "Stateless Societies in the History of West Africa." J. F. A. Ajayi / Michael Crowder. *History of West Africa* 1 (1976).

Ishaku, Jonathan Cingwe. "Re-Emergence of Civil Politics in Nigeria: Plateau State Case Study." Unpublished thesis, University of Ibadan (1979).

Joseph, Richard A. "Affluence and Underdevelopment: the Nigerian Experience." *Journal of Modern African Studies* 16. 2 (June 1978).

"Political Parties and Ideology in Nigeria." *Review of African Political Economy* 13 (1979).

"Democratization under Military Tutelage: Crisis and Consensus in the Nigerian 1979 Elections." *Comparative Politics* 14. 1 (1982).

"Nigeria at the Crossroads." *Harvard International Review* 4. 3 (1981).

"The Ethnic Trap: Notes on the Nigerian Campaign and Elections, 1978–79." *Issue* 11. 1/2 (1981).

"The Overthrow of Nigeria's Second Republic." *Current History* 83. 491 (March 1984).

"Principles and Practices of Nigerian Military Government." John Harbeson. *The Military in African Politics.* New York: Praeger (1987).

Kasfir, Nelson. "Soldiers as Policymakers in Nigeria: The Comparative Performance of Four Military Regimes." *American Universities Field Staff, West African Series* 17. 3 (October 1977).

"Explaining Ethnic Political Participation." *World Politics* 31. 3 (April 1979).

Kaufman, Robert R. "Corporatism, Clientelism and Partisan Conflict: A Study of Seven Latin American Countries." James M. Malloy. *Authoritarianism and Corporatism in Latin America* (1977).

Kilby, Peter. "What Oil Wealth Did to Nigeria." *Wall Street Journal* (25 November 1981).

Lemarchand, René. "Political Clientelism and Ethnicity in Tropical Africa: Competing Solidarities in Nation-Building." *American Political Science Review* 66. 1 (1972).

"Comparative Political Clientelism: Structure, Process, and Optic." S. N. Eisenstadt / René Lemarchand. *Political Clientelism, Patronage and Development* (1981).

Lijphart, Arend. "Typologies of Democratic Systems." *Comparative Political Studies* 1. 1 (1968).

"Consociational Democracy." *World Politics* 21. 2 (January 1969).

Linz, Juan. "The Future of an Authoritarian Situation or the Institutionalization of an Authoritarian Regime: The Case of Brazil." Alfred Stepan. *Authoritarian Brazil: Origins, Policies and Future* (1973).

Lloyd, P. C. "Political and Social Structure." S. O. Biobaku. *Sources of Yoruba History* (1973).

Lowenthal, Abraham F. "Armies and Politics in Latin America." *World Politics* 27. 1 (1974).

Lustick, Ian. "Stability in Deeply Divided Societies: Consociationalism versus Control." *World Politics* 31. 3 (April 1979).

Mackintosh, John P. "The Action Group: The Crisis of 1962 and its Aftermath." *Nigerian Government and Politics* (1966).

"Nigerian Democracy." *Nigerian Government and Politics* (1966).

Marx, Karl. "Critique of Hegel's 'Philosophy of Right'." David McLellan. *Karl Marx: Selected Writings.* Oxford (1977).

Melson, Robert / Wolpe, Howard. "Modernization and the Politics of Communalism: A Theoretical Perspective." *Nigeria: Modernization and the Politics of Communalism* (1971).

Nordlinger, Eric. "Soldiers in Mufti: The Impact of Military Rule Upon Economic and Social Change in the Non-Western States." *American Political Science Review* 64. 4 (December 1970).

Nwankwo, Asiegbu Dan. "Transition to Civil Rule in Nigeria: A Case Study of Anambra State." Unpublished thesis, University of Ibadan (1979).

Nyerere, Julius. "Democracy and the Party System." *Freedom and Unity: A Selection of Writings and Speeches, 1952–65* (1966).

O'Donnell, Guillermo A. "Corporatism and the Question of the State." James M. Malloy. *Authoritarianism and Corporatism in Latin America* (1977).

Obasanjo, General. "Convocation Address." *New Nigerian*, Kaduna (12 December 1977).

Oculi, Okello. "Dependent Food Policy in Nigeria, 1975–1979." *Review of African Political Economy* 15/16 (May–Dec. 1979).

Odinamadu, B. O. "The Dilemma of the Ibo Political Elite." *Daily Star* (4 November 1978).

Odulaja, Mojubaolu Olufunke. "A New Era? Continuity and Change in Lagos State Politics, 1954–1979." Unpublished thesis, University of Ibadan (1979).

Okigbo, P. N. C. "Ideological Perspectives of Public Sector Role in the Nigerian Economy." *Public Sector Role in Nigerian Development* (1978).

Okoli, Eukora Joe. "Causes of NPN and NPP Discord." *West Africa* (16 March 1981).

Okpaleke, N. A. "Politics of Transition in Aguata Local Government Area, 1978–79." Unpublished thesis, University of Ibadan (1979).

Olumhense, Sonala. "Twenty-four hours to triumph." *The Guardian* (5 August 1983).

"Allah-De." *The Guardian* (14 August 1983).

Olusegun, M. E. "Ogun State and Local Politics: Nigeria 1978–79." Unpublished thesis, University of Ibadan (1979).

Onogwu, Jacob Amuta. "Nigeria's Return to Democratic Rule: A Case-Study of Politics in the Okpokwu Local Government Area of Benue State in 1978–79." Unpublished thesis, University of Ibadan (1979).

Oyewumi, Oyeronke Temilola. "Continuity and Change in Nigerian Politics: The Oyo State Experience." Unpublished thesis, University of Ibadan (1979).

Panter-Brick, S. K. "From Military Coup to Civil War, January 1966 to May 1967." *Nigerian Politics and Military Rule: Prelude to the Civil War* (1970).

"Nigeria: The 1979 Elections." *Africa Spectrum* 14. 3 (1979).

Parkin, David. "Congregational and Interpersonal Ideologies in Political Ethnicity." Abner Cohen. *Urban Ethnicity* (1974).

Parkin, Frank. "Social Closure and Class Formation." Anthony Giddens / David Held. *Classes, Power and Conflict: Classical and Contemporary Debates* (1982).

Perlmutter, Amos. "The Comparative Analysis of Military Regimes: Formations, Aspirations, and Achievements." *World Politics* 33. 1 (October 1980).

Post, K. W. J. "The National Council of Nigeria and the Cameroons, The Decision of December 1959." John Mackintosh. *Nigerian Government and Politics* (1966).

Purcell, Susan Kaufman. "Authoritarianism." *Comparative Politics* 5. 2 (January 1973).

Rimmer, Douglas. "Development in Nigeria: An Overview." Henry Bienen / V. P. Diejomaoh. *The Political Economy of Income Distribution in Nigeria* (1981).

Sandbrook, Richard. "Patrons, Clients, and Factions: New Dimensions of Conflict Analysis in Africa." *Canadian Journal of Political Science* 5. 1 (1972).

Sani, Habibu A. "An Ex-Insider's Overview of the Civil Service (1966–1977)." *Nigerian Journal of Public Affairs* 6. 2 (October 1976).

Schatz, Sayre P. "Pirate Capitalism and the Inert Economy of Nigeria." *The Journal of Modern African Studies* 22. 1 (1984).

Schwartzman, Simon. "Back to Weber: Corporatism and Patrimonialism in the Seventies." James M. Malloy. *Authoritarianism and Corporatism in Latin America* (1977).

Scott, James C. "Patron-Client Politics and Political Change in Southeast Asia." *American Political Science Review* 64. 1 (1972).

Silverman, Sydal. "Patronage as Myth." Ernest Gellner/John Waterbury. *Patrons and Clients in Mediterranean Societies* (1977).

Skinner, Elliott. "Competition Within Ethnic Systems in Africa." Leo A. Despres. *Ethnicity and Resource Competition in Plural Societies* (1975).

Sklar, Richard L. "Contradictions in the Nigerian Political System." *Journal of Modern African Studies* 3. 2 (August 1965).

"Nigerian Politics: The Ordeal of Chief Awolowo, 1960–65." Gwendolyn M. Carter. *Politics in Africa: Seven Cases* (1966).

227

Select bibliography

"Political Science and National Integration – a Radical Approach." *Journal of Modern African Studies* 5. 1 (1967).

"The Nature of Class Domination in Africa." *Journal of Modern African Studies* 17. 4 (1979).

"Democracy in Africa." *Presidential Address to the Twenty-fifth Annual Meeting of the African Studies Association. African Studies Review*, Vol. 26, Nos. 3/4 (1983).

Smith, M. G. "Institutional and Political Conditions of Pluralism." Kuper and Smith. *Pluralism in Africa* (1969).

Sule, Maitama. "Discussion of the Public Service and the Political Class." Mahmud Tukur. *Reform of the Nigerian Public Service* (1971).

Szeftel, Morris. "Corruption and the spoils system in Zambia." Michael Clarke. *Corruption: Causes, Consequences and Control* (1983).

Theobald, Robin. "Patrimonialism." *World Politics* 34. 4 (July 1982).

Turner, Terisa. "Multinational Corporations and the Instability of the Nigerian State." *Review of African Political Economy* 5 (1976).

Ugolo, Manyelu. "A Case-Study of Anambra State Politics, 1978–79." Unpublished thesis, University of Ibadan (1979).

Ukegbu, Basil Nnanna. "My Political Stand." Personal Advertisement, *National Concord* (25 July 1983).

Walker, Jack L. "A Critique of the Elitist Theory of Democracy." *American Political Science Review* 60. 2 (June 1966).

Wallerstein, Immanuel. "Ethnicity and National Integration in West Africa." Pierre L. van den Berghe. *Africa: Social Problems of Change and Conflict* (1965).

Waterbury, John. "An attempt to put patrons and clients in their place." Ernest Gellner / John Waterbury. *Patrons and Clients in Mediterranean Societies* (1977).

Watts, M. "State, Oil and Accumulation: from boom to crisis." *Environment and Planning: Society and Space* 2 (1984).

Weber, Max. "Bureaucracy." H. H. Gerth / C. Wright Mills. *From Max Weber: Essays in Sociology* (1948).

Weingrod, Alex. "Patrons, Patronage and Political Parties." *Comparative Studies in Society and History* 10. 2 (1968).

Whitaker, C. Sylvester. "The Unfinished State of Nigeria." *Worldview* 27. 3 (March 1984).

Yahaya, Ali. "PRP Crisis: the Truth of the Matter." *West Africa* (15 June 1981).

Young, Crawford. "Patterns of Social Conflict: State, Class, and Ethnicity." *Daedalus* 3. 2 (Spring 1982).

Zolberg, Aristide. "The Military Decade in Africa." *World Politics* 25. 2 (January 1973).

Books

Achebe, Chinua. *A Man of the People.* New York: Doubleday and Co. (1969).

Adamu, Haroun / Ogunsanwo, Alaba. *Nigeria, The Making of the Presidential System: 1979 General Elections.* Kano, Nigeria: Triumph Publishing Co. (1983).

Adedeji, Adebayo, ed. *Nigerian Administration and Its Policy Setting.* London: Hutchinson Educational for Institute of Administration, University of Ife (1968).

Ajayi, J. F. A. / Crowder, Michael, ed. *History of West Africa.* New York: Columbia University Press (1976).

Almond, Gabriel A. / Verba, Sidney. *The Civic Culture: Political Attitudes and Democracy in Five Nations.* Princeton: Princeton University Press (1963).

Apter, David. *The Political Kingdom in Uganda: A Study in Bureaucratic Nationalism.* Princeton: Princeton University Press (1961).

Ghana In Transition. Princeton: Princeton University Press (1972).

Austen, Granville. *The Indian Constitution: Cornerstone of a Nation.* Oxford and Bombay: Oxford University Press (1966).

Awolowo, Obafemi. *Path to Nigerian Freedom.* London: Faber (1947).

The People's Republic. Ibadan: Oxford University Press (1968).

Azikiwe, Nnamdi. *Democracy with Military Vigilance.* Nsukka, Nigeria: African Book Co. (1974).

Barth, Frederick. *Ethnic Groups and Boundaries: The Social Organization of Culture Difference.* Boston: Little, Brown and Co. (1969).

Beard, Charles A., ed. *The Enduring Federalist.* New York: Doubleday and Co. (1948).

Beer, Samuel H., *et al. Patterns of Government: The Major Political Systems of Europe.* New York: Random House (1958).

Beetham, David. *Max Weber and the Theory of Modern Politics.* London: George Allen and Unwin (1974).

Bendix, Reinhard. *State and society.* Berkeley and Los Angeles: University of California Press (1968).

Bienen, Henry. *Armies and Parties in Africa.* New York and London: Africana Publishing Company (1978).

Bienen, Henry, ed. *The Military Intervenes: Case Studies in Political Development.* New York: Russell Sage (1968).

The Military and Modernization. Chicago and New York: Aldine-Atherton (1971).

Bienen, Henry / Diejomaoh, V. P., ed. *The Political Economy of Income Distribution in Nigeria.* New York and London: Holmes and Meier Publishers (1981).

Biobaku, S. O. *Sources of Yoruba History.* Oxford: The Clarendon Press (1973).

Calhoun, Craig. *The Question of Class Struggle: Social Foundations of Popular Radicalism During the Industrial Revolution.* Chicago: University of Chicago Press (1980).

Calhoun, John C. *A Disquisition on Government.* New York: The Liberal Arts Press (1953).

Carter, Gwendolyn M., ed. *Politics in Africa: Seven Cases.* New York: Harcourt, Brace and World (1966).

Clapham, Christopher. *Private Patronage and Public Power.* New York: St. Martin's Press (1982).

Clarke, Michael. *Corruption: Causes, Consequences and Control.* London: Frances Pinter Publishers (1983).

Cohen, Abner. *Custom and Politics in Urban Africa.* London: Routledge and Kegan Paul (1969).

Two-Dimensional Man: An Essay on the Anthropology of Power and Symbolism in Complex Society. Berkeley and Los Angeles: University of California Press (1974).

Cohen, Robin. *Labour and Politics in Nigeria.* London: Heinemann (1974).

Collins, Paul. *Administration for Development in Nigeria: Introduction and Readings.* Lagos: African Education Press (1980).

Dahl, Robert A. *Polyarchy: Participation and Opposition.* New Haven and London: Yale University Press (1971).

Dahl, Robert A., ed. *Regimes and Oppositions.* New Haven and London: Yale University Press (1973).

de St Jorre, John. *The Nigerian Civil War.* London: Hodder and Stoughton (1972).

de Tocqueville, Alexis. *Democracy in America.* New York: Vintage (1945).

Despres, Leo A., ed. *Ethnicity and Resource Competition in Plural Societies.* The Hague and Paris: Mouton Publishers (1975).

Dudley, B. J. *Parties and Politics in Northern Nigeria.* London: Frank Cass (1968).

Instability and Political Order: Politics and Crisis in Nigeria. Ibadan: Ibadan University Press (1973).

Eckstein, Harry. *Division and Cohesion in Democracy: A Study of Norway.* Princeton: Princeton University Press (1966).

Eisenstadt, S. N. / Lemarchand, René. *Political Clientelism, Patronage and Development.* Beverly Hills and London: Sage Publications (1981).

Evans, Peter. *Dependent Development: The Alliance of Multinational, State and Local Capital in Brazil.* Princeton: Princeton University Press (1979).

Select bibliography

Finer, S. E. *The Man on Horseback*. New York: Praeger (1962).

First, Ruth. *The Barrel of a Gun: Political Power in Africa*. London: Allen Lane (1970).

Gellner, Ernest / Waterbury, John. *Patrons and Clients in Mediterranean Societies*. London: Gerald Duckworth and Co., Ltd. (1977).

Gerth, H. H./Wright Mills, C., ed. and trans. *From Max Weber: Essays in Sociology*. London: Routledge and Kegan Paul, Ltd. (1948).

Giddens, Anthony / Held, David, ed. *Classes, Power and Conflict: Classical and Contemporary Debates*. Berkeley and Los Angeles: University of California Press (1982).

Helleiner, Gerald K. *Peasant Agriculture, Government and Economic Growth in Nigeria*. Illinois: R. D. Irwin (1966).

Homans, George C. *Social Behavior: Its Elementary Forms*. New York: Harcourt, Brace and World (1961).

Howe, Irving. *Leon Trotsky*. Middlesex, England: Penguin Books (1979).

Huntington, Samuel P. *Political Order in Changing Societies*. New Haven and London: Yale University Press (1968).

Huntington, Samuel P. / Nelson, Joan M. *No Easy Choice: Political Participation in Developing Societies*. Cambridge: Harvard University Press (1976).

Jemibewon, David M. *A Combatant in Government*. Ibadan, Nigeria: Heinemann Educational Books (1978).

Kasfir, Nelson. *The Shrinking Political Arena: Participation and Ethnicity in African Politics with a Case Study of Uganda*. Berkeley and Los Angeles: University of California Press (1976).

Kilby, Peter. *Industrialization in an Open Economy: Nigeria, 1945–1966*. London: Cambridge University Press (1969).

Kirk-Greene, A. H. M. *Crisis and Conflict in Nigeria: A Documentary Sourcebook 1966–1969*, Vols. 1 and 2. London: Oxford University Press (1971).

Kuper, Leo / Smith, M. G. *Pluralism in Africa*. Berkeley and Los Angeles: University of California Press (1969).

Kurfi, Adamu. *The Nigerian General Elections 1959 and 1979 and the Aftermath*. Lagos and Ibadan: Macmillian Nigeria Publishers (1983).

Lewis, W. Arthur. *Politics in West Africa*. Toronto and New York: Oxford University Press (1965).

Lijphart, Arend. *Democracy in Plural Societies: A Comparative Exploration*. New Haven and London: Yale University Press (1977).

Locke, John. *The Second Treatise of Government: An Essay Concerning the True Original, Extent and End of Civil Government*. New York: The Liberal Press (1952).

Mackintosh, John P., ed. *Nigerian Government and Politics*. London: George Allen and Unwin (1966).

Macpherson, C. B. *The Political Theory of Possessive Individualism: Hobbes to Locke*. Oxford: The Clarendon Press (1962).

The Real World of Democracy. Oxford: The Clarendon Press (1966).

Democratic Theory: Essays in Retrieval. Oxford: The Clarendon Press (1973).

Malloy, James M., ed. *Authoritarianism and Corporatism in Latin America*. Pittsburgh: University of Pittsburgh Press (1977).

McRae, K. D. *Consociational Democracy: Political Accommodation in Segmented Societies*. Toronto: McClelland and Stewart (1974).

Melson, Robert / Wolpe, Howard. *Nigeria: Modernization and the Politics of Communalism*. East Lansing, Michigan: Michigan State University Press (1971).

Mill, James. *An Essay on Government*. Indianapolis and New York: The Bobbs–Merrill Company (1955).

Nnoli, Okwudiba. *Ethnic Politics in Nigeria*. Enugu: Fourth Dimension Publishers (1978).

Nordlinger, Eric A. *Conflict Regulation in Divided Societies*. Occasional Papers in International

Affairs, No. 29. Cambridge, Mass: Center for International Affairs (1972).

Ojiako, James O. *13 Year of Military Rule, 1966–79.* Lagon: *Daily Times* (n.d.).

Olson, Mancur. *The Logic of Collective Action.* Cambridge: Harvard University Press (1971).

Oyediran, Oye. *Nigerian Government and Politics under Military Rule.* London and Lagos: Macmillan (1979).

Oyediran, Oye, ed. *The Nigerian 1979 Elections.* London and Lagos: Macmillan (1981).

Panter-Brick, S. K., ed. *Nigerian Politics and Military Rule: Preclude to the Civil War.* London: The Athlone Press (1970).

Soldiers and Oil: The Political Transformation of Nigeria. London: Frank Cass and Co. (1978).

Parkin, David. *The Cultural Definition of Political Response: Lineal Destiny Among the Luo.* London: Academic Press (1978).

Parsons, Talcott, ed. *Max Weber: The Theory of Social and Economic Organization.* London: Collier-Macmillan (1964).

Peel, J. D. Y. *Ijeshas and Nigerians: The Incorporation of a Yoruba Kingdom, 1890s–1970s.* Cambridge: Cambridge University Press (1983).

Pennock, J. Roland. *Self-Government in Modernizing Countries.* New Jersey: Prentice Hall (1965). *Democratic Political Theory.* Princeton: Princeton University Press (1979).

Post, K. W. J. / Vickers, Michael. *Structure and Conflict in Nigeria, 1960–1966.* London: Heinemann (1973).

Rabushka, Alvin / Shepsle, Kenneth A. *Politics in Plural Societies: A Theory of Democratic Instability.* Columbus, Ohio: Charles E. Merrill Publishing Co. (1972).

Rousseau, Jean-Jacques. *The Social Contract.* Trans. G. D. H. Cole. New York: E. P. Dutton and Co. (1950).

Sahlin, Michael. *Neo-Authoritarianism and the Problem of Legitimacy: A General Study and a Nigerian Example.* Stockholm: Raben and Sjogren (1977).

Schatz, Sayre P. *Nigerian Capitalism.* Berkeley and Los Angeles: University of California Press (1977).

Schmidt, Steffen W., *et al. Friends, Followers, and Factions: A Reader in Political Clientelism.* Berkeley and Los Angeles: University of California Press (1977).

Schumpeter, J. A. *Capitalism, Socialism and Democracy.* New York: Harper and Brothers (1942).

Sklar, Richard L. *Nigerian Political Parties: Power in an Emergent Nation.* Princeton: Princeton University Press (1963).

Skocpol, Theda. *States and Social Revolutions: A Comparative Analysis of France, Russia, and China.* Cambridge: Cambridge University Press (1979).

Stepan, Alfred. *The State and Society: Peru in Comparative Perspective.* Princeton: Princeton University Press (1978).

Stepan, Alfred, ed. *Authoritarian Brazil: Origins, Policies and Future.* New Haven and London: Yale University Press (1973).

Stremlau, John J. *The International Politics of the Nigerian Civil War, 1967–1970.* Princeton: Princeton University Press (1977).

Sullivan, Dennis G./Nakamura, Robert T./Winters, Richard F. *How America Is Ruled.* New York: John Wiley and Sons (1980).

Teriba, O. / Kayode M. O. ed. *Industrial Development in Nigeria: Patterns and Prospects.* Ibadan: Ibadan University Press (1977).

Trimberger, Ellen. *Revolutionaries from Above: Military Bureaucrats and Development in Japan, Turkey, Egypt and Peru.* New Brunswick, N.J.: Transaction Books (1978).

Tukur, Mahmud, ed. *Reform of the Nigerian Public Service.* Report of a Conference Held at the Institute of Administration, Zaria (1971).

van den Berghe, Pierre L. *Africa: Social Problems of Change and Conflict.* San Francisco: Chandler Publishing Co. (1965).

Power and Privilege in an African University. London: Routledge and Kegan Paul (1973).

Select bibliography

Welch, Claude E., Jr. *Soldier and State in Africa: A Comparative Analysis of Military Intervention and Political Change*. Evanston, Illinois: Northwestern Press (1970).

Whitaker, C. S., Jr. *The Politics of Tradition: Continuity and Change in Northern Nigeria, 1946–1966*. Princeton: Princeton University Press (1970).

Perspectives on the Second Republic in Nigeria. Waltham, Mass.: Crossroads Press (1981).

Wolf, Eric. *Peasants*. New York: Prentice Hall (1966).

Young, Crawford. *The Politics of Cultural Pluralism*. Madison, Wisconsin: University of Wisconsin Press (1976).

Zartman, William, ed. *The Political Economy of Nigeria*. New York: Praeger Publishers (1983).

Conference proceedings and government publications

The Constitution of the Federal Republic of Nigeria. Lagos: Federal Ministry of Information (1979).

Federal Military Government's Views on the Investigations of the Farms Owned by S. O. Ogbemudia and Alhaji Audu Baku. Lagos: Federal Ministry of Information (1976).

Government Views on Second Report of the Federal Assets Investigation Panel. Lagos: Federal Ministry of Information (1978).

Public Complaints Commission Decree (Decree No. 31). Lagos: Federal Ministry of Information (1975).

Public Sector Role in Nigerian Development. Proceedings of the Annual Conference of Nigerian Economic Society (1978).

Report of the Constitution Drafting Committee Containing the Draft Constitution, Vols. I, II. Lagos: Federal Ministry of Information (1976).

Report on Grading and Pay, Vols. I, II. Lagos: Public Service Review Commission (1974).

Individuals formally interviewed

Abdullahi Adamu, Haroun Adamu, Sariki Adamu, Simeon Adebo, Batoure Aga, Akinola Aguda, Datti Ahmad, G. Ajeigbe, Alu Akinfosile, Mbazulike Amechi, Mohammed Ankar, Obafemi Awolowo, Allison Ayida, Ebenezer Babatope, Nuhu Bamalli, Paul Bassi, Adamu Ciroma, Aminu Dantata, Alhaji Dantsoho, Sam Ekpe, A. A. O. Ezenwa, Joseph Garba, Abubakar Gaya, Sule Gaya, Clement Gomwalk, Ali Gummi, Francis Akanu Ibiam, Bola Ige, P. Izzah, Lateef Jakande, Mvendaga Jibo, Ayuba Kadzai, Aminu Kano, Suleiman Kumo, M. T. A. Liman, Hadjia Estar Maiduguri, Cyril Mba, Sam Mbakwe, Shettima Ali Monguno, Turi Muhammadu, Mamman Nassir, Okwudiba Nnoli, Arthur Nwankwo, Idoko Obe, H. A. Odunewu, Odia Ofeimun, Mazi Ray Ofoegbu, Femi Ogunsanwo, Chuba Okadigbo, Femi Okunnu, Josiah Olawoyin, Omo Omoruyi, Abubakar Rimi, A. Rufai, Habibu Sani, Simon Shango, Moses Tadgun, Ibrahim Tahir, Labaran Tanko, F. R. A. Williams, A. D. Yahaya.

Index

Abernethy, David, 51
Abiola, M. K., 112
Abubakar, Iya, 131, 136, 138-9
Aburi meeting, 78, 185
Achebe, Chinua, 10, 100
Action Group (A.G.): in Nigerian politics, 31-6, 38, 148-9; ideology of, 36; and party formation 1978-9, 110, 124; leadership of, 204n
Adamu, Haroun, 67, 70, 134, 155, 160
Adebo, Simeon, 136
Adelabu, Adegoke, 115
Adewusi, Sunday, 162-3, 182
Adisa, Adeoye, 115
Afolabi, S. M., 116
Agbaje, Mojeed, 103
Aguda, T. Akinola, 157
Ahmad, Datti, 137, 159
Ajasin, Michael A., 112, 167, 179
Ajayi, Jacob, 110
Ake, Claude, 75
Akeredolu-Ale, E. O., 86
Akinjide, R. A., 114-15, 119-20, 138-9
Akinloye, A. M. A., 108, 114-16, 120, 123-4, 139, 221n
Akintola, S. L., 33-4, 114-16, 120
Aku, Aper, 149, 182
Alayande, Rev., 115
Aluko, Sam, 118
Amechi, Mbazulike, 101-3
Apter, David, 4, 25, 197
Araka, Emmanuel, 177
Ariyo, Ayo, 173, 182
Asiodu, Philip, 78, 88, 210n
Awolowo, Obafemi: and consociationalism, 32-6; pre-independence politics, 32-4; and the NPC, 34; and Aminu Kano, 35; party formation and campaign for Second Republic, 44-5, 110-25; Yoruba solidarity, 44-5, 111-16, 122; UPN leadership, 66, 94, 122-5; and class, 116-21; political associates, 117-18, 121-5; free education, 118-19; political opponents, 123-4; 1979 election results, 116, 156; and Adewusi, 163; 1983 election results, 176, 180; and state creation, 204n
Ayida, Allison A., 77-8, 86, 88, 211n
Azikiwe, Nnamdi: and the NCNC, 33; party formation, Second Republic, 66, 94-6; Igbo solidarity, 94-108; and C. C. Onoh, 98, 108; and Sam Mbakwe, 99; and Igbo "progressives," 100; and Mbazulike Amechi, 102-3; and Jim Nwobodo, 102-4; formation of NPP, 102-4, 144; and the NPN, 66, 105-6, 178; and Awolowo, 108; attempted electoral disqualification, 154

Babalola, B. Olusegun, 158
Babatope, Ebenezer, 118
Badie, Bertrand, 188
Balewa, Abubakar Tafawa, 34, 124
Balogun, Ola, 158
Bamalli, Nuhu, 131, 136, 138
Barth, Frederick, 46, 51, 68
Belabo, Paul, 140
Bello, Ahmadu (see Sardauna of Sokoto)
Biafra, 78, 95-6, 105, 122
Bida, Makaman, 66, 106, 131, 136, 138
Birnbaum, Pierre, 188
Braithwaite, Tunji, 166
Brazil, 19, 22, 30
bureaucracy (see Civil Service)
Burke, Edmund, 187
Burrage, Michael, 187

Calhoun, John C., 24-5
Cardinal programs (UPN), 118

233

Chubb, Judith, 59–60
Ciroma, Adamu, 103, 131, 134, 136, 138–9, 146
Civil Service (servants), 76–90
Civil War (*see* Biafra)
Clapham, Christopher, 190, 196
class: and ethnicity, 5–7, 48, 53–4; and clientelism, 58–9; and political mobilization, 116–21, 146, 165
clientelism: and prebendal politics, 55–68; definition of, 57; and corruption, 189–92
Club, 19, 102, 122, 140, 144, 146
Cohen, Abner, 6
Collins, Paul, 129
Collins, Randall, 186
Committee of Friends (UPN), 122, 124
Conglomerate Society, 52
consociationalism, 4, 24–9, 31–8, 44–5, 62, 76, 202n
Constituent Assembly, 97, 102, 131, 140–1
Constitution Drafting Committee (CDC), 38–9, 43, 47, 75
corruption, 83, 86, 87–90, 189–95
cultural sections, 45–7, 51, 53, 195
CUS (Council for Understanding and Solidarity), 132, 140–1, 149

Dahl, Robert A., 15–16, 19–20, 22, 25, 31, 37
Danjuma, Theophilus, 141
de Tocqueville, Alexis, 187–8
democracy: general, 3–5, 15–29; in Nigeria, 30–40, 187–8, 198; consociational democracy (*see* consociationalism)
Diarchy, 179
Dikko, Umaru: formation of the NPN, 106, 136, 138–9; selection to Constituent Assembly, 131; and the "Kaduna Mafia," 134; in Shagari government, 160; role in 1983 elections, 160–1, 163–4
Dudley, Billy J., 187
Durkheim, Emile, 50

Egbe Omo Oduduwa, 112
Egbunike, Engineer, 101
Ekeh, Peter, 193–6
Ekwueme, Alex, 98, 148, 157, 178
Elections: of 1957, 34; of 1959, 33; of 1965, 32, 34; of 1979, 94, 147, 154; of 1983, 153–83, 220n
Electoral Act, 176, 181
elites: and consociationalism, 27, 38; and ethnicity, 51–2; strategic elites, 80–3, 88; northern, 77, 95, 100, 130; Igbo, 105, 107

Enahoro, Anthony, 138–9
Entrepôt state, 10, 83–7
ethnicity: and politics, 47–9, 107–8; ethnic missionary, 51, 97; ethnic system, 51–2, 98; and clientelism, 58–63; sub-ethnic identities, 111–15

Fani-Kayode, R., 159
Federal Electoral Commission (FEDECO), 153–8, 162–9, 172–82
Federal Executive Council (FEC), 36, 79, 88
feudal, 56, 65
Flynn, Peter, 58
Furnivall, J. S., 32–3, 46

Garba, Joseph, 130, 141
Gaya, Sule, 131, 136
Goni, Mohammed, 181
Gowon, Yakubu: military government of, 72–3, 76; and Ojukwu, 72, 78; nine-point program, 73–4; and Aburi talks, 78; and higher civil servants, 87–8; state creation, 96, 130; and Middle-Belt, 141; Tarka's resignation, 149; overthrow of, 31, 35, 76, 87
Great Nigerian People's Party (GNPP), 66, 144–7, 166
Gusau, Yaya, 135

Hausa-Fulani, 50, 62, 69
Hobbes, Thomas (*see also Leviathan*), 153, 188
Hodgkin, Thomas, 17
Huntington, Samuel, 22–3, 210n

Ibiam, Akanu, 96, 215n
Ibrahim, Kashim, 106, 145, 166
Ibrahim, Waziri, 122, 144, 179
Igbo, 47, 50, 62, 69, 94–107
Ige, Bola, 115, 118–19, 179
Ijekebe, 98
Ikoku, S. G., 101, 142, 165
indigenization, 86, 107
Ironsi, Aguiyi, 76–7
Islam, 130

Jakande, Lateef, 112, 117, 119, 123–4
Jemibewon, David A., 70
Jibo, Mvendaga, 139, 149
Joda, Ahmed, 78
judiciary, 176–81

Kaduna Mafia, 133–6
Kadzai, Ayuba, 140–1
Kano, Aminu: and Awolowo, 35; and Igbo
  politics, 101, 214*n*; in Northern Movement,
  131; and northern politics, 131–2, 142–4;
  formation of the PRP, 142–3; relations
  with NPN, 144–5; political thought of,
  143; attempted disqualification of, 155;
  PRP faction, 144, 165; and Shari'a, 214*n*
Katagum, Sule, 138
Kirk-Greene, A. H. M., 50
Kumo, Suleiman, 134, 136–7
Kuper, Leo, 46
Kurfi, Adamu, 153, 155–6

Lar, Solomon, 140
Lemarchand, René, 58–60, 68
Leviathan (*see also* Hobbes), 157, 167, 174,
  180, 182
Lewis, W. Arthur, 17, 21, 24, 26, 35, 43, 186
liberalism (liberal democracy), 5, 23, 157,
  187–8, 193
Lijphart, Arend, 21, 25–8, 34, 39, 202*n*
Linz, Juan, 19–20
Lloyd, P. C., 196
Locke, John, 23

Mabolaje Grand Alliance, 115
Mackintosh, John P., 36–7
Macpherson, C. B., 16, 20
Madison, James, 17, 23
Maitatsine, 162
majority rule, 23–6
Mbadiwe, K. O., 95, 99, 139, 148
Mbakwe, Sam, 99–100, 102, 107, 138
Melson, Robert, 48
Middle-Belt, 140–1, 209*n*
military rule: and Nigeria's "minorities,"
  69–70; and civil society, 70–1; and
  prebendal politics, 71–6; and the civil
  bureaucracy, 76–80; and corruption, 72–3
Mill, John Stuart, 21, 25
Modakeke, 177, 179
Mohammed, Murtala: regime of, 31, 74; and
  civilian rule, 35, 38–9, 121, 158; critique
  of Gowon regime, 73; anti-corruption
  drive, 87–8; and higher civil servants, 88;
  northern background, 130
Muhammadu, Turi, 134, 184
Musa, Balarabe, 143

Nakura, Ali, 121
national cake, 3, 9, 11, 44, 74, 84, 147,
  207–8*n*

National Unity Council, 122, 144, 146
NCNC (National Convention of Nigerian
  Citizens, formerly National Council of
  Nigeria and the Cameroons): in Nigerian
  politics, 31, 33–4; and Yoruba politics
  1978–9, 110, 113–15
NEPU (Nigerian Elements Progressive
  Union), 35–6, 142–3
Nigerian Advance Party (NAP), 166, 219*n*
Nigerian National Alliance (NNA), 131
NNDP (Nigerian National Democratic
  Party), 110, 114, 119
Nordlinger, Eric A., 26, 37
NPC (Nigerian People's Congress): in
  Nigerian politics, 31, 34, 36; and the NPN
  1978–9, 131, 133
NPN: in Nigerian politics, 34–5, 129–50;
  formation of, 44, 58; political strategy of,
  44, 60; and sectional identities, 44, 58, 60,
  62; and Dr Azikiwe, 66, 94, 102–3; Grand
  Patron of, 66; and Igbo politics, 94, 98,
  105–6; and Yoruba politics, 109–10,
  115–16, 120; Accord with NPP, 164–5;
  relations with the PRP, 165–6; 1983
  electoral maneuvering, 166–8; 1983
  electoral fraud, 172–81
NPP: in Nigerian politics, 44, 93–108; and
  ethnic consolidation, 44, 104–8, 116; and
  Dr Azikiwe, 66, 99, 103–7, 114, 122, 144;
  and Sam Mbakwe, 99; and Jim Nwobodo,
  103–5; and Yoruba politics, 113–16;
  origins, 140; and the Middle-Belt, 141–2;
  and Club, 19, 140, 144; Accord with the
  NPN, 164–5
Nwankwo, Arthur, 100
Nwobodo, Jim, 101–4, 108, 177, 214*n*
Nyerere, Julius, 17
Nzeogwu, Kaduna, 71–2, 158

Obasanjo, Olusegun: and party politics, 3;
  regime of, 71, 74–5, 130; and prebendal
  politics, 75; transition to civilian rule, 93;
  state creation, 97
Obeya, Ignatius, 182
Odenigwe, Godwin, 98
Odujno, Soji, 113
Ogunsanya, Adeniran, 123–4, 176
Ojukwu, Odumegwu (or Emeka): on
  corruption, 72; and Gowon, 78–9; Aburi
  talks, 78, 185; attitude to civil servants,
  79, 211; and Igbo politics, 96, 105, 178;
  and the NPN, 105, 178; on con-
  federalism, 185
Okadigbo, Chuba, 97, 105, 138–9
Okafor, R. B. K., 95, 103

Okezie, J. O. J., 105, 148
Okoro, Nwakamma, 99, 105
Okpara, Michael, 96, 99, 124, 178
Okunnu, Femi, 89, 123
Olawoyin, Sunday, 123
Olson, Mancur, 53–4
Olunloyo, Omololu, 179
Omoboriowo, Akin, 167, 179
Onabanjo, Bisi, 113
Orizu, Nwafor, 95, 105
Osadebay, Dennis, 102
Otegbeye, Tunji, 113, 117
Ovie-Whiskey, Victor, 157, 167, 173, 182, 220*n*
Owelle (*see also* Nnamdi Azikiwe), 104
Oyebola, Areole, 113
Oyo Empire, 110–11, 114

Parkin, David, 6
Parkin, Frank, 192–3
patrimonialism, 63–6, 189
patronage, 9, 57, 66–7
patron–client (*see* clientelism)
Peel, J. D. Y., 196–8
People's Progressive Party (PPP), 100–1
Perlmutter, Amos, 69
permanent secretaries, 76, 78–9, 88
plural society, 21, 24, 32–3, 45–7, 84, 186, 193, 201*n*
polyarchy, 15, 19
Post, Ken, 37, 52–3
prebendalism: illustrations of, 1, 9, 67, 70; definitions of, 8, 55–6, 66–7, 75; and democracy, 10–11, 172; impact of, 10; and clientelism, 55–68; and Max Weber, 63–5; contrast with patrimonialism, 63–8; and insecurity, 68; and the state bureaucracy, 83–4; and civil servants, 84, 90; and party formation, 125, 129, 147–50
primordial, 5, 47–8, 193–4
Progressive People's Alliance (PPA), 166–7
Progressive People's Party, 166
PRP (People's Redemption Party): in Nigerian politics, 44, 141–6; and Igbo politics, 101; and Dr Azikiwe, 102–3; and the Mabolaje, 115; formation of, 142–3; and Aminu Kano, 142–4; factions of, 143–4, 165–6, 178; and the NPN, 142–4, 165–6
Public Complaints Commission, 88
publics, *see* Ekeh, Peter

rational behavior, 6–7
revenue allocation, 4
Rimi, Abubakar, 143, 176, 181

Rimmer, Douglas, 8–9
role expansion, 69, 77
Rosiji, A., 34

Sandbrook, Richard, 59, 194
Sani, Habibu, 83–4
Saraki, Olusola, 138–9
Sardauna of Sokoto, 130, 132, 135, 142
Schatz, Sayre, 86
Schumpeter, J. A., 18, 23
Scott, James C., 57–9, 68
sectionalism, 43, 47, 49, 76, 93, 108
segmentation, 43, 46, 49–54
Shagari, Shehu: and Dr Azikiwe, 103, 106; and Yoruba politics, 115–6; on free education, 119; formation of NPN, 131, 136–7; campaign for presidency, 136; NPN leadership, 137–8, 148; political abilities, 137; and prebendal politics, 147–8; selection of Vice-President, 148; 1979 elections, 154; 1983 elections, 157, 168, 176–7; government of, 165, 187
Shari'a, 101, 133, 135, 141, 149–50
Skinner, Elliot, 46–8, 51
Sklar, Richard L., 36, 48, 74, 157, 160
Skocpol, Theda, 82, 186
Smith, M. G., 21, 25, 33, 46
social closure, 192–5
social science, 2, 5, 8, 47, 189–97
Socialism, 114, 117–19
Soyinka, Wole, 158, 172
State: prebendalized, 56–7; and the economy, 73, 85–7; and civil society, 80–4; and prebendal politics, 83–4
Steiner, Jürg, 45
Stepan, Alfred, 186
strategic elite (*see* elites)
Sule, Maitama, 138–9
Supreme Military Council (SMC), 75, 78, 107, 204*n*
Szeftel, Morris, 189

Tahir, Ibrahim, 106, 131, 133–4, 137–9
Tarka, Joseph, 66, 131–2, 137–9, 149
Theobald, Robin, 66
Tiv, 46, 66, 96, 148–9
Trimberger, Ellen, 82
Turner, Terisa, 10, 82, 85–6

Udoji, Jerome, 105
Umeadi, Philip, 117, 124
Unification Decree, 77
Unongo, Paul, 140–1, 149, 178
UPE (Universal Primary Education), 118–19

UPN (Unity Party of Nigeria), 34, 44, 66, 94, 144
Usman, Bala, 134

van den Berghe, Pierre L., 50
Vickers, Michael, 37, 52-3

Wachuku, Jaja, 95
Wada, Inuwa, 131, 142
Waterbury, John, 68
Wawa, 97, 113
Wayas, Joseph, 139, 148
Weber, Max, 18, 56, 63-5, 83, 186, 192, 210n

Weingrod, Alex, 57, 61
Whitaker, C. S., 58, 159, 184-5, 187-8
Wolf, Eric, 189
Wolpe, Howard, 48

Yahaya, Ali D., 134, 143
Yar' Adua, Shehu, 88, 130
Yoruba, 47, 62, 69, 94, 97, 105, 109-24, 195-7
Young, M. Crawford, 4, 6-7, 50-1

Zie (see Azikiwe, Nnamdi)
zoning, 136-40